JACK

JACK

A Biography of Jack London

ANDREW SINCLAIR

HARPER & ROW, PUBLISHERS

NEW YORK, HAGERSTOWN, SAN FRANCISCO

LONDON

An article in the August 1977 issue of *American Heritage*
on Jack London includes illustrations from this book.

JACK: A BIOGRAPHY OF JACK LONDON. Copyright © 1977 by Andrew Sinclair. All rights
reserved. Printed in the United States of America. No part of this book may be used or
reproduced in any manner whatsoever without written permission except in the case of brief
quotations embodied in critical articles and reviews. For information address Harper & Row,
Publishers, Inc., 10 East 53rd Street, New York, N.Y. 10022. Published simultaneously in
Canada by Fitzhenry & Whiteside Limited, Toronto.

FIRST EDITION

Designed by Sidney Feinberg

Library of Congress Cataloging in Publication Data

Sinclair, Andrew.
  Jack : a biography of Jack London.
  Bibliography: p.
  Includes index.
  1. London, Jack, 1876–1916—Biography. 2. Novelists,
American—20th century—Biography. I. Title.
PS3523.046Z876   818'.5'209 [B]   76-57899 √
ISBN 0-06-013899-8

77 78 79 80 10 9 8 7 6 5 4 3 2 1

TO
Mrs. Patrick Eve

CONTENTS

ILLUSTRATIONS

I am a parcel of vain strivings tied
　　By a chance bond together,
Dangling this way and that, their links
　　Were made so loose and wide,
　　　　　　　　　Methinks,
　　　For milder weather.

HENRY THOREAU

FOREWORD

After the Civil War there was a restlessness in the land. That restlessness was greater on the distant edge of the land which drew the wanderers. The three thousand miles of the new railroad track across the continent to San Francisco put an end to the weary months on the wagon trail or the voyage round the Horn. Yet it did not satisfy the westering lust in the terminal city before the Pacific Ocean. When the travellers arrived there, they found no end to their journey. The Orient waited beyond the Golden Gate. Unprospected territories lay this side of the northern and southern poles. The immigrants to the promised land of California brought their discontent and their greed with them. San Francisco was the new place of unsatisfied desire.

More reckless than Topsy, the city just growed like an outrage to justice. Wealth flaunted its turrets from the hills at the growling slums beneath. Charles Crocker spent more than a million dollars on his four-storied palace—"a delirium of the wood carver." Its ostentatious ugliness was surpassed by Mark Hopkins, who lived in a castle of towers and gables. Old San Francisco—as Jack London was to write—"incontinently inter-mingled its slums and mansions as did the old cities of Europe. Nob Hill arose, like any medieval castle, from the mess and ruck of common life that denned and laired at its base."[1]

Down at the bottom round Embarcadero and Market Street lived the rootless and shifting work-beasts, ready to revolt from their toil and rend the few masters of the new feudalism. They were not united against the rich, for they also hated the rival Chinese workers from Asia and the new immigrants from the Old World. The turmoil in the slums bred a fierce radicalism and racism, the protests against frustrated desires and losing hopes. Mob violence flared with unemployment, casual murder was common-place on the waterfront and in the vice district called the Barbary Coast.

Outside the raw city, a greater disappointment grew. The land of California had been settled in a rush—and a Gold Rush. The state had only joined the Union in 1846, and its population of less than twenty thousand had increased fifteen times in the next thirty years. The chief motive of this speedy immigration had been the greed which is called opportunity. To Emerson on the East Coast, California was settled by "a rush and a scramble of needy adventurers."² To Thoreau, who wanted western migration to be a return to the innocence of the wilderness, going to California seemed only going three thousand miles nearer to hell. The new state attracted those in search of a quick dollar and social status, the peddlers of suspect stocks and instant salvations, bonanza farmers and placer miners —the looters of the soil and the plunderers of other pioneers.

Even the traditional settlers of the west had caught the fever of specula-tion. The small farmers acquired land easily, mortgaged it, exploited it, lost it to the banks, and moved on. Between the Gold Rush and the great slump of the 1870s, the promise of easy money and free land proved a Mohave Desert for the many, an Eldorado for the few. Half of the fertile acres of the state were soon controlled by five hundred people and a few railroad trusts.

With the exception of the Santa Clara Valley and Napa and Sonoma counties, the land looked exhausted and barbarous after three decades of overworking for quick profits. It was peopled by subsistence farmers and migrant laborers, "the most shiftless, thriftless men of the class that can be found in the Union."³ The best of the first pioneers were mostly dead or scattered, their hopes withered. "And where are they now?" Mark Twain asked in Roughing It. *"All gone, or nearly all—victims devoted upon the altar of the golden calf—the noblest holocaust that ever wafted its sacrificial incense heavenward. It is pitiful to think upon."⁴*

By 1875, this was the heritage of the wanderers to California—a wasted earth, a radical discontent, a new state divided so brutally between rich and poor that injustice was visible on the exhausted tenant farms and the very streets of San Francisco. Yet that raw deal, that tooth-and-claw battle to earn a living wage, also encouraged a ferment of ideas. The frenzies of the old Burned-Over district of upper New York State, the revivals and prophecies, the confessions and mental confusions, the spiritualism and the free love had come across the continent with many of the new Californians. They had brought with them a longing for utopia as well as for mere things. They had kicked over the social traces to head for a wider liberty for their appetites.

One of these unstable migrants was the tiny spiritualist Flora Wellman, who had run away from the respectability and wealth of her family in small-town Ohio. Under five foot in height, partially bald and short-sighted from an attack of typhoid, she had to assert herself to deny her handicaps. She had fled from her home at the age of sixteen, drifting from boardinghouse to the charity of family friends, giving lessons in music. She had reached her early thirties when she met the magnetic William Henry Chaney, an experienced vagabond and astrologer in his fifties, originally born in a log cabin in Maine. Their temporary alliance proved profitable in the lecture halls of San Francisco, then looking for novelties and sensation.

The two wanderers lived together in the same boardinghouse. "A very loose condition of society was fashionable at San Francisco at the time," Chaney later wrote, "and it was not thought disgraceful for two to live together without marriage. I mean, the Spiritualists and those who claimed to be reformers."⁵ If this liaison was as transient as the times, it was a liaison of likes. Chaney himself was a jack of all trades in his drifting career, at times a sailor, an editor, a politician, and an attorney before settling for astrology, an art that engaged his talents for speaking and fantasy. His life was one of wasted gifts and evaded responsibilities. He was a dabbler whose westering was never done.⁶

The crisis of the relationship was caused by Flora Wellman's pregnancy. According to her, Chaney insisted that she have an abortion under the threat of leaving her. Childlessness was the condition of his many marriages and vagabondage. She refused to abort and made two sensational attempts at suicide, first taking an overdose of opium and then giving herself a flesh wound in the forehead with a revolver. These actions were reported in the San Francisco newspapers.⁷ The result was not to keep Chaney in town, but to provoke his flight to Oregon. Flora Wellman continued to give her lessons in music and lectures on spiritualism, supported by public sympathy and curiosity. On January 12, 1876, she gave birth to a boy, who was given the name of John Chaney.

JACK

1

LOST BOYHOOD

I never had a boyhood and I seem
to be hunting for that lost boyhood.

JACK LONDON

A small boy of three sat alone in a room of a house behind a grocery
store in Oakland. There was the sound of blows from the yard.
People were beating carpets out there. The small boy was afraid of
being alone, he was afraid of the noise, he was afraid of the evening
and the light going out of the room. Then the noise stopped and
the people went away and he was wholly alone. He was full of
primitive fears.

Later he sat in the still warm kitchen of the house. There was
another noise. The flies were buzzing, trapped against the window.
The small boy had a feeling of terrible calamity.[1]*

The child was called John Griffith London. One of the reasons
he often felt afraid was that his mother Flora hardly ever touched
him. She was always busy. She made up in energy what she lacked
in inches. Dwarfish and blinking through round glasses, she scur-
ried from a music lesson to a spiritualist séance to a scheme for
getting rich quickly and poor surely. The impatience of the new
Californians, the dream of instant wealth drove her. They would be
rich soon, but for the moment, they must scrounge and scrape and
save, they must eat off newspapers and count the pennies until they

*Notes begin on page 257.

1

had hoarded enough to invest in something which would make their fortune.

The small boy watched his small mother, too busy for him, too determined to succeed, slowly becoming bitter and bent as failure dragged down the golden dream. She often complained of heart trouble; she pretended she was dying when she was thwarted. Usually angry and melancholy and preoccupied at the same time, she ruled the home through her hysteria. Her small son shrank from her tantrums as from unforgotten blows.

The man the boy believed to be his father, John London, was kind—very kind. His health was not good, because he had suffered from lung trouble since the Civil War. Yet this huge, bearded man was willing to work when he could. He had been a farmer and an Indian fighter across the west, a carpenter and a sewing machine salesman in San Francisco. He had married once before and had been widowed. His five elder children had been left in Iowa with neighbors, but he had kept with him the two youngest, Eliza and Ida. He had married Flora Wellman eight months after her son's birth and had given the boy his name—the boy was always called Jack to distinguish him from his stepfather. When diphtheria nearly killed Eliza and Jack in their slum apartment in San Francisco, John London had taken his household across the Bay to West Oakland, away from disease and gossip about his wife. He ran a grocery store there and was working a small holding. At the time of Jack's first memories, the family was at last beginning to thrive.

If the small boy was sometimes afraid, he was not wholly deprived of love. Eliza was already nine years old, and she mothered him and her younger sister. Because her stepmother was so busy with music lessons and séances, Eliza had to mind Jack and help in the household as soon as school was over for the day. When the little boy was four, she was even allowed to take him to school with her, because there was nowhere else to leave him. He sat with his picture books in a box in front of the other children, trying to understand the words. His ambitious mother may have neglected his yearnings but not his education. If she could not succeed, he must. She herself had come from a wealthy home in Ohio, and she

Flora Wellman, Jack London's mother.

John London, the stepfather who gave Jack London his name.

resented her slow descent into poverty. Education was the way up, so she taught the little boy to read.

Mother love had come from his black wet-nurse, Virginia Prentiss, a woman who had two little children of her own. She had brought him up through his babyhood when his mother had neglected him, and she loved him as if he were her own golden-haired child. Whenever Flora could not cope with him, she left the boy with "Mammy Jennie," who even moved across the Bay to Oakland to be nearer her Jack. Color-blind as children are, he saw only her warm holding arms and certain love.

His own mother taught him to feel apart from many of the other boys. She told him that he was from an old American family. He was better than the Chinese, whom the other small boys taunted in the streets. He was better than the Irish and the Italians and other people who had recently come to the United States. He had a birthright which he must defend from them.[2] He did not forget the lesson.

At the age of six, Flora put him on a table at a séance, and the table floated in the air. The other boys called his home "the spook house" because his mother screamed and war-whooped when she was possessed by her Indian control Plume.[3] He himself became nervous from her example, and the Oakland teachers found him difficult. He knew that the mothers of the other boys were not like his own. He even heard his parents arguing in the back of the grocery store about a child born out of wedlock. He did not know they were talking about him.

Not knowing the source of his sense of loss, he confused his hunger for his mother's love with a hunger for food. He became avid for meat. Although the family was not rich, there was a fair amount of steak to eat, as well as vegetables and all the clams that anyone cared to dig.[4] Yet the boy's hunger without a name made him steal meat from the lunchbox of a girl at school. He was to brood about the theft all his life. He knew he was deprived of something that other children had, and he called it meat. No matter that millions of other American children were more deprived of food and security than he was and did not hold it against their parents. He always would exaggerate the hardships of his childhood to dramatize his great leap forward from his origins.

The grocery store failed. The family moved on to a 20-acre farm in Alameda, then on again to a 75-acre pasture on the bleak coast of San Mateo County. The boy began to have his first nightmares, both times when he drank too much by mistake. Once at the age of five, he was carrying beer to the men in the fields and he swallowed a bellyful of it. Once at the age of seven, he was given wine at an Italian wedding, and he could not refuse it. "I was a sick child," he wrote later,

> and, despite the terrible strain on my heart and tissues, I continually relapsed into the madness of delirium. All the contents of the terrible and horrible in my child's mind spilled out. . . . All the inconceivable filth a child running at large in a primitive countryside may hear men utter was mine. . . . My brain was seared for ever by that experience. Writing now, thirty years afterwards, every vision is as distinct, as sharp-cut, every pain as vital and terrible.[5]

Living on the barren land seemed a sad business to the boy after the playground of the city. It was a long walk to the schoolhouse on top of the hill at Colma, and there was the stock to feed. Often the days were fogbound from the sea mist, yet freedom also lay toward the Bay. When John London had the time, he took his seven-year-old stepson to collect clams and mussels from the marshy shore, and to watch the duck fly away across the salt water. Eliza remembered Jack as a good and healthy child at the time, who found his idol in her father, yet had a sensitivity that showed in his soft mouth and made him cry when he was frustrated.

The farmhouse at San Mateo was no more a home than any of the other places in San Francisco and Oakland and Alameda. The family moved on to its grandest dream, a small ranch in the Livermore Valley. There, John London tried to become an independent farmer with an orchard and new barns for his horses, with incubators for chickens and coops for laying hens. He mortgaged his land to pay for all these improvements in the hope of quick profits, for Flora had arranged to sell the chickens and the eggs to a hotel in

San Francisco. All prospered briefly, or waited for calamity.

The boy found himself in a burning valley without friends of his own age. He withdrew more and more into an imaginary world of dime novels and romantic history. From the dime novels he developed an appetite for fantasies of adventure and villainy, of bold strong men and remote beautiful women. There was also the bright vision of Ouida's novel *Signa,* the first book he owned. He had found it by the roadside with its last forty pages missing, and he read it again and again. Ouida told of the illegitimate child of a peasant girl and an artist, who dreamed of escaping from the drudgery of Italian village life through his skill on his violin, until eventually he became a great composer. Jack on the Livermore ranch dreamed of the same escape. Ouida's novel, he later wrote, was the star to which he hitched his child's wagon.[6]

The other book that dominated his imagination was borrowed from school. It was Washington Irving's *Alhambra.* Jack built in the dust of the ranch a miniature Moorish palace from fallen chimney bricks and plaster and beads, and he wept all the way home from school when he returned his copy of *Alhambra* and was not given another book to replace it. The African adventures of Paul du Chaillu and a life of Garfield, *From Canal Boy to President,* also inspired him to visions of travel and success . . . the usual ambitions of an American child.

But his was a tumbleweed family, blowing with the winds of failure, and when he was ten years old, the little world of the ranch ended as all his little worlds had ended. Eliza had had enough of being the slave of the household, and at sixteen she married an elderly widower with several children of his own, Captain James H. Shepard. She could not take Jack with her, so he lost the chief support and comfort of his life. With Eliza gone, there was no one to do the hard work in the ranchhouse, the chickens died of an epidemic, the bank called in the mortgage. Once again Flora's hopes of a quick fortune had encouraged overexpansion and disaster. Defeated, the family returned to an eight-room home in Oakland, which Flora ran as a boardinghouse. Her husband went back to the vegetable trade, fell ill, grew older, and ended up as a night watchman and a special constable on the docks.

Jack at the age of ten with his dog Rollo. He gave this portrait to his stepsister Eliza on her birthday.

The boy was again on his own, back near the raw waterfront and San Francisco Bay. He had no relief from his sensitivities or his nightmares now. He must put on a bold face, earn his keep, learn an inner reticence, repel intruders, hide a sense of difference. One of the earliest photographs of him showed him already dressed like a young workingman. With his faithful dog Rollo by his side, he proudly wore one of his first store-bought shirts. Suspenders kept up his trousers and his blond curls were slicked down onto his skull. His body was sturdy and well nourished, his mouth open and loose, the eyes in his square face staring lopsided and intent into the camera. He looked like any strong child from the Oakland high schools, which were rough and mauling places. His classmates were "pretty tough kids," one of his schoolmates wrote later, "who would have shied a brick at any long-nose who might have suggested we write or draw."[7]

At school he was sometimes aggressive and rebellious, for formal education seemed to bore him. Yet he fought only when he was attacked. He made his first friend at the time, Frank Atherton, who was impressed that Jack was so well organized. He had a paper route morning and evening, and he gave his mother the $3 a month that he earned. He worked on an ice wagon and in a bowling alley for his pocket money. He insisted on taking out two books a week from the Oakland Public Library, and he concentrated on reading them rather than playing. He was a methodical and stubborn boy with a private world which he defended fiercely.[8]

Part of his defensiveness was due to knowing that he was badly dressed and lived in the slum area of Oakland. He could not even attend the graduation ceremony at the Cole School because he did not have a suit to wear, and he had to leave school at thirteen because his mother had ruined them again by a speculation in real estate. His family was slipping even further down the social scale. They moved into a ramshackle house by the estuary. Jack felt obliged to go to work in a cannery for fourteen hours a day at a wage of 10 cents an hour. He gave all his earnings to his mother.

At this point, Jack could see no future for himself or his dreams. He had fallen into the trap of duty and obligation. It was the trap that keeps children going to school because they think that all children go to school, so therefore they must. It was the trap of expectation and gratitude, that because parents have paid for a child, the child should pay back the parents. Jack toiled at the cannery and hated the loud machines, the interminable repetition of his movements. "I was up and at work at six in the morning," he raged later to his first love.

> I took half an hour for dinner. I took half an hour for supper. I worked every night till ten, eleven and twelve o'clock. My wages were small, but I worked such long hours that I sometimes made as high as fifty dollars a month. Duty—I turned every cent over. Duty —I have worked in that hell hole for thirty-six straight hours, at a machine, and I was only a child. I remember how I was trying to save the money to buy a skiff—eight dollars. All that summer I saved and scraped. In the fall I had five dollars as a result of absolutely doing without all pleasure. My mother came to the machine where I worked and asked for it. I could have killed myself that night. After a year of hell to have that pitiful—to be robbed of that petty joy.[9]

His stepfather had been too weak, his mother too remote and hysterical, to bind the boy with a sense of duty for long. They had taught him rootlessness by their own moving from place to place, they had taught him recklessness by their contradictory scrimping and waste of their petty resources. By hard trading with the Oakland junk dealers, he saved enough to buy an old center-board skiff. He threw in the job at the cannery, and spent nearly all his time sailing on the bright treacherous seas of San Francisco Bay. His happiest hours as a child had been with John London, rowing and fishing in the vast sea-shell of the waters pent within the inlet through the Golden Gate. Now he taught himself to sail dangerously on the choppy and foggy waters, crashing the rollers made by the sidewheel steamers, beating against the wind to Goat Island, yearning at the clippers that tacked toward the west and the other side of the world.

"What do I want?" the boy asked in Jack's later novel, *The Valley of the Moon,* as he looked past Alcatraz to the Golden Gate.

Jack as a youth in his delinquent days.

Don't you sometimes feel you'd die if you didn't know what's beyond them hills an' what's beyond the other hills behind them hills? An' the Golden Gate! There's the Pacific Ocean beyond, and China, an' Japan, an' India, an' . . . an' all the coral islands. You can go anywhere out through the Golden Gate—to Australia, to Africa, to the seal islands, to the North Pole, to Cape Horn. Why, all them places are just waitin' for me to come an' see 'em. I've lived in Oakland all my life, but I'm not going to live in Oakland the rest of my life, not by a long shot. I'm goin' to get away . . . away. . . .[10]

As John London's strength and purpose failed, as Jack became the stronger of the two, he turned into a delinquent. Petty crime was the obvious way for him to make money. It was not a much worse way than the petty business and sharp dealing that had so often ruined his mother. "Begin at the beginning," he wrote later in notes for his autobiography. "How loneliness made him observant and perceptive. How he wanted to be good; not to swear, not to do this, not to do that. How he became a miserly collector, and first went oyster-pirating, and had to drink beer when he wanted candy, and then turned over to a wastrel. Plastic, fluid, flowed into any environment."[11] It was a true enough self-analysis of the youth, still wanting to be a child loved by his family, but ready to be molded and finding the mold at home cracked and cold. Also true was the remembrance of the child with his avid appetite for candy hiding inside the young man who had to play the drunken bully to impress the waterfront.

So Jack at fifteen became a rebel against everything he had been taught. He was "a pretty good boy when you come to figure it all out," his mother later told an Oakland reporter, "but he fell in with bad company. He used to have terrible fights with the boys of the neighborhood. He got to going down to the waterfront. He became awfully bossy in the house. We couldn't stand him sometimes."[12]

Flora London did not recognize or admit a growing cause of her son's resentment. His younger stepsister Ida had also left home to marry as soon as she was old enough, but because she could not support her child, Johnny Miller, she left him more and more with

Flora, who lavished on Johnny all the love she had withheld from Jack. Jealous and bitter, her own son stayed on the waterfront, struggling and surviving through his fists and cunning.

Later, Jack never wished to talk of his sense of betrayal at home, so he made a dime novel adventure out of his delinquent days. A children's book, *The Cruise of the Dazzler,* and his confession of his drinking in *John Barleycorn,* are the only records of this time. According to them, he borrowed $300 from Mammy Jennie to buy a sloop, the *Razzle Dazzle.* With the sloop went an oyster-pirate's girl called Mamie, won from the jealous French Frank by Jack's good looks and held by Jack steering the sloop with his feet, a loaded shotgun in his hands to keep off his rival's boat. Thus he became "the Prince of the Oyster Beds" when he was only sixteen, the fearless looter of the guarded preserves controlled by the big companies. He was also the most open-handed of the drinkers at Johnny Heinold's First and Last Chance Saloon, the leading buccaneer and fighter and carouser of the Oakland wharf. Mammy Jennie was soon repaid; Flora and his stepfather were supported in style. After the *Razzle Dazzle* was burned by rivals, Jack teamed up with a blond Viking, Young Scratch Nelson, and sailed on more perilous raids of piracy against the inoffensive oysters. Only once did the backwash of a debauch craze the young man enough to make him decide to drown himself, slipping away on the tide through the Carquinez Straits until he sobered in the dawn and was saved from his suicidal folly by a Greek fisherman.

This was the myth Jack recorded about his waterfront days; but there was too much of Paul Bunyan and boys' romance in the tale. Jack certainly knew how to tell a good story at the bar of the First and Last Chance Saloon. He was not so much a liar as an improver upon the truth, the heir of Mark Twain and Bret Harte and the frontier tradition, which held that the story of a stranger should never deny the pleasure of others for the sake of the facts. Boasting of his fantastic exploits was a man's job in the west. So was hard bargaining, treating to drinks, lethal practical jokes, false praise of the fair sex, and an absolute belief that the white man could outfight and outsmart any lesser breed.

The truth of the waterfront days was that Jack was briefly lucky as a thief on his sloop, then so unlucky as to lose his boat because of the cutthroat competition of his rivals. After that, drink and fighting nearly killed him off, as they killed off most of the dockside gangs. Fortunately, he was ready to revert to his conscience when that suited his convenience. He joined the Fish Patrol, set up to catch the pirates he knew so well. Blithely he decided to use the law on his rivals instead of lawlessness. It was the other side of the same coin. Adventure was all.

Jack was to make another book and myth out of his days with the Fish Patrol, writing in the first person of taking "the swart Mongols" from their junks back to jail on the *Reindeer* with a pistol in his hand, or running down the murderous King of the Greeks with his illegal sturgeon-fishing line with its thousand hooks, or catching thirty oyster-pirates at a time by stranding them on a shoal, or using a steamer to tow ten Greek fishing boats with their unlawful gill-nets upriver to the sheriff. *Tales of the Fish Patrol* are the only record of those days, and they were written for the *Youth's Companion* as a serial for boys. Jack later admitted privately that the sole weapon he had carried with him was a table fork, and he had had to use it only once to keep off an amorous Greek sailor.[13]

He had realized the influence he had over people and his dangerous power of persuasion. Without the public library and his love of books, his future seemed to lie in being a gang leader. Yet the possibilities of the world were opening in front of him. America began to call its footloose child. He teamed up with the Road Kids —the gangs of homeless boys who lived like young wolves. They hunted in a pack and dragged down their victims in a rush. Jack learned from them how to beg, how to steal and roll workingmen for their money, clothes, and boots. He called himself 'Frisco Kid and jumped the freight trains, riding the rods up to the Sierras, and living free and wild and perilous.

It was still aimless delinquency. When a last drunken night after an election rally nearly killed him, he decided that he must get away. His friends on the waterfront were all on the death road, moving quickly or slowly. His family disapproved of his rebellion.

The harshness of existence was crippling his imagination just as the fighting was breaking his knuckles and the drink was gutting his body. He decided to take the other way from California. Like the boy on the skiff in *The Valley of the Moon,* he could point to the further west and say, "Oakland's just a place to start from, I guess." Eight days after his seventeenth birthday, he signed as an able seaman on a three-masted schooner of some 150 tons, the *Sophia Sutherland.* The ship was bound for Japan and the Bering Sea on a sealing expedition. Oakland was just a place to start from, he guessed.

At the time he sailed, there seemed to be little special about Jack except for his physical presence, his conviction that somewhere there was a way for him and a better place to be. He was bursting with potential, but in the raw mess of the new town of Oakland nothing was further from achievement than potential. He was distinguished in only a few ways from the violent horde of youths struggling to survive in the slums about him. He loved books and took them wherever he went, as if a string of right words might guide him through the labyrinth of his fierce desires. He was still a child in his appetites for candy and meat and instant gratification. He had never been tamed by the authority of love or fear. Yet he could pretend to self-control and obedience for a while, when he needed to hide his inner sense of his own superiority.

His very sociability was a disguise for his feeling of isolation. He was easy with groups of men because they obscured his private self. He could seek, but never find, the love of the mother he desired and denied. Yet he could not avoid her. She had given him her ambition and her urgency, her unbalance and her nightmares. Either he must get on in life or move away from her.

LAWLESS AS SNOW-FLAKES

The friendly and flowing savage, who is he?
Is he waiting for civilization, or past it and mastering it?

. . . Is he from the Mississippi country? Iowa, Oregon, California?
The mountains? prairie-life? bush-life? or sailor from the sea?
Wherever he goes men and women accept and desire him,
They desire he should like them, touch them, speak to them,
stay with them.

Behavior lawless as snow-flakes, words simple as grass,
uncomb'd head, laughter, and naïveté,
Slow-stepping feet, common features, common modes and emanations,
They descend in new forms from the tips of his fingers . . .

WALT WHITMAN

Jack had no experience as a seaman. He had only been a small-boat sailor. All the same, he learned as quickly as a fish on the water. He was pleasant and ready to obey orders, and he made discipline seem easy to bear. If another sailor attacked him, he fought back with his quick, small fists. If he was not tall—only 5 feet 7 inches in height —he had broad shoulders and hit hard. He fitted well in the cliques and divisions of the packed forecastle, split between the Irish and the Scandinavians. He took two of the younger Vikings as his mates, but he also cleared a small space around himself for his reading. He was at his books as often as he was able, keeping the oil lamp burning through the nights. When the despised and complaining cockney called the Bricklayer died in a storm, Jack took over the dead man's bunk, ignoring the superstition of the other sailors. The bunk was nearer the light, and he could read more, even if he was haunted by the memory of the badly weighted corpse of the Bricklayer bobbing on wave after wave in the wake of the ship, unable to sink and lie down in the deep.[1]

He was given the wheel on the voyage to the Bonin Islands. A storm was blowing, and he learned to battle against nature. His veins swelled to the surge of power that comes from the struggle, his mind delighted in mastery of the elements. "In my grasp the wildly careering schooner and the lives of twenty-two men," he wrote later.

> With my own hands I had done my trick at the wheel and guided a hundred tons of wood and iron through a few million tons of wind and waves. . . . When I have done some such thing, I am exalted. I glow all over. I am aware of a pride in myself that is mine, and mine alone. It is organic. Every fibre of me is thrilling with it. It is very natural. It is a mere matter of satisfaction at adjustment to environment. It is success.[2]

It was the first success for a young man used to failure. He was proud of being a sailor among sailors, and he caroused like a sailor among sailors when the *Sophia Sutherland* put in at the Bonin Islands for ten days. He survived the debauch and dried out on the voyage to Siberian waters to hunt the seal herds. Then the bloody business began, month after month of killing and stripping the skins and flinging the carcasses to the sharks that followed the boats for their share of the massacre.

"It was wanton slaughter, and all for woman's sake," Jack was to write in *The Sea-Wolf.*

> No man ate of the seal meat or the oil. After a good day's killing I have seen our decks covered with hides and bodies, slippery with fat and blood, the scuppers running red; masts, ropes, and rails spattered with the sanguinary color; and the men, like butchers plying their trade, naked and red of arm and hand, hard at work with ripping and flensing knives, removing the skins from the pretty sea creatures they had killed.[3]

This wholesale murder, this daily slaughterhouse was the young sailor's first sight of nature red in tooth and claw. The men were more bestial than the beasts they killed. It was a crude commercial struggle to survive, dictated by the market in furs. Jack began to see that the struggle to live among humans was part of the struggle to live among animals. The men got the wages, the captain took the profits, the women wore the furs, the sharks devoured the meat, the herds of seals suffered. He began to understand the connection between nature, man, and the market before reading Darwin or Marx. His memory recorded as his body and his hands toughened. After a hundred days of the killing and the laying away of the pelts, the *Sophia Sutherland* put back for a last debauch in Yokohama. Jack survived that drinking bout, too, swimming back to his ship at night while the police looked for his drowned body. On the long voyage home, he nearly died of an attack of shingles. It was the first time his splendid body had let him down, and he did not like to admit to it. When the *Sophia Sutherland* docked in San Francisco, he was well enough to treat his shipmates to one round of drinks before slipping across the Bay to see his family with some of his wages still left in his pocket. The sea might be his escape, but he would not make it his life. It did not appease his hunger.

When he reached home, he thought of writing of his experiences, and he was soon fortunate. The San Francisco *Morning Call* announced a competition for a descriptive sketch written by a young reader. Jack's mother was so proud to see her wandering son at work at an old typewriter that she herself took his story to the newspaper office to meet the deadline. The sketch won the first prize of $25, even though it was full of literary effects, with the spray like molten silver, the yawning precipices of water, the forecastle as dark as Erebus. Yet Jack was obviously a born narrator, and the story drove forward through the sudden return of the seal-boats in a snowstorm and the death of the Bricklayer under the fitful glow of the oil lamps.[4]

This lucky success began to change the relationship of mother and son. She saw in him the instrument of her ambition. If he became a writer, she might rise with him back to the comfort and position of her youth, so treasured and so long lost. Yet there was little time for his writing now. John London's health was failing, Jack's sailor's wages had only paid the family debts and left him enough for some second-hand clothes, the prize money was spent almost before it was received. Now secure in his mother's approval, he was ready to accept her standards. He would work his way up like a good American boy and support the household. He found a job in a jute mill, making burlap on a ten-hour shift for $1 a day. He was earning no more than he had at the age of fourteen. It was a time of international slump and depression, as he read in the newspapers. The employers could cut wages and break strikes without difficulty. When a man walked off his job, two pressed forward to take his place.

Jack was glad to find any work at all in 1893. He still believed in the inspirational world of Horatio Alger, that a canal or water-front boy could rise to be President. By hard work, he wanted to make himself part of the aristocracy of the working class on his way to riches. He became the friend of a young blacksmith's apprentice called Louis Shattuck, and he went courting. The young sailor with his rolling walk and his tam-o'-shanter and his golden grin was successful with the factory girls, particularly with one named Lizzie Connolly, who gave her fellow her cameo ring. He ate taffy and red-hots all the time, claiming that the candy was a substitute for the beer he could not afford.

He became thrifty again, following his mother's example. The few dimes he could spare from his pay were spent on double dates with Louis at Blair's Park, where the balloons went up on Sundays, and two ice creams cost 30 cents, two tamales only 20. The free-spending days of the oyster-pirate and the sailor were over, the miserly days of the newsboy were back. He tried to step over the barrier that seemed to stand between girls of his own sort like Lizzie and the unapproachable maidens of the middle class and dime novels. At a Salvation Army meeting he fell in calf-love with a fifteen-year-old girl. He was to call her Haydee in *John Barleycorn,* and he described her slender oval face, beautiful brown eyes, and mouth hinting of petulance. "Never did girl have more innocent boy-lover than I who had been so wicked-wise and violent beyond my years." It was weeks before he kissed her on a park bench. Only once in a year of trying to be good did a waterfront woman take him back for a night of the "old sad savagery."5

He was so determined to become the respectable workingman his mother wanted him to be that he aspired to learn a trade. The jute mills had not raised his pay as agreed; the lint from the burlap was choking his lungs; he decided to become an electrician. He thought he would learn on the job, as he did not believe much in technical schools. He was a practical man in a practical world, in his opinion. So, ripe for exploitation, he presented himself to an electrical company. He was set to work as a cleaner in the engine room. Soon he was promoted to shoveling coal for the boilers. He was young and strong, but the dirty work nearly broke him. His wrists were so swollen that he had to wear leather straps to support them. His determination kept him heaving coal beyond his strength.

Later, he was told that he was doing two men's work as a scab. For his pay of $30 a month, he was saving the management the wages of two workers, each of whom had been getting $40 a month. His grit and sweat meant $50 a month saved for the company. It was Jack's first lesson in practical socialism. He was indignant, but as he was a proud American boy, he did not walk off the job until the evening after he had heard the truth. Fortunately, he had not labored long enough to cripple his body, only to mutilate his childish myth of success through hard work. He never learned to be an electrician, merely to be a coal-heaver.

Sickened by this work orgy, Jack escaped again. He had exhausted himself, he needed to renew his body in the pursuit of liberty. An army of sorts was leaving Oakland in the spring of 1894. It was made up of 2,000 militant men who were out of work. They were loosely grouped under the leadership of a man called Kelly, who styled himself a general. They wanted to join up with Jacob Coxey's army of the unemployed, which was marching on Washington to protest the lack of jobs and to seek the Commonweal of Christ. This movement proved what the Socialists already knew to be true, that the new millions of tramps riding the freight cars and living in hobo jungles were not idle men, but workless men. They were forced to move to find a job. The seasonal demands of agriculture and industry required a huge pool of the unemployed. Many wanted work and could only get it from time to time. So they migrated in want and hope.

The frightened citizens of Oakland ran Kelly's army out of the city in boxcars during the night. Left behind, Jack and a friend paid the fare on a train to Sacramento the next morning. Then they began jumping the overland freight cars bound for the east. Jack started to keep a diary for the first time in his life. It served as the notes for the first major work on tramping in American literature, *The Road.* In that later serial for the Hearst newspapers, Jack wrote that he did not become a tramp to study sociology, but to satisfy his wanderlust. Like any modern beat or hippie kid, he went on the road because he could not keep away from it; because he had not got the price of the fare in his jeans; because he was so made that he could not work all his life on one same shift; "because—well, just because it was easier to than not to."[6]

His diary told of him holding down the train to Truckee and sending back his suitcase by Wells Fargo to Oakland. Sidetracked on the next freight to Reno, he watched the Indians gambling and listened to the Salvation Army and the unemployed talking on the street corners. A new detachment was being formed to chase after Kelly's army, which had already moved on. Jack's face was so peeled by the sun that it looked as if he had fallen in a fire, while the nights were so cold that he froze. Scores of people were going east as he was; only one man was going west. At last, he caught a freight out of Reno to Humboldt, then he rode the bumpers on another special to Winnemucca. Unfortunately, a spark from the engine set fire to his overcoat and jacket; both were ruined before he could put out the flames.

At Winnemucca, his friend turned back while Jack went on. The reasons he recorded for the parting were boyish. They showed him still determined to be middle class in his values. The road had no more charms for his friend.

The romance and adventure is gone and nothing remains but the stern reality of the hardships to be endured. Though he has decided to turn West again I am sure the experience has done him good, broadened his thoughts, given a better understanding of the low strata of society and surely will have made him more charitable to the tramps he will meet hereafter when he is in better circumstances.

That night, Jack continued jumping the overland freight trains to catch up with Kelly's army. He had to surrender the cameo ring which Lizzie Connolly had given him, because a conductor and a brakeman demanded a bribe for letting him ride the freight. He reached Ogden, Utah, with $2 still left in his pocket, then beat in a blind baggage car to Evanston, Wyoming, and on to Rock Springs. That town seemed to him to be the "wild and woolly west with a vengeance. The soldiers, miners, and cowboys all seem to be on the rampage." On through Laramie and a blizzard until he caught up with the Reno detachment of Kelly's army in a refrigerator car in Grand Island, Nebraska, where he was served with breakfast and a good dinner. The townspeople were both sympathetic and scared of the traveling workingmen, so they provided food and policemen to help them on their way.

In Iowa, Camp Kelly had been set up in the Chatauqua Park of Council Bluffs to serve as a cachement for the army. Jack was assigned to a company, but he found the marching wearisome, particularly as his shoes had worn out and he was helping a sick man along the way. Kelly himself rode a fine black horse, being a general; Jack was barefoot and scarcely able to walk. He hitched a ride on one of the twelve commissary wagons and bummed a pair of boots, for he had discovered that "the fat cats" were the people who collected and distributed the food to the army. Although there were sing-songs nearly every night on the way south, the discipline of the ragged men was falling apart. "All along the line it resembled a rout or retreat."

At Des Moines, he bluffed his way onto one of the leading flatboats which were floating the army downstream. It usually tied up first at the end of the day, attracting most of the food begged from the people on shore. Jack and his companions on the flatboat did not turn over these supplies to the commissary, and they ate well at the expense of the army. They were in danger of a kangaroo court-martial by the time they reached Mark Twain's home town of Hannibal, Missouri. Like Huckleberry Finn, Jack went supper-less to bed on May 24 in his camp on an island on the Illinois side of the Mississippi. And like Huckleberry Finn, he decided to pull out in the morning. His words were: "I can't stand starvation."

Abandoning Kelly's army, which would disband when Jacob Coxey was arrested in Washington, Jack beat his way on the rail-roads to Chicago. There he found $4 from his mother waiting for him at the post office. He bought a new outfit and visited the World's Fair. Then he took a ship to the other side of Lake Michi-gan, where his aunt Mary gave him a hearty welcome and he met a cousin called Ernest Everhard. There his tramp's diary ended, almost bare of social comment, the mere record of some wandering weeks.[7]

So far, his days on the road were random and aimless and innocent, as lawless as snowflakes. He deserted the cause of the workingman when he found the food short and the march no longer a jaunt. But he had heard the talk by the campfires. The words of socialism had become familiar, although they meant little to him. He was too preoccupied with his own wants to see a pattern in society, for he had not yet felt personal oppression.

He soon did. Until now, his war with authority had been a game. He had looted orchards and oyster beds, and he had run away from furious owners and patrolmen. He had ridden the rods, playing games with the railroad bulls who tried to pull him off the trains. But he heard now of vindictive brakemen who killed road kids by bouncing a coupling pin on a chain up from the rails against the body clinging to the rods under the boxcars. He learned of the murders done by Pinkerton detectives and strikebreakers. He him-self met with random violence in New York City, when a police-man bloodied his head just because he looked shabby and was holding a book. He learned to avoid the law, because it carried a club.

Finally, he suffered from the injustice of the law. He was arrested for vagrancy in Buffalo after visiting Niagara Falls. He knew the reason for it. When John London had been a special constable in Oakland, he had lived on the fees paid him for arresting tramps. Now Jack was given thirty days in jail, and was cut off by the judge in mid-sentence as he tried to speak up for his rights as an American citizen. Once in jail, he found himself in a nightmare more terrible than any of his dreams. Later, in *The Road,* he would refuse to describe in detail what happened to him in the penitentiary. He would not deal with the sexual side of life as a tramp, although he would dedicate *The Road* to Josiah Flynt, "the real thing blowed in the glass."

Flynt did describe the underside of tramp society in an article for a book by Havelock Ellis, which Jack later bought for his library. Flynt declared that about 1 in 10 of the 60,000 professional tramps was an invert. Such a man would pick up a slum boy between the ages of ten and fifteen, then seduce him into traveling the road as a virtual slave. These boys were called "prushuns," their masters "jockers."[8] In the chapter in *The Road* on "Road-Kids and Gay-Cats," Jack London was careful to state, "I was never a prushun, for I did not take kindly to possession. I was first a road-kid and then a profesh. . . . And be it known, here and now, that the profesh are the aristocracy of The Road. They are the lords and masters, the aggressive men, the primordial noblemen, the *blond beasts. . . .*"[9]

In his eight months as a tramp, Flynt had seen some bestial scenes, including the gang rape of a black boy in a freight car. He claimed that the inversion of the "jockers" was largely due to the absence of women on the road. In jails, the situation was even worse.

> In the day-time the prisoners are let out into a long hall, and can do much as they please; at night they are shut up, two and even four in a cell. If there are any boys in the crowd, they are made use of by all who care to have them. If they refuse to submit, they are gagged and held down. The sheriff seldom knows what goes on, and for the boys to say anything to him would be suicidal.

Jack was no longer a boy when he was put in jail, but he was a good-looking young man of eighteen. He cleverly made up to an old prison hand on the way to jail, a squat and powerful man with kind eyes, although Jack also saw in him a brute-beast, wholly amoral. He was Jack's "meat" and Jack held on to him avidly. This old lag had Jack made a hall man within the jail in two days, one of the thirteen hall men who dominated and exploited the other 500 prisoners. They were the privileged trusties of the system, the middlemen between the warders and the convicts. They ruled by fear, the fist, and the club.

As he had the run of the prison, Jack saw the intolerable excesses of the jail. "They were unthinkable to me until I saw them," he affirmed in *The Road,*

> and I was no spring chicken in the ways of the world and the awful abysses of human degradation. It would take a deep plummet to reach bottom in the Erie County Pen . . . filled with the ruck and the filth, the scum and the dregs, of society—hereditary inefficients, degenerates, wrecks, lunatics, addled intelligences, epileptics, monsters, weaklings, in short, a very nightmare of humanity.[10]

Desperate to stay apart from these horrors of the flesh, Jack joined the oppressors to survive with the fittest. He watched a handsome young mulatto thrown down five flights of steel stairs because he had stood up for his rights. Jack did not intervene. He only wished to get out of jail without injury. He did so, protected by his pal and his physique. Once outside, he knew his pal expected him to join in a life of petty crime and the intimacy of two on the road. He jumped the first freight train alone and got away. He beat back across Canada and regained his home in Oakland. He had learned, as a sailor and a tramp and a prisoner, to be tolerant of homosexuality; but he remained a woman's man and never seems to have slept voluntarily with men.[11]

Economically as well as sexually, Jack's jail experience taught him about the viciousness of trying to survive among the degraded. He had been a middleman like any petty capitalist, taking commissions on the trading between the convicts, ruling by fear and hard dealing. When he later became friendly with the hobo Socialist orator Frank Strawn-Hamilton, he would plan to construct a book round their tramping experiences. In his notes for the work, he would see in the Erie County Penitentiary the microcosm of racism and capitalism. He would want to show "how white tramps, trusties, kept the negroes in subjection. The whole Buffalo situation, described analytically, made into generalizations. Particularly describe the hall-men, tramps, they were virtually masters."[12] For them, the easy times; for them, the making of money.

Jack would never bring himself to write that book or the truth of his experiences on the road. He preferred to present those times in tales of adventure, only hinting at the horrors and the vices. The best of his future Socialist lectures, however, would deal with the subject of "The Tramp" in order to prove that the vagrant hordes of hoboes and discharged criminals were necessary to society. The road was one of the vents through which the waste of the social organism was given off. The unfit were eliminated because they could not breed. Sterility was the tramp's fate as it was the prostitute's. "They might have been mates, but society has decreed otherwise." While it was not nice that these people should die, they must die out. And the tramp must not be blamed for who he was. "As the scapegoat to our economic and industrial sinning, or to the plan of things, if you will, we should give him credit. Let us be just. He is so made. Society made him. He did not make himself."[13]

Even though it was Jack's own whim of iron that had made him into a tramp and he could choose to return to his home and education, he perceived that the degradation of the jailbirds was not always their fault. Some were born failures, but some were the victims of exploitation or bad luck. Among the hoboes on the road and the scum in jail, he had found all sorts of men. Many of them had been just as good as he was, "and just as *blond-beastly;* sailor-men, soldier-men, labor-men, all wrenched and distorted and twisted out of shape by toil and hardship and accident, and cast adrift by their masters like so many old horses." He had begged and slammed back gates with them, or shivered with them in boxcars and city parks, listening to life histories which began as well as his. Their digestions and bodies might be even better than his, and yet they ended before his eyes in the shambles at the bottom of the Social Pit.

This basic inability of the physically strong to control their own destiny began to change Jack into a Socialist, of his own special persuasion. The nightmare that he had seen in fact turned him toward radicalism. Since his delirium of a wine-dream at the age of seven, he had imagined himself "immured in madhouses . . . beaten by keepers, and surrounded by screeching lunatics."[14] Yet these were only nightmares. In Erie County Penitentiary, he had seen worse things than he had ever imagined. He had indeed been immured in a madhouse. He had watched keepers beat and mutilate innocent victims. The dregs of society had screeched insanely around him. He must never return to the evil dream that was the end of the road. Never, never, never, never, never.

3

A FRANTIC PURSUIT
OF KNOWLEDGE

I had been in the cellar of society, and I did not like the place as a habitation. The pipes and drains were unsanitary, and the air was bad to breathe. If I could not live on the parlor floor of society, I could, at any rate, have a try at the attic. It was true, the diet there was slim, but the air at least was pure. So I resolved to sell no more muscle, and to become a vender of brains.

Then began a frantic pursuit of knowledge. I returned to California and opened the books. . . . Other and greater minds, before I was born, had worked out all that I had thought, and a vast deal more. I discovered that I was a Socialist.

JACK LONDON

If Flora had denied her son her love when he was a child, she repaid him when he came home from the road to study in earnest. She had given up her tantrums and accepted failure, settling down into a dour persistence at making ends meet. Her small figure was stooped and thickish, her hands out of shape. Yet she gladly gave her son a room at the back of the cottage in Oakland, when he went back to high school. He had dropped out of the educational system for six years, and he intended to make up that lost time in two. He attached himself to a program of study as if it were a lifeline, working nineteen hours a day in his room, which was just big enough to hold his bed and work table and shelves for his books. He was so quiet and his reading light burned so late through the nights that some of his neighbors thought his mother had set out a lamp to guide her wandering boy home.

At the local high school, Jack at nineteen found himself in a class of sixteen-year-old boys and girls, the only one among the boys who wore long trousers. They seemed so young to him that he felt he was in a kindergarten. One of his schoolmates remembered him as unbelievably shabby and careless, in an old blue suit, wrinkled and ill-fitting, his face ruddy and sunburned, his tawny and disheveled hair looking as though he constantly ran his fingers through it. He chewed tobacco to stop the pain of his rotten teeth until his stepsister Eliza bought him his first toothbrush, sent him to the dentist, and paid for a plate to hide his missing front teeth. The other students found him distant and unapproachable, and their fear of him increased his own sense of isolation. He was crippled with shyness and spoke his answers to the teacher in such a low voice that he could hardly be heard. He fled from the children in the classroom the moment the lesson was finished, reaching into his pocket for his shabby cap and leaving the room in a rush, swinging his arms as though to increase his speed.[1]

In fact, he was swinging his arms to hide his sailor's roll. He was trying to stop his shoulders swaying by developing a short, quick step. Once again he was determined to learn manners and rise from the working class. Although he had the frame of a man, he was still at the social stage of the adolescent; terrified of choosing the wrong knife and fork when invited out; scared of using a swearword to an educated girl; aware to an unusual degree of his defects in breeding and education. Yet he had all the enthusiasm of a young man and the belief that enough energy, willpower, and application could remedy every lack.

His year at high school passed conventionally enough. He took an A in English and B's in French, history, and mathematics, his weakest subject. Although he had to act as a janitor in the school building to earn his pocket money, he was not spending much. He had given up drinking altogether, only going into Johnny Heinold's First and Last Chance Saloon to raise a small loan from time to time. Eliza had trained herself to work with her elderly husband as a team of pension attorneys, and could afford to buy Jack his first bicycle to get him to school and to the countryside near Oakland.

His liberation was no longer his sloop in the Bay, but "his wheels." Only the sharpest pinch of debt could make him pawn them.

Although he made no friends at the high school, he did contribute ten sketches and stories to its magazine, the *Aegis*. They were a shock to his fellow students, tales of his sealing and tramping days. He was floundering as a writer. Rudyard Kipling and Robert Louis Stevenson were his models, but he had not yet assimilated what they had to teach him. In two of the more interesting stories about 'Frisco Kid, there was something of Kipling's slang and of Mark Twain's plots and style. Just as Huckleberry Finn went off with Tom Sawyer, so did 'Frisco Kid aim to team up with the rich boy, who was eventually drowned. "Somehow, I cudn't tell why, I kinder took ter dat kid. He wuz so pritty an' innisent like, jest as if he wuz a girl." And just like Huckleberry Finn, 'Frisco Kid wanted to leave "sivilization." "I cudn't stand it no longer, so I guv me adopted parents the ditch, an' hit the road onst more."[2]

Jack's new companions were no longer oyster-pirates or blacksmith's apprentices, but young people in search of an education like himself. First of his new friends was Fred Jacobs, who worked at the public library and went to night school to prepare for the entrance examinations to the University of California. Jacobs was engaged to Bess Maddern, a plumber's daughter, who also wanted to go to college, and who made money by coaching high school pupils in grammar and algebra. Bess was a well-built girl with broad hips and dark hair and a face as handsome as a figurehead. In Jack's evolutionary terms, she was an earth mother, the backbone of the race. She did not particularly attract him; he left her to his friend.

He also grew to know Edward Applegarth and his sister Mabel. They were the children of English immigrants, a father who was a mining engineer and rarely at home, a mother whose prettiness hid a will of marble under a smile of rectitude. Jack went with Ted Applegarth to the Henry Clay Club, a debating society for high school students. He was invited frequently into the Applegarth home, where he learned about chess from the brother, and about music and poetry from the sister. He fell head over heels in love with Mabel, whose frail beauty appeared to be the dream of her favorite Victorian romantic poets in the flesh. In Jack's works, Browning and Swinburne on the bookshelves would always mean a touch of class.

Mabel Applegarth was as beautiful and superficial as a tea party in an English summer garden. Her young lover found her more refined and perfect than any girl of his fantasy, an ethereal creature with wide blue eyes, "a pale gold flower upon a slender stem."[3] She was not a heroine from Ouida, more a spirit hardly touching this earth. In return, she did not see Jack as the slovenly ogre of the classroom, but as a rough charmer and a physical danger. His adoration of her made him receptive to the lessons she gave him in English grammar, manners, and chivalry. She often felt faint or fell ill from unknown causes, and her weakness made Jack act the gentleman.

Later, to the second love of his life, he wrote of Mabel Applegarth: "Did I love her? There was no love greater, so I thought. She was more than mortal. I remember, we were eating cherries one day. Lying on my back and looking up I saw that the black juice had discolored her lips. I hailed it with delight. An omen that we were drawing closer together, that she was stripping off her immortality. . . ." Physical love and food always went together in Jack's memory, just as he associated the threat of death with the thrill of the body. For he also remembered sailing with Mabel in a storm:

> We were in danger once, a day of danger; and often and often her life lay in my grasp. The slip of a hand, the crash of a rock, the snap of a rope, and she had been gone. And often and often and just so often did I swear to myself, should it so happen, that I would follow her in the plunge. Loose my grip on all life, on all joy, on all the future, and follow her; for life and joy and future were embodied in her, were her—at the time. It was a great love.
>
> But see! Time passed. I grew. I saw immortality fade from her. Saw her only woman. And still I did not dream of judging. Time passed. I awoke, frightened, and found myself judging. She was very small. The positive virtues were hers, and likewise the negative vices. She was pure, honest, true, sincere, everything. But she was small. Her virtues led her nowhere. Works? She had none. Her culture was

a surface smear, her deepest depth a singing shallow. Do you understand? Can I explain further? I awoke, and judged, and my puppy
love was over.[4]

Yet during the time when he loved Mabel Applegarth, he was
trying to adopt the values of her class and leave his own. He had
grown up believing in the double standard. Good girls were remote and worthy of worship and marriage; other girls were little
better than whores and should be treated as such. And never the
twain should meet, at least not socially. Jack had neither the experience with women nor the rigor of thought to break down this social
fiction. His socialism was still incoherent and inconclusive. Commu-
nists, nationalists, populists, idealists, and utopians all seemed to be
Socialists to the young man. So did anyone who strove for a better
form of government, which would keep him and other men and
women from falling back into the Social Pit.

His dread of the Pit drove him into a fever of study, which
gradually began to take on patterns in his mind. He was sleeping
little more than five hours a night, reading almost at random
through the shelves in the public library, trying to cram into his
mind the knowledge of every subject under the sun. Like any
brilliant adolescent, he thought he could acquire the whole of
human wisdom if he read enough. Certainly, he read *The Communist
Manifesto* soon after returning to Oakland. Certainly, he read
Proudhon and Saint-Simon and Fourier, and discovered that the
private ownership of property could be considered theft. Certainly,
he joined the new branch of the Socialist Labor Party in Oakland
in April 1896, and learned about the class struggle and the coming
revolution, which would end poverty for ever.

His isolation also ended. Not only did he believe in the brotherhood of man, but he found men to act as his brothers in the party
in Oakland. They were not militant, but middle-class, under the
reformist English influence of Ruskin. They taught Jack about Marx
and William Morris, and they found out his value as a speaker, his
power of friendly persuasion. Soon he was talking of socialism to
a little crowd in the triangular park behind the old City Hall. Later

the Oakland police arrested him for speaking from a soapbox, but the judge released him with a caution. He was ignorant enough to demand in an Oakland newspaper that all should read "Carl Mark's *Capital*," although he had not read it himself since it was not available in English translation. Yet he had acquired the passionate belief that only a form of socialism could deal with "the increasing distress of the masses, divorced from land, capital and machinery."[5]

Marx did not become the key to all the mysteries of heaven and earth for the young student so much as did a popular philosopher of unrestricted capitalism, Herbert Spencer. That disciple of Darwin had the gift of presenting a cosmic catch-all, and through him Jack came to understand that the laws of the universe and of nature must work themselves out, whatever individuals might do. He felt the perverse satisfaction of knowing that he was irrelevant to the destiny of the species. He could do anything he wished, and yet it would not affect the grim logic of Darwinian selection. His revelation told him that all was law:

> It was in obedience to law that the bird flew, and it was in obedience to the same law that fermenting slime had writhed and squirmed, and put out legs and wings, and become a bird. . . . All things were related to all other things, from the farthermost star in the wastes of space to the myriads of atoms in the grain of sand under one's foot.[6]

Jack's problem was to reconcile the irrelevance of the individual and the inevitability of the revolution with a personal belief in his own destiny and willpower and right to succeed. He wanted to be protected from the Pit, but equally he wanted to rise to a peak of fame. His own life might be insignificant to the human race, but it was all he had. Yet the very contradictions of elementary Marxism and social Darwinism suited his divided nature. His fears of failure were assuaged by the prophecy of perfectibility through certain revolution, while his need to escape and his flights of irresponsibility could be explained and excused by the inevitability of natural selection and Marxist dialectics. His insatiable appetites and hunger for fame could be justified in terms of the inexorable rise of the white race to dominance in world affairs. As an old-stock

American in the supreme age of imperialism and capitalism, he should join in their triumph and achieve their goals, while working to replace them.

So Jack believed in both an evolutionary and a revolutionary socialism. He wanted a white aristocracy of the intellect to take over the running of the state for the good of all. Given a reasonable opportunity, those natural noblemen would prove themselves the fittest to survive. He himself would benefit, for he had risen from the lower depths. He would later end his credo, "How I Became a Socialist," with the bitter lesson of his experience in jail. "No economic argument, no lucid demonstration of the logic or inevitableness of Socialism affects me as profoundly and convincingly as I was affected on the day when I first saw the walls of the Social Pit rise around me and felt myself slipping down, down into the shambles at the bottom."

Jack was most a Socialist when he was depressed and the nightmares rode him. The theory of socialism protected the unlucky and the unfortunate. It seemed an efficient way of getting more food and more decent jobs for more people. It was both charitable and logical. He recognized that all men could not have his determination or abilities, and that unions helped the exploited, even if the strong could sometimes make it on their own. Yet when he felt confident, he decided that the survival of the self and the race determined all human behavior. At those times of his assertiveness, the first principle of his socialism was not Marx's class consciousness or even the brotherhood of man, but "selfishness, pure, downright selfishness."[7]

So Jack achieved his personal version of socialism. His pessimistic belief in biological determinism, his overview of man's spirit struggling against inexorable forces, gave him his dark power as a thinker and writer. It was a tribute to his sense of logic that he explained his support of imperialism by saying that it was the vanguard of the proletarian revolution. When the working classes took over the governments of the imperial powers, they would bring socialism to the conquered lesser breeds. And evolution came before all. Like it or not, history was a form of biology. "Nature has no sentiment, no charity, no mercy," he wrote in one letter.

> We are blind puppets at the play of great unreasoning forces. . . . These forces generated the altruistic in man; the race with the highest altruism will endure—the highest altruism considered from the standpoint of merciless natural law, which never concedes nor alters. The lesser breeds cannot endure . . . I cannot but hail as unavoidable, the Black and the Brown going down before the White.[8]

With such a harsh belief in natural selection as the basis even of the brotherhood of man, Jack determined to force himself more and more, to prove that he should survive among the fittest. Finding the curriculum in his high school too boring and progress too slow, he left after one year and went to a cramming school in Alameda to prepare himself for the university entrance examinations. Although the fees were high, he could borrow them from Eliza. He worked hard cramming at the academy, but he dropped out after five weeks, claiming later that the principal found his advance too rapid because it made the other pupils appear backward. At any rate, there was an agreement to disagree between Jack and the principal. The fees were refunded, and Jack returned to study at home.

Helped by Fred Jacobs in physics and Bess Maddern in mathematics, Jack worked nineteen hours a day for the three months before the university examinations. His body and his mind grew weary, his eyes began to twitch and fail, but he persevered. His mother and John London did not discourage him and kept him fed somehow—better a student than a hobo. He also felt that they owed him some support in exchange for the times when he had supported them. He was no longer sensitive to the prick of the job ethic, the virtue of earning money. He cast aside that duty for the duty of educating himself, and he was glad of it. If he always worked with his muscles for his living—he asked Mabel Applegarth —whose company would he be fitted to enjoy? "Tennyson's? or a bunch of brute hoodlums on a street corner?"[9]

After three months of study and nervous exhaustion, he sat for the university entrance examinations in August 1896. He had managed to learn within sixteen months enough English, history, physics, algebra, and geometry to pass into Berkeley as a special student. He celebrated the end of the examinations by spending a week sailing in a salmon boat between San Francisco and the saloons and arks of Benicia, the old headquarters of the Fish Patrol. The survivors of the waterfront fell on his neck and went on a glorious drunk with him, mourning the dead like his mate Young Scratch Nelson. He forgot his books in the whiskey and steered back through the fierce ebb, exulting in the spray and chanting his disdain for the schools. It was his one reversion to alcohol—his frolic after the brain-fag.

He had vast hopes when he reached the university in the fall. Yet he had studied so hard that he expected too much of the place. To him, the pleasure was in the achieving, not the possessing of the goal. One of his later friends, James Hopper, described the charisma and ambition of the new student with his curly mop of spun-gold hair, his strong bronzed neck, and eyes like a sunlit sea. "His clothes were flappy and careless; the forecastle had left a suspicion of a roll in his broad shoulders; he was a strange combination of Scandinavian sailor and Greek god, made altogether boyish and lovable by the lack of two front teeth, lost cheerfully somewhere in a fight." He looked more like the superman of all the possibilities than he ever would again. He was full of gigantic plans, as he would be until the end of his life. He intended to take all the courses in English, most of the courses in the natural sciences, and many in history and philosophy.[10] He would do ten times as much as the average student. He knew that he was capable of everything.

In fact, he hardly went to the courses in which he enrolled. One of his teachers, David Starr Jordan, did influence him by giving a series of lectures on evolution; to Jordan, Jack appeared a person of great physical strength and endurance as well as decided individuality.[11] Yet Jack's three courses in English and two in history meant little to him. He did not even bother to earn any credits in the English courses. Most curiously, he did not go to listen to the radical economist Thorstein Veblen, who was teaching on the campus.

After his second semester, Jack dropped out of Berkeley with an honorable dismissal. Although later he made a virtue of his leaving, although he was to attack "the passionless pursuit of passionless knowledge," he remained in awe of scholarship all his life. If he had the braggadocio of the self-taught, he also felt the secret hunger of the deprived. Yet stronger than his wish to be educated was his will to succeed as a writer. Spending four years at a university was too long for a working-class student who felt that his time was limited. And there were other reasons for dropping out. There was very little money at home, and he had learned for certain that he was a bastard.

Berkeley was a small enough place and near enough to Oakland and San Francisco for the rumors about Jack's birth to reach his ears. There were also relatives who envied the young man's efforts to gain an education and chose to enlighten him. He understood at last why he had reached out for love and had reached in vain. "From the hunger of my childhood," he wrote to Mabel Applegarth, "cold eyes have looked upon me, or questioned, or snickered and sneered."[12] He learned of the scandal of his birth in the files of the San Francisco newspapers; his mother had made two suicide attempts in an effort to prevent her lover, a vagabond astrologer called William Henry Chaney, from deserting her. Discovering the name of his probable father, Jack wrote to him. Chaney eventually replied evasively and libelously. He claimed that he had been impotent because of hardship, privation, and too much brain work during the two years he spent with Flora, whose reputation had never been good.[13] In point of fact, there were many similarities between Chaney and Jack London—intellectual vigor and physical strength and a charming plausibility that could convince any audience. Yet Chaney feared responsibility so much in his wandering life with his many wives that he denied the young man who was probably his only son.

The effect of this denial on Jack was as violent as the effect of his jail sentence. He could hardly admit to himself the blow of finding out that nobody would own up to fathering him. Yet a fierceness came into him at this time, a stubborn insistence that he was self-made. He owed nothing to anyone; he had created the man he was. He could feel no gratitude in the face of such a denial by his presumed father, such a false start from his true mother. He began to go against every influence they might have had on him. For their worlds of spiritualism and astrology, mysticism, and nonsense, he substituted his own positivism and rationalism, trying to be as down-to-earth in his manner and speech as the three people of his childhood who had loved and accepted him, his stepfather, his stepsister Eliza, and his wet-nurse. He would remain generous toward them, because they had always been generous toward him. He even attempted to forgive his mother. She was the wronged woman, after all, and she had tried to make up for her coldness in his childhood. So he went home to his den in her cottage, where gossip could not reach him. He was more proud and isolated than ever, absolutely determined to impose his sense of his identity on an indifferent world.

His desperate endurance in his first months as an author was a tribute to his persistence and his ignorance. He would have liked to become a composer like Ouida's Signa, but even he recognized such a career was impossible without any musical training at all. So he decided to become a poet, a magazine pundit, and a writer of fiction, in that order. He wrote frantically and continuously for fifteen hours a day, often forgetting to eat. He borrowed an old Blickensdorfer typewriter at nights; it had an evil spirit and could only type in capitals; its wayward keys had to be hammered until the blisters burst on his fingertips. The sound that came from his room was like distant thunder or the breaking of furniture. His shoulders grew rheumatic, his spine bent like a pipe-stem. Yet still he pounded onward—ponderous essays, scientific and sociological short stories, humorous verse, triolets and sonnets, blank verse tragedies, and even an elephantine epic in Spenserian stanzas on "Gold."[14]

Most of what he wrote was unreadable and hardly worth reading. The erratic capital letters of the typescripts made him appear illiterate. The machine banged awry what grammar he knew. And as a poet, Jack was better off as an oyster-pirate. He put on the fashionable straitjacket of the minor decadent poets, imitating their

archaic language without achieving their grace. He thought he was
sending the magazines what they wanted; but they did not want his
unsolicited mimicry and they returned it. In his case, imitation was
the sincerest form of beggary. In the market, pseudo-Swinburne
found no takers.

> For a whim of bubble-blowing,
>   Perhaps to while an empty day,
> For a whim of stubble-sowing,
>   For a game at godlike play.
> Shall the bubbles in the drifting
>   Pay the whim of Him who played?
> Shall the seedlets in the sifting
>   Of the sifter be afraid?[15]

Such facile rhyming was the opposite of Jack's economic and
political essays, which were solid and serious and socialistic. Yet as
he had no reputation, he found no publisher for them either. He
did not know what an editor looked like, and he had not met
anyone who had ever tried to publish anything. He had nobody
else's experience to profit by. So, impetuous and headstrong, he sat
and wrote, as if hacking away at it were training enough.

The experience that he bought with his blistered fingers was
worth nothing at all. The typescripts were all returned, read or
unread, with rejection messages or slips. The process seemed to
him like the working of another soulless machine in the cannery of
literature. The manuscript fell into the mailbox from his hand.
Time passed. It was brought back by the postman. A part of the
machine, some cunning arrangement of cogs and cranks at the other
end, transferred the manuscript to another envelope, took the
stamps from the inside and pasted them on the outside, and added
the rejection slip. There could not be a human being involved in
such a process of continual rejection.[16]

Energy was not enough. The excess of desire, the pressure of
hunger did not force acceptance on the magazine factories of the
east. Later Jack would admit that his early efforts were too wide-
spread. He would feel like weeping at that first waste of his creative

drive. He would know that he was "the greenest of tyros, dipping my brush into whitewash and coal tar, and without the slightest knowledge of perspective, proportion or color . . . without a soul to say, 'you are all wrong; herein you err; there is your mistake.' "[17] His greatest strength and weakness, indeed, was always to be his refusal to take advice gladly. He needed to discover the obvious as if it were his Newfoundland.

He was writing for the market at the wrong time. He was not acceptable to a Mauve Decade, in which Ambrose Bierce was thought too bitter by the magazines and Stephen Crane could only publish *The Red Badge of Courage* as a newspaper serial. It was the period in which one letter of protest from a prurient nobody raised more hell in an editorial office than ten letters from enlightened people.[18] The stranglehold of the genteel and the uncontroversial on the monthly magazines provided bad models for Jack's efforts as a beginner.

Faced with poverty and paranoia if he persisted much longer, Jack gave up trying to live as a writer in the spring of 1897. He could not borrow more money from Eliza, he could not continue to live off credit and his stepfather, who was now peddling picture frames in the streets. Through a relative, he was offered a job in the country laundry of the Belmont Academy. His pay was still what it had been as a coal-heaver, $30 a month, but his board was included. But now that he was more educated, he was more aware of his slavery. He worked with his partner for six days a week like a steam engine, boiling the shirts and pressing the white ducks of the schoolboys. Once again, he was a work-beast. Once again, he was selling his brawn, not his brain. On his Sunday of rest, he was too exhausted to read the trunkful of books under his bed, while out on the verandas, the cool youths sported their clean linen.

He lasted three months in this new stupor of brainless labor before he gave up his job just as he had given up his other laboring jobs. He was still determined not to return to the treadmill of the working class which ended in the Pit. In his later myth of himself, he liked to present his two years as a work-beast as a titanic struggle against the grinding machines of society. In fact, he spent six years as a delinquent and sailor and wanderer compared to the two years spent as a manual worker. Yet in that short time of hard labor, he could feel, with the passion of William Blake against the dark satanic mills, how the factory system deformed and stunted and murdered its victims. For him as for Blake, the unceasing mental fight and the arrows of desire.

Kelly's army had sent him off on the road, and now the gold strike in the Klondike lured him to the northland, a way out from the California of wages and work-beasts and failures. Eliza grub-staked him and her husband to the $500 they needed for their outfits. Their agreement was that the young man would help carry the burdens of the old man. They sailed on the *Umatilla* from San Francisco on July 25, 1897, the boat loaded with gold-seekers, some of the quarter of a million men who were to try their luck at another Eldorado or Bonanza Creek. Of that horde, only 50,000 would reach the interior and 1,000 return richer than they were when they started. But at the beginning of that final westering dream turned northward, who would reckon the waste?

Frank Norris, the Californian novelist with a bleak belief in biological determinism even darker than Jack's own, wrote of the sailing of one of the boats for Alaska. On that July day at the San Francisco docks, he saw 20,000 people packed sardine fashion on the wharves, caught up in the thrill of the same Gold Rush that had founded the first American California, "a ferment of emotion, a very fever heat of cupidity and desire." The excitement in the air verged upon hysteria as the new pioneers set out to the mines of the far north. The mob expectancy that had made Kelly's army from Oakland the largest of the marching armies of the unemployed now sent off the dispossessed and the dreamers on one last fling. With them went Jack on "this last Argo, loaded with gold seekers from a land of gold," which he had never found, which he believed was his due because of his hunger.[19]

4

KLONDIKE AND PAYDIRT

I never realized a cent from any properties I had an interest in up there. Still, I have been managing to pan out a living ever since on the strength of the trip.

—JACK LONDON

There was something gallant, greedy, and childish in the scramble for the gold of the north. It attracted the visionaries and the failures, the bold and the immature. "There is a splendid uncertainty about the whole affair," Frank Norris wrote, "that invests it with a quality of dignity like a charge of cavalry or a dash for the pole." So the gold-seekers imagined, crammed together on the *Umatilla* and the *City of Topeka* with their outfits, each weighing nearly a ton, littering the decks. Jack was used to the packed masculine society of the forecastle; the conditions were no hardship to him. He also knew the temptations of the waterfront saloons, so he did not fall victim to cardsharpers and fleecers in the boom ports on the journey, Juneau and Skagway.

His problem was his ailing partner, Captain Shepard, who had suffered a mild heart attack even before they left the dock. He would have to pack the 4,000 pounds of their combined outfits on his own. So he joined forces with three other men on the boats—a small adventurer called Merritt Sloper; a hunter and miner, Big Jim Goodman; and the recorder and cook of the party, thin Fred Thompson with orange whiskers, a man who was both pompous

41

and visionary. Thompson's laconic diary is the tally stick for mea-
suring the myths Jack was to pan from his trip to Alaska. It shows
that the party of five reached Juneau in the rain, then paddled
onward 100 miles with Indians and hired canoes to Dyea Beach,
arriving on August 7. They must hurry on, if they wanted to have
a chance of reaching the Klondike before ice made the highland
rivers impassable.[1]

The scene at Dyea Beach was a brutal hurly-burly. Thousands
of men cursed and struggled with stacks of deadweight stores and
crazed horses. Outfits had to be dumped from the dugout canoes
onto the shore, then dragged out of the new shanty area. There had
only been one shack at Dyea a year before; it would be a ghost town
two years later. Meanwhile, all was shouting and trading, with the
Siwash Indians of the Tlingit tribes putting up their prices as port-
ers, while the tenderfeet, called *cheechakos,* counted out their money
or carried their own stores. Fred Thompson had to pay the Indians
22 cents a pound to have his outfit of 3,000 pounds carried to the
summit of the Chilkoot Pass, but the price soon reached 50 cents
a pound. A man without money or strength in his shoulders never
got beyond Dyea Beach.

So Jack found himself a work-beast again. He had escaped the
dumb labor of the laundry only to become his own pack animal
over the Chilkoot Pass. Joaquin Miller, the old poet of the Sierras,
was already strolling toward the pass, playing his flute and carrying
little more than an onion and a pad of paper; he reported back to
his readers in San Francisco that the summer scene reminded him
of the California woods near his home, only there were great gar-
dens of snow instead of grapes on the hillsides.[2] Jack and his party
did not rhapsodize as they hauled their 6 tons of stores on a hired
boat upstream to the approach to the pass. After that, they must
backpack all the weight up the canyon to Sheep's Camp, then they
would have to plod in the Chilkoot lock-step under the threatening
glaciers up to the Scales, then finally they needed to perch and cling
onto the handholds and toeholds hacked out of the ice on the sheer
rocks before the height of the summit, where the squalls and vapors
swirled round the human donkeys who had struggled so far.

Jack was strong, but his skin was tender and he had to carry the weight for two men. But luckily Captain Shepard lost his nerve. When the elderly man saw the straining line of gold-seekers on the 14 miles up to the peak of the pass, he complained of a bad attack of rheumatism and turned back for California, leaving Jack to dispose of the spare outfit. His place as cook and packer was soon taken by an old man called Tarwater, who became a mythical Argus in Jack's memories. Although Shepard's going lightened Jack's load, he still had to take up the white man's burden. His belief in the superiority of the Anglo-Saxon race over all others forced him to prove his strength. He was determined to do what the Indians could do, and to do it better.

The heat was so intense on the lower slopes of the Chilkoot that Jack stripped to his underwear and sweated along like a "puffing, steaming, white human engine in scarlet flannels."[3] As, load by slow load, the outfits were lugged up to the summit of the pass, the late August weather changed from sun to cold to driving rain. Underfoot, the dust gave way to the swamp of Pleasant Valley, then to a stretch of brittle tundra leading to broken shale. After these hazards, there was still the fearful bruising of the boulders and the slippery risks of the ice-steps and packed snow of the last trudge to the summit, which the party reached at the end of the month.

All the way from the top of the pass down to the shores of Lake Lindeman ahead, there were abandoned cities of stores, the outfits piled as high as houses, the alleys between them thronged with their despairing owners. To survive the elements of earth and thin air, to lift a ton of food and equipment into the heights, was not enough. The ordeal by water was to come, and it demanded a quick building of boats that could withstand the sudden storms of the lakes and the roaring rapids on the rivers that flowed down to Dawson City. This journey meant death by drowning for the ignorant and an impasse for the unskilled. Jack and Merritt Sloper were both expert in the world of small boats, and the party had brought along its whipsaws and nails, ropes and canvas. There were plenty of spruce trees round Lake Lindeman to provide the timber. Time was the enemy, for the freeze would begin in October. So Jack and his party spent only a fortnight in making their boat, the *Yukon Belle.* They also lent a hand in building a sister ship, *Belle of Yukon,* joining forces with another party that had a woman attached to it. The two boats survived the first passage and portage onto Lake Bennett, where the alternative trail up from Skagway met the Chilkoot trail.

There Jack saw the confirmation of his dark biological beliefs and nightmares of cruelty. The fate of the horses used on the Skagway trail showed man's inhumanity to his most useful beast as well as to himself. The bodies of hundreds of dead pack animals littered the shores of the lake, shot after they had been flogged almost to death to reach that height. Their carcasses would haunt Jack's Alaskan stories. The tale told Fred Thompson was that there were so many dead horses and mules along the trail, that if they were laid side by side, a man might walk on horseflesh all 50 miles to the lake.[4]

On September 23, the party reached Lake Tagish, where the Canadian customs officials had set up another barrier. By scheming, Jack and his companions only paid little more than $20 tax on their outfits, although many others had their stores confiscated when they could not afford the heavy duties. There were rumors of approaching famine among the immigrants to Dawson City. Those who did not carry 700 pounds of flour and beans and bacon for the winter were turned back. Jack helped old Tarwater to slip through without any provisions, for he had learned to wheedle on the road. Then fair winds took the square-rigged *Yukon Belle* across Lake Marsh to the upper Yukon River, where the first flurries of snow heralded the freeze. The water route now lay through the terrors of Box Canyon.

Many carried their boats for two days round the canyon, while Jack steered the *Yukon Belle* through the rapids in two minutes, then returned to take the next boat through the churning waters. His courage and timing were superb as he stood lashed to the steering oar, riding the hogback of the race, the rock walls dashing by like twin lightning express trains, until the wallowing boat burst through a smoking comber into the whirlpool midway along the

canyon, forcing the steersman to ride the curving wall of water onto
the second rush of the rapids beyond. Jack repeated his feat 3 miles
downriver by taking both boats along the Mane of the White Horse
Rapids at racetrack speed. So they reached Lake Laberge. Jack left
behind him a myth which he never denied, that he had piloted
dozens of boats through the rapids to make a grubstake of $3,000.
In fact, he had only done the job twice, the second time out of the
kindness of his heart.⁵

A cold north wind nearly stopped the adventurers by the
shores of bleak Lake Laberge. It blew for three days. The men must
force their stiff bodies and sluggish boat through the thin ice already forming on the lake, or they would have to spend the winter
months by that desolate wasteland. Once through, the way down
to Dawson City was helter-skelter along the Yukon current. Mush
ice was already throwing its broadsides at the *Yukon Belle* from
tributary rivers. Even if the sun of an Indian summer broke through
the chill dawn fogs, winter was only weeks away, and there were
hundreds of miles to travel past shoals and split currents and more
rapids and canyons. Anchor ice rose from the river bottom and
coated the surface, while the rim ice stretched out its long grip from
the cold shore.

After Five Finger Rapids and the 6-mile dash along Rink Rapids, past the trading post at Fort Selkirk where Jack probably saw
his first huskies and wolf dogs, a choice had to be made. Old
Tarwater transferred to the *Belle of Yukon,* as its crew intended to
winter in Dawson City. Jack and his three original companions
decided to occupy an abandoned cabin of the Hudson Bay Company on an island at the mouth of the Stewart River, about 80 miles
upstream from the city. They were afraid of famine at Dawson and
of the high prices there. They were also anxious to begin prospect-
ing, even in the winter. They had come for gold and they meant
to stake their claims at once. The Stewart River was said to be a
lodestone.

Two days after they had established themselves in their cabin,
Big Jim Goodman set out for nearby Henderson Creek to look for
likely ground. He returned that same evening with the news that

he had struck paydirt. Jack went out with him to the creek, while the other two men prepared the cabin for their winter stay. At the creek, Jack and Goodman panned for gold and staked eight claims. The records in Dawson City still show that Jack London applied for placer mining claim Number 54 on the left fork ascending Henderson Creek, solemnly swearing that he had discovered therein a deposit of "gold."[6]

Although Fred Thompson always maintained that Jack had discovered only fool's gold, his sneer hid his own sense of failure. Modern gold dredges have recovered much of the precious metal from Henderson Creek. What Thompson had to regret was that, like most of the Klondikers, he had wasted his money on the folly of getting there and existing there, taking nothing out. During the rush of 1897 and early 1898, some $60 million was spent on outfits and transport by the gold-seekers, while only $10 million worth of gold was actually grubbed from the soil.[7] By the normal methods of panning, sinking shafts, and sluice mining, the individual miners could only scratch the frozen surface for the metal and break the ground for the professional mining companies, which were to follow with their ore-extracting machines. The story had been the same in California, where the small farmers like John London had only served to clear the land for the professional ranchers. The little speculators were the skirmishers of profit, mere cannon fodder for the organized regiments moving in their rear.

Just as the dream becomes the nightmare, the excitement of the rush to the gold became the cold sweat of extracting it. Jack did not mean to break his back at that. Thawing the frozen gravel with spruce fires, sifting the black soil to find occasional grains of the precious metal, were no quicker ways of making money than working in a cannery or a laundry. He had already decided to become a writer, he had already refused to slave as a work-beast. Adventure was one thing, drudgery another. He would not linger for the will-o'-the-wisp of the lucky strike while the body wore down with its hopes. Faced with the dull facts of gold mining, Jack had to recognize another empty illusion. From the waste of his energy and his outfit, he had to pan out the glitter of his struggle, the gleam of some sort of victory over himself. That is why he began to understand the Gold Rush so well. He, too, must soon go home and make a brave show of the last of his series of failures.

Immediately, he went downriver to Dawson City with Fred Thompson and two other men on the *Yukon Belle.* They cached their food in the cabin of two brothers, Marshall and Louis Bond, who owned the crossbred St. Bernard and Scots shepherd dog called Jack which would be the model for Buck in *The Call of the Wild.* To Marshall Bond, Jack looked like a hobo with his cap pulled low over his forehead. All that could be seen of him was a thick stubbly beard above some square broad shoulders.[8] He looked as tough and uninviting as the other Klondike pioneers.

In the six weeks which Jack spent in the raw, chill, and ramshackle frontier town, where 5,000 people feared to starve that winter, he haunted the saloons and buttonholed the old-timers. He might have been avoiding work at the gold claims, he might have been collecting material. Certainly, he wanted to hear all the yarns of the place, told with that blend of fantasy and fact that formed the frontier tale. One Klondiker later remembered that he had never seen Jack on the trail or working for gold, only in a Dawson bar —a muscular youth of average height with a shock of yellow hair, unkempt and slovenly. He was always in conversation with some veteran sourdough or notorious character, and he himself loved to talk.[9] So he absorbed the legends and background of Dawson City —the Elkhorn and Eldorado Saloons, the Tivoli and the Opera House dance halls, the street scenes of the dog-sleds and the occasional stampedes to stake a claim near the latest strike.

Marshall Bond also remembered one night in his cabin, with Jack outside the circle of the conversation and the lamplight, a confusion of cap and coat and moccasins. The men were speaking of socialism, which some of them mixed up with anarchism. Then, from the shadow of the lamp and the blur of beard and cap, they heard a quick, sympathetic voice. Jack expounded the subject and hypnotized the audience by his knowledge and his enthusiasm. "Intellectually he was incomparably the most alert man in the room, and we felt it. Some of us had minds as unresilient as putty, and some of us had been educated and drilled into a goose step of conventionalism. Here was a man whose life and thoughts were his own. He was refreshing."[10]

In the tedious confines of the winter cabins, Jack began to develop his powers of analysis and persuasion. Yet first he and Fred Thompson must return with supplies from Dawson for the cabin on the island in the Stewart River. Either the two men backpacked all the way or they pulled their own sled, for they owned no team of huskies. Then they were cooped up for five months in a trap of cold and boredom, short rations and scurvy: Jack's most severe test of endurance and his personal triumph. He settled down to absorb the books that became the bedrock of his thought and writing, underlying even the socialism which was his faith. These were the works of Darwin, Huxley, Herbert Spencer, and Kipling, Milton's *Paradise Lost* and Dante's *Inferno.*

The dualism in his thought and nature became ingrained that winter. Intellectually, he continued to perceive that his own life was insignificant to the human species or to the wilderness. Yet he had a superb body and a mind as devouring as a wolfpack. His vigor denied his philosophy. From the close study of Kipling, he derived and improved a style packed with terse detail and short sentences, as direct and necessary as conversations gasped in the freezing air. From reading Milton and Dante, he could conceive of himself as a Lucifer defying all creation in his pride, or treading his way in horror through the circles of hell. Above all, he learned to describe the trials of the spirit through the tortures of the flesh.

In that winter, survival was all. Jack had little time to reflect upon his visions. Writing later about housekeeping in the Klondike, he told of a life with three other men in a cramped space on a diet of sourdough bread, doughnuts, beans, and bacon grease, where a cook's pride depended on his gravy or his vinegar—concocted from dried apples, water, and brown paper. Food reigned supreme in the minds of the confined men. The cold, the silence, and the darkness were not their chief woes. The one deprivation that overshadowed all was the lack of sugar.[11] At least, that was true for Jack with his youthful craving for candy.

Halfway through the winter, Jack fell out with Merritt Sloper. He was too generous with the common store of food, and he blunted the edge of Sloper's ax while hacking out the ice to melt for their water. Sloper's rage was excessive, because fatigue and confinement had made him half-mad. So Jack left to join another trio of companions, a Dr. Harvey, a Judge Sullivan, and a young hero-worshipper, Bert Hargrave; but he would remember the intolerable togetherness of cabin life in his finest story of the north, "In a Far Country." There the two men could not adapt to their winter confinement, and they ended by killing one another.

Hargrave was Jack's first disciple. He was convinced that he was in the presence of a genius, and he knew Jack well. To Hargrave, Jack seemed to be an idealist in pursuit of the unattainable, as a man both intrinsically kind and irrationally generous. In close quarters and among friends, he showed a refinement and a gentleness that had survived his rough life. Sometimes he became silent and reflective, but he was never morose or sullen. He always listened. When he was winning an argument, he often stopped to allow his opponent to tangle himself up in his own words. Then Jack calmly rolled another cigarette, threw his head back, and laughed infectiously, because he did not want to humiliate his opponent with his superior powers of logic. Above all, he had a mental craving for the truth. He applied one test to religion, to economics, to everything. "What is the truth? What is just?"[12]

Thus he cast his spell on those who were attracted to him. He loved conversation, and he disciplined himself to be consistently cheerful throughout the tedium of the winter. If he suffered from the general melancholia, he never showed it, even when he fell sick of the scurvy. The disease crippled his body. His joints swelled so that he had to bend double to walk. His gums softened until the few good teeth left in his mouth were loose. His face puffed up so that he could poke a finger into his cheek and the dent would remain for hours in his chapped skin.

Spring came in May with the great break-up of the ice on the waterways. Huge cakes of ice piled up until their rearing hillocks threatened to destroy the cabins on the river islands. As soon as the dark current of the Yukon opened, the ailing Jack and Dr. Harvey tore down the logs of their dwelling and used them to build a raft to float downstream to Dawson. The odd craft was nearly lost when Jack's steering oar cracked, but it reached Dawson where the sale of its timber netted $600. Jack made enough to have his scurvy treated—raw potatoes and a lemon worked wonders on the disease. He spent the end of May and early June 1898 in the dreary and desolate city, built on a swamp, flooded to the second story, and inhabited by mosquitoes, dogs, and gold-seekers. Then he found two companions to share a trip 2,000 miles downriver to the mouth of the Yukon and the sea. He knew he had failed; his body was in bad shape; he wanted to get back to California as soon as possible.

Jack kept a log of the journey, which he hoped to work into something. He did not think of using the Klondike as a literary asset until he was penniless and leaving it. Yet consciously or unconsciously, he had endured the hard breaking of the tenderfoot by the wilderness, he had listened to the tales of the old-timers. The diary of his voyage downriver was only a postscript to his full memory. The boat he used was as cramped and exposed as the cabin he had left. It was home-made and leaky, but it did not look out of place in the wasteland and the wild river. The bow was a woodshed, the middle of the boat a pine lean-to for sleeping. Then there was a bench for the rower, and aft, a galley for the cook. In the stern the steersman stood, although the current would take the boat all the way.

The 2,000 miles of their monotonous journey lasted only three weeks. There were flats by the river, where hordes of mosquitoes nearly ate them alive. They lived on goose eggs until they were sick of the taste, and on the flesh of raw duck. For once in his life, Jack satisfied his craving for uncooked wild game by the surfeit of it.

By Anvik, the scurvy and the diet of wild game had crippled him again. He was saved by a kind stranger who gave him some raw potatoes and a can of tomatoes. These things were worth more to him "at the present stage of the game than an Eldorado claim." The boat threaded the labyrinth of channels of the Yukon Delta and reached the port of St. Michael's, stinking of dead fish in its mudflats. Jack shipped as a stoker on a ship bound for British Columbia, but he was badly burned on the hand after eight days and had to give up the job. Although he was prone to accidents, this mishap was caused either by his weakness from scurvy or by the bad whiskey given the stokers to keep them working in the boiler room. When the ship reached Vancouver, he had just enough money to pay for a steerage ticket back to San Francisco. He arrived there early in August 1898, a year after he had left with the other argonauts.

In all, Jack brought home $4.50 worth of gold dust, which he pledged to a pawnbroker in Oakland. He was as broken in health and as penniless as most of the other Klondike adventurers. His only excuse for his folly was the value of the hardship to his character. He must make a myth of his experience, presenting himself as a frail hero who had outlasted the worst of the winter and the wild, not a short-winded young man who had come home with his tail between his legs at the first opportunity. He even believed that the Indians who lived in Alaska could endure the hardship there less well than the white pioneers. They were the necessary victims of the march of civilization. His diary recorded that the "Indian seems unable to comprehend the fact that he can never get the better of the white man."[13]

Jack did not confess that the wilderness had got the better of him, although not of the Indian, nor did he concede that his sense of racial superiority was only a cover for his unspoken failure. The terrible conditions of the Klondike justified his return. "As for the hardship," he wrote later, "it cannot be conveyed by printed page or word of mouth. No man may know who has not undergone. And those who have undergone, out of their knowledge, claim that in the making of the world God grew tired, and when He came to the last barrowload, 'just dumped it anyhow,' and that was how Alaska happened to be."[14]

MAKING A NAME

Don't loaf and invite inspiration; light out after it with a club, and if you don't get it you will nonetheless get something that looks remarkably like it. . . . WORK all the time. Find out about this earth, this universe; this force and matter, and the spirit that glimmers up through force and matter from the maggot to Godhead. And by all this I mean WORK for a philosophy of life. It does not hurt how wrong your philosophy of life may be, so long as you have one and have it well.

JACK LONDON

At the cottage in Oakland, Jack learned that he had lost one of the three people he had loved closely. His stepfather had died, and his mother had taken in Johnny Miller to live with her all the time. Her doting on the small boy, who was not even her blood relation, made Jack decide to get his ounce of support from her as well. She was not penniless, since she had a widow's pension because of John London's service in the Civil War. So her son looked only for odd jobs, not for steady labor. He would try his hand at writing again. All the same, under pressure from the Applegarths, who still wanted him to marry Mabel, he took the civil service examinations for a job as a mailman and came out high on the list. No place was immediately open for him at the post office, and he settled down to wait and live by his pen.

He set his sights lower and aimed at a quick dollar. His piece taken from his diary, "From Dawson to the Sea," was returned by the San Francisco *Bulletin* with the comment that Alaskan stories were a drug on the market. He took seven days to write a 21,000-word serial for boys, but the *Youth's Companion* returned it. He resurrected his old stories and articles and poems and jokes, and sent them on their rounds once more. He kept a notebook to record his success; between August 1898 and May 1900, 15 of his submissions were accepted at once, while the other 88 were rejected more than 400 times. The pile of his rejection slips skewered on their piece of wire reached 5 feet high.[1]

Still he persevered, as if determination would crack the wall of indifference. "Some are born to fortune," he wrote later in *John Barleycorn,* "and some have fortune thrust upon them. But in my case I was clubbed into fortune, and bitter necessity wielded the club."[2] This does not seem to have been true. Every time he had a steady job, he had given it up to return to writing. Yet his mother approved of his effort to better himself and her. She would support him, and while she did, he would try and try again. His sense of dependence on her and his bitterness at the continual rejection of his work made him dramatize his persistence into a heroic struggle against fate. "If I die I shall die hard, fighting to the last," he wrote to Mabel Applegarth, "and hell shall receive no fitter inmate than myself. . . . If I were a woman I would prostitute myself to all men but that I would succeed—in short, I will."

The inadequate Mabel felt the force of his unrewarded and solitary labor, of his disgust at depending on his family for bed and board, of his unstated fear that he might fail again at writing as he had failed in the Klondike. She was his only confidante. Yet she shared the genteel standards and spurious morality of the East Coast magazines, which found the strength of his best writing too crude for their readers. As he absorbed Kipling and found his own fierce and direct style, she showed her distaste for it and provoked an outburst from him. "The time is past when any John Halifax, Gentleman, ethics can go down with me," he thundered at her failure to understand him. "I don't care if the whole present, all I possess, were swept away from me—I will build a new present; if I am left naked and hungry tomorrow—before I give in I will go on naked and hungry."[3]

At the point when he was about to give in for the time being, a local magazine, the *Overland Monthly,* offered $5 for his Alaskan story, "To the Man on Trail," and $7.50 for the next seven Alaskan tales. Another obscure magazine, the *Black Cat,* also bought an old science fiction story, "A Thousand Deaths," for $40—enough for Jack to pay his debts and redeem his bicycle from pawn. The story seemed to him a penny's worth of rot, but its plot reveals his despair at his denial by his probable father. The hero of the tale is drowning in the sea, when he is saved by the father who has ignored him all his life. The father is a sadist and a scientist of the occult, who tortures his son to death a thousand times, resurrecting his victim each time in order to torture him again. Finally the son kills his cruel father and is free to live his own life. The story was written when Jack was at Berkeley, at the time that Chaney repudiated him.[4]

When the post office finally did offer him a place as a mailman, he refused it. Although he was again in debt, he still insisted on trying to write, and his mother continued to support his decision. He spurned the first magazine editor who bothered to advise him not to try to live by his pen. "No, no," Jack replied. "I have seen too much labor and too many laborers, not to understand the game. Some day I shall hit upon my *magnum opus.* And then, if my struggling expression at last finds tongue, I will not have to go to the poor house because my muscles can no longer work."[5] To justify this determination, he made a philosophy out of his chosen path. He suggested that all young writers should do what he had made himself do, as though willpower and expertise could always conquer literature without benefit of genius. The chief market for a writer was the magazines, and they depended upon printing what would be popular in order to attract readers and advertisers. Without cynicism, Jack wrote: "The deepest values in life are today expressed in terms of cash. That which is most significant of an age must be the speech of that age. That which is most significant today is the making of money." The man who feeds another man is his master. Readers feed writers, and readers demand literature that is immediate. Of course, the critics ultimately appraise an author, but their choice is not the choice of the public nor of the magazine editors. For the young writer, bread and glory are divorced. Where he dreams of serving one master, he finds two masters. "The one master he must serve that he may live, the other that his work may live."

The way out of the dilemma was to secure a literary name. Once secured, the magazine editors would print any work of any quality that had the name attached to it. This was just, since every known writer was once an unknown, struggling in the crowded lists for a chance of recognition. He had drummed up his trade, he deserved his pay. If he was not secured in the position he had won, what was the use of his striving? "And further, what incentive would there be for the unknown? If nothing goes with a name, why strive?"

So competition was rough justice, and success in the marketplace became its own proof of worth. The writer needed to oscillate between hackwork and work for the good of his soul. Then he would earn a name and keep himself well. But it was not enough to imitate successfully. Originality, tempered to the market, had to be hammered out. A personal philosophy had to be forged as a weapon to test thought and prose. Every famous writer had possessed a view peculiarly his own, something new, as well as something the world wished to hear. No writer could be individual or great without the intensive and daily study of history, biology, evolution, ethics, and the thousand and one branches of knowledge. There was enough time to do everything, if time was divided carefully. "Time! When you speak of its lack you mean lack of economy in its use. . . . If you cannot find time, rest assured that the world will not find time to listen to you."[6]

If this rule of thumb sounded crass and exhaustive and materialistic, as if literature were some base metal which any blacksmith could batter into shape, it was Jack's advice on how to achieve success. He overrated his pleasure in the struggle, he underrated the inborn power of his genius as a maker of myths. Yet this distorted view was truly democratic. It implied that any wordsmith from as poor a background as his own could forge as commercial and renowned a career as his would be. Success was its own virtue; endurance won its just reward.

This working philosophy forced the young writer through the first fifteen difficult months after his return from the Klondike. Then, in October 1899, the *Atlantic Monthly* sent him a check for $120 for "An Odyssey of the North." During those fifteen months, he cannot have earned more than $10 a month from writing, mostly from the worst sort of hackwork. He churned out trashy or falsely erudite articles for obscure magazines, and he invented racial jokes which a music-hall comedian would blush to deliver:

Tommy—If a Filipino eats his father and his mother, what is he?
Tommy's Papa—A cannibal, of course.
Tommy—Naw. He's a orphan.

Such a joke was worth half a dollar to the San Francisco weekly, *Town Topics*. Jack was prepared to turn out anything, if he thought there was a market for it. His most extraordinary effort was to enter for the $10 prize offered by the local Fifth Ward Republican Club for a campaign song. He might be a Socialist, but one verse of his winning entry was imbued with true Republican principles:

> We ask that right be given,
>   And justice where 'tis due;
> Reward for those who've striven—
>   And did the best they knew.
> But punish those, who lying,
>   Have wrought thee evil deeds;
> And pardon those denying,
>   Who follow other creeds.

The pardon of the Republican Ward did not extend to paying the red winner of the competition all of his prize money, although he threatened to sue for it. This led him to expiate his apostasy by writing "The Socialist's Dream" of true equality:

> He saw the soil enriched by men
>   Who gloried in such honest life,

Ranking with those of greater ken
Who pleasure took in mental strife;
But who as comrades true and bold
Were in man's brotherhood enrolled.

Such trivial hackwork and hypocrisy became less necessary
when the check from the *Atlantic Monthly* was followed in 1900 by
an offer from Houghton Mifflin to publish his Alaskan stories in
volume form under the title of *The Son of the Wolf.* Overnight, he
had won a name and now, as he had predicted, the magazines
wanted him. He sent out most of his rejected manuscripts, and they
were accepted. This seemed to prove his point, even if it did not
help his reputation as a writer of quality. He also accepted an offer
to begin contributing articles to the Hearst press, the bugaboo of
the Socialists. Income was one thing, politics another. He insisted
on making money in every way he could, while keeping the flame
of his faith to himself. He was still working for the cause and
attending Socialist meetings. At one of them he met the second
passion of his life, Anna Strunsky.

She was seventeen and intensely vital, from a Russian-Jewish
family proud of knowing Emma Goldman and other leading radicals. Her father's house was open to all the intellectuals near the
Bay, and a long table was always laid for unknown guests. The
warm, inclusive bourgeois family expressed its devotion to liberty
and thought and brotherhood, and also looked after its own. With
a mind that darted and teased, with a passionate and loyal heart,
Anna attracted the discontented and the inquiring through her
beauty—brown and burning eyes, generous mouth, throaty voice.
She was, however, as high-principled and ultimately cautious as she
was attractive and intelligent. If her heart led, her head decided.

Anna did not disguise the impact of the young writer on her,
the physical shock of his presence. At their first encounter on the
speaker's platform of the old Turk Street Temple after a Socialist
meeting, they shook hands and talked. She felt a wonderful happiness, as if she were meeting the young Lassalle, Marx, or Byron.
She was certain that Jack would become a character known to

The young writer at the time of his first marriage.

Bess Maddern, Jack's wife, in 1902.

history. His face was pale from study now, but it was illuminated by large blue eyes fringed with dark lashes, and a beautiful mouth which laughed easily. The brow, the nose, the contour of the cheeks, the massive throat, were like those of a Greek statue, while the body gave an impression of grace and athletic strength. He was a little under the average height for California and he wore a gray suit with a soft white shirt and collar.[7]

A passionate friendship began, tempestuous and almost terrible, stormy with intellectual and physical differences. Anna was quick to see the truth behind the young man's apparent belief in a crass materialism and a driving ethic of success at all costs. He was, as she knew, "more often man against himself instead of man for himself," and had imposed upon his life a value system of work and even love which was opposed to his natural gifts and emotions. His contempt for romanticism and aesthetic standards hid a yearning and delicacy at the core. His nature was gentle and emotional, yet he forbade himself to deviate from the course he had chosen. "He systematized his life," Anna later wrote of him. "Such colossal energy, and yet he could not trust himself! He lived by rule. Law, Order and Restraint was the creed of this vital, passionate youth."[8]

Her opinion of Jack was shared by other radical girls, who all recognized his charisma. To Elsie Whitaker, the beautiful daughter of the English writer and Socialist Herman Whitaker, Jack's projection of his beliefs was so powerful that she felt there was never anyone whose struggle in life had been such a conflict, as he tried to fit his rugged individualism into the mold of materialism.[9] He appeared much the same to Jessie Peixotto, who thought him a Marxist only on occasion, for in the days of his self-confidence he was obviously not one. Jack was a brilliant person, she knew, but his theories were his own.[10] His intelligent friends mostly agreed that he deceived himself about his consistency, because of his simplistic theory of social evolution by which every contradiction could be reconciled as part of the grand process of the universe. He would not admit to his uncontrollable desires and his fierce appetites, which still made him wolf "cannibal sandwiches" of raw beef on the waterfront whenever he had the money to pay for them. And he spoke too much of his candor and honesty, when he was at pains to paint a false picture of his background and breeding.

No doubt, his inventions about his origins were based on his insecurity and genuine pride of race. When Ninetta Eames, the wife of one of the editors of the *Overland Monthly*, decided to write an article on the magazine's young discovery, Jack forged a genealogy for her and for his East Coast publisher. He claimed John London as his father, and he asserted that both his parents were descendants of families that had come to America before the Revolution. He stated that he could trace his ancestors through four generations, and that they mingled the blood of the English, the Welsh, the Dutch, the Swiss, and the Germans—all Nordic people in his way of thinking. Yet in a private letter to Ninetta Eames, he asserted that he was self-made, that he owed nothing to anyone, that he had rejected all family ties. "As regards brothers and sisters, they are only half, and are of little importance, as you some day may chance to learn. I do not mean that they themselves are of little importance, but insomuch as they concern me they are."[11]

With this careful construction of a false identity for the public, Jack began to make a coherent myth out of his own life. Perhaps he assuaged his sense of betrayal by his own blood in shouting that he was self-made. Nobody had struggled so much, nobody had gone so far from a worse start. He was already presenting himself, in the words of a friend, as the public's male Cinderella.

Yet those who knew him responded to his true inner pain and his sense of injustice. There was some sense in his doctrine. Drawn as he was to Anna Strunsky, he could not marry her because he did not have the money. He might not keep her in the style in which her father kept her. It was all very well to talk of romance, but he could not afford it. There was a real disagreement between his materialism and her idealism, despite the physical attraction which surged between the courtesies of their correspondence. Faced with his desire for her, even he admitted to a softening in his self-discipline. If he presented himself to the world as a man caught by the melancholy of materialism, there was a reason to hide what was in his heart.

"I, too, was a dreamer," he confessed to Anna,

on a farm, nay, a California ranch. But early, at only nine, the hard
hand of the world was laid upon me. It has never relaxed. It has left
me sentiment, but destroyed sentimentalism. It has made me practical, so that I am known as harsh, stern, uncompromising. It has taught
me that reason is mightier than imagination; that the scientific man
is superior to the emotional man. It has also given me a truer and
deeper romance of things, an idealism which is an inner sanctuary
and which must be resolutely throttled in dealings with my kind, but
which yet remains within the holy of holies, like an oracle, to be
cherished always but to be made manifest or be consulted not on
every occasion I go to market. To do this latter would bring upon
me the ridicule of my fellows and make me a failure.[12]

Jack had noticed among the Applegarths that rich people could
be entertained by his tales of hardship, but they would not offer him
a job, and not even for Anna Strunsky would he put aside his
striving for commercial success. The nightmare of the Social Pit was
real to him, as it was not to her. He must continue on his course,
she on hers. She was a young student who had just registered at
Stanford. An immediate marriage was impossible for both of them.
And a love affair was equally impossible, given the conventions of
the time. It was an age before efficient contraception, when marriage normally came before mating. The muddle of Jack's birth,
indeed, made him determined that his own children should be
approved by society. If he desired a woman to share his bed, bear
his sons, look after his household, type out his manuscripts, and
leave him alone to study and write most of the day, he could not
choose Anna. He must find a woman who had lived poorly enough
not to expect too much from him. If she was also educated and
strong and handsome, an earth mother of the right racial type to
suit his basic theories on evolution, so much the better.

As it happened, he knew a woman of that breed, Bess Maddern, who was free because his friend and her betrothed, Fred
Jacobs, had died on his way to fight in the Filipino War. Jack now
had the money to move his mother Flora and Johnny Miller into
a rented villa in a better part of Oakland. There were rooms to
spare, and as Bess was helping him to settle into the new house, he

proposed to her. It would be a companionate marriage, for both loved other people, alive or dead. There was room enough for each of them to live better together than worse apart. Bess accepted the loveless proposition coolly; she liked Jack and could help him in his writing career by making a home for him.

Jack was pressed to defend his decision to marry in haste without repenting at leisure. "It was rather sudden," he admitted to Anna Strunsky on the day before his marriage on April 6, 1900. "I always do things that way. . . . For a thousand reasons I think myself justified in making this marriage. It will not, however, interfere much with my old life or my life as I had planned it for the future."[13] To Ninetta Eames, he explained the element of make-believe in his quick decision:

> Sunday morning, last, I had not the slightest intention of doing what I am going to do. I came down and looked over the house I was to move into—that fathered the thought. I made up my mind. Sunday evening I opened transactions for a wife; by Monday evening had the affair well under way; and next Saturday morning I shall marry. . . . I am already tied. Though single, I have had to support a household just the same. Should I wish to go to China the household would have to be provided for whether I had a wife or not. As it is, I shall be steadied, and can be able to devote more time to my work. One only has one life, you know, after all, and why not live it? Besides, my heart is large, and I shall be a cleaner, wholesomer man because of a restraint being laid upon me in place of being free to drift.[14]

The marriage was an affirmation of Jack's belief that he could logically control all the wild impulses of his nature; its restraint would prevent his breaking loose and wasting his energies. But not all his friends believed in the marriage, particularly not his new confidant, Cloudesley Johns, an aspiring young writer who recognized Jack's genius in his first short stories. Johns had received a letter from Jack only a month before, saying that he hoped to go abroad soon, or else he "might mismate at home and live miserably till the game was played out."[15] So Johns refused to congratulate his friend. He would, he wrote, wait until ten years after the marriage. He found Bess likable enough, but she had little in common with Jack. Above all, she did not have her husband's sense of play and fun.[16]

Love is play, to a certain extent. And Jack did love play and was always ripe for a woman who knew how to play with him. He had met one of that kind several weeks before his marriage, Charmian Kittredge, the emancipated niece of Ninetta Eames, a lithe and athletic woman with a wide mouth and lidded eyes and a pile of brown hair. Their meeting had not gone too well; Charmian was looking for more elegant suitors who had already made their way in the world. Plain but lively, shallow but versatile, she was a stenographer, one of the new "liberated" women of California, but in fact as conventional, outside her few clandestine affairs, as most Californian women. Her type would be common enough in the 1920s, the lone woman making a career among men; but she was uncommon at the turn of the century, more attractive because of her rarity. At any rate, whatever plans Ninetta Eames may have had for her unmarried niece of thirty and her young author were canceled by his sudden marriage. Charmian had to wait her time and went off on a trip to Europe.

Jack and Bess were happy enough, especially after he moved his domineering mother and Johnny Miller out of his household into a cottage nearby. Bess wore her bloomers when they went out on their bicycles to visit their friends, spinning along the roads, full of the physical satisfaction of exercise and sex. "Ever bike?" Jack asked a friend.

> Now that's something that makes life worth living! I take exercise every afternoon that way. O, to just grip your handle bars, and lay down to it (*lie* doesn't hit it at all), and go ripping and tearing through streets and roads, over railroad tracks and bridges, threading crowds, avoiding collisions, at twenty miles or more an hour, and wondering all the time when you're going to smash up—well, now, that's something."[17]

Bess began to love him and he began to feel fond of her, determined to make a success of this marriage of reason. Certainly she satisfied the want in him for the love and contact which he had never had from Flora—he called Bess "Mother-Girl" and she called him "Daddy-Boy." But something was missing. He soon relegated her into the role of pregnant woman and housekeeper, and she seemed to want this minor key.

His suppressed emotions kept on pricking at him. Within four months of the wedding, he was writing to Anna Strunsky more passionately than ever, suggesting that they meet and collaborate on a book. They had a union of intellects which he could never have with his wife. Too late, he recognized the strength of his feeling for Anna.

"For all the petty surface turmoil," he wrote to her,

> which marked our coming to know each other, really, deep down, there was no confusion at all. Did you not notice it? To me, while I said, "You do not understand," I none the less felt the happiness of satisfaction—how shall I say?—felt, rather, that there was no inner conflict; that we were attuned, somehow; that a real unity underlaid everything. The ship, new-launched, rushes to the sea; the sliding-ways rebel in weakling creaks and groans; but sea and ship hear them not: so with us when we rushed into each other's lives—we, the real we, were undisturbed. Comrades! Ay, world without end![18]

Yet if he had married for reason and regretted his lost love, his life was stable and his career progressed. No eastern gang of critics was waiting to ambush the young western writer. The fashion for Rudyard Kipling and Social Darwinism had begun to whet the appetite of the reading public for something more raw and natural than the niceties of the Mauve Decade. The stories in *The Son of the Wolf* were well received, and Jack was sometimes called the Kipling of the Klondike or the Bret Harte of the Yukon. S. S. McClure, always seeking new talent for his magazine and publishing house, put Jack on a retainer of $125 a month to keep him for a year while he wrote his first novel. All at once, Jack seemed to have achieved a marriage, a career, and a regular wage.

Two years before, he had returned penniless from the Klondike. He had not loafed, he had lit after inspiration with a club, he was making a name, he was becoming a brain merchant. He had quite easily achieved the fame he wanted at twenty-four—an age when many other young writers had suffered nearly as much and were still battling for any recognition at all. He saw this incredible success in such little time as proof of his superhuman power of will. He stressed how hard he had worked, how hard he would work, to achieve so much so young so swiftly; but he would not admit the compelling force of his obsessive terror of degradation. The paradox is that he had achieved success because he was a born writer, a natural myth-maker, and a man of haunted dreams and split desires, of unconscious ferocity, divine discontent, and some genius.

6

THE CROWD AND THE CRACK

I have the fatal gift of making friends
without exertion. And they never forget me.

JACK LONDON

Before Jack had proposed to Bess, he already knew that marriage must interfere with his old life. They were on a ferryboat together one day, when he saw a gang on the deck below skylarking and behaving badly. He wanted to join them, to show off, to shock the other passengers. But he was with Bess and he could not. He had a duck-out-of-water sort of feeling. "While I cultivate new classes," he confided to Cloudesley Johns, "I hate to be out of grip with the old."[1]

Yet that was the price of marriage and literary success. He might remain a boy at heart, but he could not remain a boy in behavior. He still had the fatal faculty of making friends, but his home could no longer be the Mecca for every returned Klondiker, sailor, or soldier of fortune he had ever met. He had dropped the waterfront gangs and the young workingmen and the students for the brotherhood of the Oakland Socialists, and now he felt he must change his friends again to suit his profession. He was quickly rising in the world, from his Oakland villa to an Italianate chalet called *Capricciosa* to a rented bungalow by a poppyfield in the Piedmont Hills. The Socialists were already beginning to fall away, except for those he saw in his occasional visits to the Ruskin Club, run like a school meeting by his friend Frederick Bamford.² Only Herman Whitaker joined Jack up in the hills, for Jack was generously helping his friend to become a writer, but Whitaker appeared in Jack's new literary circle like a specter at the feast and reported back on Jack's misbehavior to the old comrades. Anna Strunsky always explained Whitaker's treachery by quoting a remark of the playwright Molnar, who heard that a friend was speaking ill of him: "Is that so? Why! I don't remember ever to have done him a favor."³

Jack's new circle of friends called themselves the Crowd. They were the smart bohemians of the San Francisco area. He had met some of them with Anna Strunsky, but his real contact with them was through George Sterling, who became the third love of Jack's life. Sterling was a young man of shy ambition, an envious hero-worshipper of literary success. He was already the protégé of the old Ambrose Bierce, who overpraised his pupil's cautious Georgian lyrics. Sterling earned his keep by working as the secretary of his uncle, F. C. Havens, a speculator who was making a fortune in Oakland real estate. Jack had once shoveled coal for one of Havens's companies, and he did not want to be patronized by George. So when a meeting was arranged between the two of them in San Francisco, each tried to dazzle the other. George introduced Jack to gourmet cooking and the conscious artiness of Coppa's restaurant, with its murals of black cats and the fat man bearing the motto —*Paste makes waist.* In his turn, Jack introduced George to the raw whiskey and Chinese whores and prizefights and gambling of the Barbary Coast. The poet tried to impress the Klondike writer with his breeding and taste; the Klondike writer tried to bludgeon the poet with his knowledge of low life.

It was to be the pattern of their relationship. George Sterling was always accused of making a hedonist out of Jack, whilst Jack was always accused of debauching George. Yet each supplied what the other man lacked. George gave his new friend an insight into a mocking nature that genuinely did not care for the material world. Jack gave his new friend an entrance into a physical world of sport and women and rough pleasure and intellectual vigor, which that timid Puritan poet had craved and never dared to touch.

Yet Jack showed his delicacy in his manner of coming close to his George. Only after knowing the poet for more than a year, and at the time of telling Cloudesley Johns that his marriage with Bess made him "a hypocrite grinning on a grid,"[4] could he bring himself to write a letter to George Sterling which ran in part:

> You know that I do not know you—no more than you know me. We have really never touched the intimately personal note in all the time of our friendship. I suppose we never shall. And I speculate and speculate, trying to make you out, trying to lay hands on the inner side of you—what you are to yourself, in short. . . . So I do not know you, George; and for that matter I do not know how I came to write this.[5]

George's reply was warm enough to start a relationship in which the two men admitted their love of each other. Jack called the poet "Greek" and was called "Wolf" in return. Their fond names for each other perfectly suited the image each had of himself. Many of the Crowd had already compared Sterling's lean body and profile to a Greek coin, although a crinkle on his nose and a receding forehead made some say it was a Greek coin run over by a Roman chariot. As for the name Wolf, the success of Jack's Alaskan stories and *The Call of the Wild* identified him with his heroes, both animals and men. And there was something of the lone wolf in Jack, even inside the Crowd.

Twenty years later, the love of the Wolf and the Greek would have been called latent homosexuality, yet at the time both men would have resented furiously any such inferences that might have been drawn from their closeness.[6] Their bodily contact was limited to boxing and wrestling, as in a Greek stadium. Their nakedness together was for the beach or the swimming hole. They were not exclusive, but throve in the company of others. They loved games and practical jokes; no gathering of the Crowd was without roughness and horseplay. Jack was determined to enjoy now the boyhood he claimed he never had. He even liked boxing with the women of the Crowd, and he would put on the gloves with anyone who dared. Padded against bruising, Charmian Kittredge went to Piedmont on Sundays to spar with Jack with a foil or the gloves. She impressed him enough to make him tell Anna Strunsky that Charmian was charmingly different from the average kind in her relish for sports and equality with men.[7]

The picnics at Piedmont became famous, particularly those held at the old Dingee place. It was, as George Sterling liked to say, as beautiful as a wreck of paradise. The park and mansion had long been abandoned. Cherry trees grew in the tall wild grass. Riotous garden flowers strangled the broken statues of nymphs and goddesses. Squirrels chattered from the marble arms of Diana, and birds nested in the unpruned rose bushes.[8] There the Crowd met on Sundays: the three lovely Partington sisters and their painter brother; Ambrose Bierce's son and his beautiful wife, standing in for their disapproving father, who sent along his spy and new protégé, the poet Herman Scheffauer; the flamboyant and plump Spanish painter Xavier Martinez, who married Elsie Whitaker, and the editor Harry Lafler; James Hopper, athlete and war correspondent, and sometimes the aged Joaquin Miller, still making melodrama out of his poetry; Jim Whitaker until he was excluded and Charmian Kittredge, who included herself; and Anna Strunsky, who was always asked but rarely came, while a score of hangers-on came unasked.

Jack invited his wife Bess to the first of the picnics, and George Sterling's distinguished wife Carrie made an effort to include her. Yet Bess remained withdrawn and disapproving. With the birth of her second daughter in the fall of 1902, she dropped out of the Crowd, which had already begun to intrude upon her marriage. She would not compete with the mob of Jack's friends. She would devote herself to bringing up her two little daughters, Joan and Becky, and she would try to hold her man through his children, for he loved them. "Behold, my seed comes after me," he wrote to Anna of his elder daughter. "I am joyed with it, satisfied."[9]

Yet Jack had never seen a reason not to indulge all his urges at the same time, if he could. While his wife looked after the babies, he studied and wrote, or he reveled with the Crowd in the first carefree days of his fame. He and the Greek led in the romping and

At Fifteen Months Joan Argufies with her Mammy Jennie, who was likewise her Daddy's Mammy Jennie.

And her Mammy Jennie Settleth her Hash in Short Order.

Jack's own photographs and captions for the family album.

the sports, the wild-berry or buckeye-ball fights, the foot races and the watermelon trials. As soon as there was a wind, Jack broke loose his kites to fly them over the poppies on the hills. Then there were the Wednesday evenings in the huge room of Jack's bungalow, with its views over the pines down to Oakland and distant San Francisco and the Golden Gate with the clippers leaving for the Orient. The room was so large that Jack said four of the poor cottages of his boyhood would fit into it. On these evenings, after the card games, there was the quiet reading of poetry or chapters from work in progress. These were the dreamlike days, as silver-gilt as the wild barley, never to come again.

Jack's magnetism and power imposed themselves on the Crowd. He seemed to radiate light and strength. One woman remembered him sitting on a chair, talking to George Sterling, on a late November afternoon. His face had a transparent quality, as if light were leaking through it. His whole head, unruly hair and all, looked phosphorescent, as though it had been dipped into some southern sea.[10] He had the gift of burning his image into people's memory, of transmitting his energy in an aura of electricity about his person. Those who met him felt that he must be a genius, however little of this he might convey in his words.

Behind the scenes, a battle was being fought to break the bond between the leaders of the Crowd. George Sterling's wife and mother were both jealous of Jack, who was accused of teaching the Greek to run after other women. He was also accused of inciting the Greek to leave his safe job as secretary to his uncle. For the poet was talking more and more of living the wild life preached by Jack, of retiring to a cabin in the woods by the sea. Ambrose Bierce was fighting too, for the soul of his lost acolyte. Jack and Bierce had always been gall and wormwood to each other, a quarrel that had begun with Bierce's first remark, that Jack wrote as if his digestion, like his politics and rhetoric, were out of order.

Bess and Flora and the Oakland Socialists were also fighting against the influence of the Crowd on their Jack. Flora had already been excluded from the Crowd, after trying to give her favorite performance as Cleopatra, dressed in her Egyptian costume. Bess resented losing her husband on his only holidays from writing, when he could have been with the children. She accused the Greek in reverse of debauching her husband by feeding him a hashish sandwich. Jack did eat this, "as a matter of scientific investigation," and had more terrible nightmares than usual as a result. But he refused to share the search for mysticism, sensuality, and horror of the Greek's experiments in drugs and poetry.[11] Alcohol and prose were good enough for him.

Although Jack did not quarrel with Sterling or the Crowd, he did begin to separate himself from them. Success was changing his manner. He was more assertive, and their frivolity irritated him. He started to lay down the law with the insistence of the self-taught, making universal truths out of his dogmas and selective education. In a revealing letter to Cloudesley Johns, he wrote: "If I see a man with a good brain who simply won't get down and dig, who won't master fundamentals, I cannot help but pity him. So it is with you. You refuse to systematize yourself; refuse to lay a foundation for your life's work; say that such is not your temperament, etc.; and in short are cowardly.''[12] Jack used his principles like a pick, his prose like a fist. If his presence was persuasive, his arguments were bullies.

His own master continued to be Rudyard Kipling, the most highly paid short story writer of his day, whose short and simple sentences had the force admired in Herbert Spencer's *Philosophy of Style*. "There is no end of Kipling in my work," Jack admitted to a friend in 1900. "I have even quoted him. I would never possibly have written anywhere near the way I did had Kipling never been. True, true, every bit of it. And if several other men had never existed, Kipling would never have written as he did.''[13]

Initially, Jack had copied his master's prose. He had rewritten and absorbed it until he could turn out a fair facsimile of the stories in *Plain Tales from the Hills*. "The Scorn of Women," for instance, transposed to a Klondike setting the fight between Mrs. Hauksbee and Mrs. Reiver in Kipling's "The Rescue of Pluffles." "While I shall surely develop expression some day," Jack used to complain when he was struggling for his own style, "I lack in origination." In the event, he digested the lessons of his master and surpassed him in the Alaskan tales. He was a more powerful writer, a maker of universal myths in which he intermingled his own little experiences. "Knowing no God," he boasted, "I have made of man my worship; and surely I have learned how vile he can be. But this only strengthens my regard, because it enhances the mighty heights he can bring himself to tread. How small he is, and how great he is!''[14]

In the first three books of the Alaskan tales, *The Son of the Wolf, The God of His Fathers,* and *Children of the Frost,* the rule of Kipling is under a law of diminishing returns. The rough-hewn characters, who speak dialect and group round Malemute Kid in imitation of the three soldiers in India telling their barrack-room tales, become the archetypes of mankind faced with the struggle against the White Silence and the Law of Life. The nightmares that haunted Jack's little sleep become the dying visions of Cuthfert, trapped "In a Far Country," dreaming like Jack of the lost comfort of sugar and "squares of honey, streaming liquid amber." But even in the best of the northern stories published in 1902, "The Law of Life" and

"The League of the Old Men," the aboriginals are given little character, just a role to play in the losing game of survival. Resistance to old age and the cold is as useless as resistance to the coming of the white race. The abandoned and aged Koskoosh is resigned to his fate, as his fire burns low and the wolves wait to feed on him. All men, all animals, must eat and be eaten. Both the struggle for survival and the acceptance of death are biological necessities. "Nature did not care. To life she set one task, gave one law. To perpetuate was the task of life, its law was death."[15]

If Jack transcended Kipling in his dramatic vision of the conflict between the individual and the wilderness, he demeaned Kipling by making him the mouthpiece of his own Anglo-Saxon racism. In 1903, after the three books of Alaskan tales had been published and he knew his style was all his own, Jack wrote a generous and red-blooded defense of Kipling which revealed more of his own racial beliefs than the Englishman's. In "These Bones Shall Rise Again," he praised Kipling's name as imperishable because he had been the bard of the genius of his race. Surely the Anglo-Saxon was a pirate, Jack wrote, a land robber and a sea robber. Under his thin coating of culture, he was still the freebooter he had been in Drake's day, and Hengist's and Horsa's. "In battle he is subject to the blood-lusts of the Berserkers of old. Plunder and booty fascinate him immeasurably. . . . He possesses a primitive brutality all his own." In the name of God, the Bible, and Democracy, he had ruthlessly conquered all lesser races and had imposed his law upon them.[16]

This was Jack's mistaken defense of Kipling. Although he was right in saying that Kipling's reputation would rise again, he was imposing his own fierce theories of race on his teacher. He even tried to explain Kipling's success and his own in racial terms. According to him, literature itself was determined by evolution. What the Anglo-Saxon race wanted at the time was short episodes told in a terse, bald, jerky, disconnected, but essential way that excited the fancy. This Kipling had done in Jack's eyes, and this Jack was doing, giving the race what it wanted, "the passing thing done in the eternal way."[17] The master would hardly have recognized his pupil's use of his name, as Jack tried to graft his own crude imperialism onto socialism.

If Marx was said to have stood Hegel on his head, Jack's evolutionary socialism stood Marx on Darwin's feet. To Jack, the survival of the fittest race must precede the victory of the fittest proletariat. Imperialism must therefore run its full course and should be supported.[18] This belief enabled him to write yellow journalism for the Hearst newspaper, the San Francisco *Examiner*. His first piece was a flag-waving welcome to the S.S. *Oregon*, returning through the Golden Gate after a spell of duty in the war against Spain:

> Up, up she swept grandly on the breast of the flood tide, this huge gun platform, this floating fort, this colossus. . . . Fang after fang was exposed till she fairly bristled with teeth which have tasted. In truth, one tingled at the sight, and the hot blood rushed backward through all the generations of culture and civilization to things primordial and naked. . . . The knowledge that such a splendid fighting machine was ours, made by us, and fought by us, was us—was a good knowledge. Tomorrow?—Ah, yes, tomorrow, when the lion shall lie down with the lamb, we shall beat our *Oregons* into automobiles and electric railways; but today it were well that we look to our *Oregons* and see that they be many and efficient.[19]

Such sentiments appealed to the Hearst editors and readers, while they disgusted many of Jack's friends.[20] He maintained to Cloudesley Johns that the magazine editors who used him wanted their stories tailored for their readers just as the Hearst press did, so where was the difference if he was to sacrifice his art?[21] And he continued to write newspaper articles that patronized the Washoe Indians for trying to become like the white men, and that praised the German-American sharpshooters at their annual festival. He even began to report prizefights. At Jim Jeffries's massacre of Gus Ruhlin, he despised Ruhlin for lying down so soon. "O why, did this man who elected to play the animal, why did he not play it out? It was inconsistent."[22]

Ruhlin's inconsistency did not discourage Jack's own. His

hackwork for Hearst in San Francisco did not stop him from practicing his socialism on the other side of the Bay. Even if his Socialist comrades distrusted the heresy of many of his opinions, they knew the value of a name and recognized the depth of feeling with which he preached socialism, the insistence of his low and vital voice. So he was twice chosen by the Social Democratic Party to run for mayor of Oakland. In 1901, he opposed John L. Davie, the wealthy populist, who had once employed John London as a ferryboat watchman and a strikebreaker; but Jack won only 245 votes in the election.

On the stump as well as in his writing, Jack pushed his version of socialism through natural selection. He wanted every worker to have the equality of opportunity to become, not his own boss, but the boss of other workers. He wanted labor leaders to be able to rise to the top of industry without owning the means of production, which the state should own. The increasing Socialist vote for Eugene V. Debs in 1900 made it clear to Jack that within a decade there would only be a capitalist and a Socialist party in the field. "In the meantime commercial expansion against the ultimate marshalling of the races."[23]

He believed in efficiency before brotherhood, in equal opportunity before fair shares for all. In one essay, he argued that the community was penalized by the high cost of the competitive system and its waste of resources. The logic of unrestricted commercial selection with its slumps and booms and unemployed masses was this: either kill off half the laborers or destroy all the machinery. In the end, the struggle of capitalism would lead to race prostitution and destruction unless men learned to cooperate rather than compete. The health of the workers was ultimately more important for the species than the fortunes of the lucky few.[24]

Other of his Socialist essays were based on similar themes. The class struggle was a reality, not because Marx said so, but because Darwin said so. "No, I am not a revolutionist or Marxist," Jack would sometimes confess. "I've read too much Spencer for that."[25] To him, the class struggle was the result of the ending of the frontier. There was no more opportunity for the aristocrats of the working class to pile up their own fortunes. They must therefore fight to replace the millionaires, since they could no longer become rich themselves. Then the proletariat would conquer under its new leaders as certainly as the sun also rose.[26]

In the battles before that inevitable victory, the working class would have its traitors, its Judases. These were the scabs. Nobody desired to scab, to give most for least. But in a tooth-and-nail society, the scab, desperate for a job, was the employer's weapon just as the union, ready to terrorize the scab, was the workers' weapon. Jack even approved of labor violence against scabs. The "will to live" of the scab recoiled from the menace of broken bones. Terrorism was a successful policy for labor unions. It probably won them more strikes than all the other weapons in their arsenal. A battle to the death was being waged between labor and capital, and all the weapons of open war should be used.[27]

In his confident moments, Jack could claim in his compelling way that some sort of logic held together all his contradictions— his sale of himself to Hearst and his attacks on capitalism, his marriage of reason and his urge to love, his solitary writing and his larking with the Crowd, his simple prose style and his savage yearnings, his insistence on logic when most compelled by his dark unconscious. If he occasionally admitted that he was careless and irregular and melancholy by nature, he soon reacted by imposing more work upon himself and by laughing at inspiration.[28] He insisted on trying to run his writing life like the steam room in the laundry.

It could not work. Jack's new publisher at Macmillan's, George Brett, had to warn him that daily writing might be the enemy of good writing. "There is no real place in the permanent world of literature for anything but the very best a man can do."[29] Jack should only do his best work, and nothing else. In principle, Jack agreed with his publisher; but in practice his new style of life needed a greater income than his best writing could support. In reaction from his meager childhood, he was generous. He did not like to stint the Crowd. He paid for two households, his own and his mother's. He was permanently in debt, as if, like Balzac or Dostoevsky, he needed the threat of his creditors to keep him at his desk.

Under their pressure, he accepted the worst proposition of his life, an outright offer from Macmillan's in 1902 of $2,000 for *The Call of the Wild*. The royalties on his first best-seller, which would be printed and reprinted in millions of copies, would have been enough to solve many of the financial problems of his life. Yet he needed the money at the time, he took it, and he held no grudge against his publishers. They did advertise the book as they had promised and they did help his reputation.

Permanently overspending, Jack seemed to find in struggling with his debts an excitement that he could not find in the increasing boredom of his marriage. He hated and condemned the bourgeois style of life, and yet he was living it in Piedmont. His wife was not his companion nor his intellectual equal; she was a good mother at the expense of being a good wife. He craved a mate of the sort that he could only find in Anna Strunsky and George Sterling. He continued to brood over his marriage, and he broke out. There were sprees in San Francisco and efforts to find another person to love. A crack in his confidence had begun. Later, he would set out notes for "A Great Novel" that he would never write. It would deal with his marriage to Bess. His complaints would be the familiar ones of a tired husband, the usual excuses of a man who has married a woman he does not love, and who hates domesticity.

"His faith and tolerance," the notes read,

> lack of nagging, never a scene. He early discovered how microscopic she was. . . .
>
> She was an egomaniac; her mother was, and so was his. So the three could not get along together.
>
> Her peasant mind. The band across her brows.
>
> In her talk, it was always herself—what she had done, what she was doing, her sacrifices; how she had slaved for her husband; how he lacked consideration. . . .
>
> His horror, later, when he learns there was nothing too sacred

for her to gossip about, and that she lied about those things as well. . . .

How he loved elsewhere before he knew she lied, how he looked on her sleeping face, and the child's, and cursed himself for a cur. His "long sickness."[30]

HIS LONG SICKNESS

I have experienced the greater frankness, several times under provocation, with a man or two, and a woman or two, and the occasions have been great joy-givers, as they have also been great sorrow-givers. I do not wish they had never happened, but I recoil unconsciously from their happening again. It is so much easier to live placidly and complacently. Of course, to live placidly and complacently is not to live at all, but still between prize fights and kites and one thing and another I manage to fool my inner self pretty well. Poor inner self. I wonder if it will atrophy, dry up some day and blow away.

JACK LONDON to CHARMIAN KITTREDGE

Jack had thought his hunger was for fame as a writer. Now he had that fame, and the hunger was still in him. He had endured the lonely struggle for success because of his fantasy of breaking down a wall of eastern indifference. The wall was breached, Boston and New York were won, yet there was no pleasure in the work any more, just the getting of money. He had kicked open the doors of smart society in San Francisco; now smart society began to repel him.

There was also something wrong with his obsessive discipline. It had forced him to deny his passions, to warp his nature. Perhaps universal ideas were not everything. Besides the survival of the fittest and the brotherhood of man, what about the supremacy of self? Jack began to hear of Stirner and Nietzsche and their praise of the egotist and the superman. He began to sink into what he

Anna Strunsky, the first great love of Jack's life.

called the "long sickness," that reassessment of himself which most people undertake when their marriage fails and their dreams are achieved too quickly. As in the Irish fairy tale, Jack had reached the crock of gold at the end of the rainbow. He felt sick when he found it full of dry leaves.

His loss of control first showed in his pursuit of Anna Strunsky. As early as 1900, he had proposed that they collaborate on a book, writing fictitious letters to each other. It would be a dangerous collaboration, in point of fact, an opposition of two minds. He would take the part of Herbert Wace, a young economics professor with a belief in logic and evolution. She would take the part of his older friend, Dane Kempton, with a tempered faith in romantic idealism. They set to work. In the first of the letters, Anna as Kempton congratulated young Wace on his engagement to be married—only to receive the cool reply that marriage was a mere institution to perpetuate the species. For Wace, there need be no distorting element of love in such a practical and biological relationship.

As Dane Kempton, Anna immediately challenged such an unnatural view of marriage. She had not understood Jack's relationship with Bess, and she saw his growing disillusionment. During the two years of their working on the book, they would grow closer and closer, provoking the jealousy of Bess by their obvious intimacy. In the fictitious letters as in his life, Jack might protest that love was a mere blind prejudice, but the collaboration would revive his old love of Anna and convince her that their intellectual differences might be less important than their mutual passion.

Before the writing of the book started, Jack tried to present the idea coolly to his friends, hiding his desire in his usual shroud of reason. "A young Russian Jewess of 'Frisco and myself," he wrote to Cloudesley Johns,

> have often quarreled over our conceptions of love. She happens to be a genius. She is also a materialist by philosophy, and an idealist by innate preference, and is constantly being forced to twist all the facts of the universe in order to reconcile herself with herself. So,

finally, we decided that the only way to argue the question out would be by letter. Then we wondered if a collection of such letters should happen to be worth publishing. Then we assumed characters, threw in a real objective love element, and started to work.[1]

As the project progressed, their passions and their disagreements grew. Their coolness melted in the frustration of their thwarted love for each other. "You are a fanatic of a text," Anna complained as Dane Kempton. "You are in the toils of an idea, the idea of selection, as I well know, and you exploit it like a drudge. . . . Nature spares the type, but the individual must spare himself." A great man like Herbert Wace or Jack himself should stay alone like an aristocrat. He should not settle for the dull convention of marriage with a woman he did not love. "Slave to your theory and rebel to the law, you lose your soul and imperil another's."

Jack countered this assault in the words of Herbert Wace. There was nothing cramped or narrow or incompatible about him and his partner. It would be a marriage of doers, not wonderers; of thinkers, not feelers; of intellects, not emotions. In the end, a man had to breed and breed well. "The slug must procreate its kind or its kind will perish; and so I. The need being the same, the only difference is in the expression." Man should practice sexual selection upon himself to beget healthy children as carefully as he used it on fish and fowl, the beast and the vegetable.

The Kempton-Wace Letters defined the intellectual conflict between Anna and Jack—their stated reason for not staying together in the first place. Actually, class expectations and lack of money had separated them, but Jack had now joined Anna's class and he was earning money. She was close to his literary success and new power, she knew his suppressed passion and thrilled to it. "I care because I know you to be of those who are capable of love," Anna declared as Dane Kempton, but describing her Jack. "Probably it was one little twist in your development that has turned you into alien ways of thinking and living."[2]

Privately to Anna, Jack began to admit his apostasy, although his mouthpiece Wace still defended biology above romance. The

day after Christmas, 1900, he wrote to her that he was suffering
from a bad attack of the blues:

> Just when freedom seems opening up to me, I feel the bands tighten-
> ing and the riveting of the gyves. I remember, now, when I was free.
> When there was no restraint, and I did what the heart willed. Yes,
> one restraint, the Law; but when one willed, one could fight the Law,
> and break or be broken. But now, one's hands are tied, one may not
> fight, but only yield and bow the neck. . . .
>   I could almost advocate a return to nature this dark morning. A
> happiness to me?—added to me?—Why you have been a delight to
> me, dear, and a glory. Need I add, a trouble? For the things we love
> are the things which hurt us as well as the things we hurt. . . . The
> things unsaid are the greatest. Surely, sitting here, gathering data,
> classifying, arranging; writing stories for boys with moral purposes
> insidiously inserted; hammering away at a thousand words a day;
> growing genuinely excited over biological objections; thrusting a bit
> of fun at you and raising a laugh, when it should have been a sob—
> surely all this is not all. What have you been to me? I am not great
> enough or brave enough to say. This false thing, which the world
> would call my conscience, will not permit me.[3]

Jack's yearning toward Anna grew, declared itself. Three
months after the birth of his first daughter in 1901, he was writing
to Anna, "Large temperamentally—that is it. It is the one thing that
brings us at all in touch. We have, flashed through us, you and I,
each a bit of the universal, and so we draw together." By October
1901, he was writing to her as "Dear You" and thanking her for
a glowing review of *The God of His Fathers,* in which she had insisted
on the Promethean quality of Jack's work.[4] By January 1902, he
wrote to her as "Dear, Dear You"—both of them could only look
back on a tumultuous and bankrupt year. By February, he was
confessing the difficulty of keeping himself under control. "For one
of my mold," he admitted, "I realize how easily I may go to pieces."
He was on the point of declaring himself. "You are the world's
desire, you proud-breasted woman. . . . To you I have stuttered and
failed to tell my inmost thoughts."[5]

The writing of *The Kempton-Wace Letters* continued as their love
grew. By the end of March 1902, they had completed 50,000

words of one of the rare deliberate courtships by literary device. The book did not end with the conversion of Herbert Wace, "the Werther of science," weeping over his rational folly, but with a wish fulfillment of its authors, in which Wace's woman, balking at a loveless marriage, leaves him to his self-sufficiency and the passionless pursuit of passionless knowledge.

In the spring and early summer of 1902, Jack declared his love, signing himself by a pet name, "The Sahib." One letter to her ran: "Dear, Dear You, I shall be over Friday afternoon. I am doing 2000 words a day now, and every day, and my head is in such a whirl I can hardly think. But I feel. I am sick with love for you and need of you."[6] He took candid photographs of her, although it was Bess who had taught him how to use a camera. He threw caution to the winds of the Bay. Their association reached the edge of scandal.

Then, out of nowhere, another way of escape from his marriage came to Jack. It was a call from the American Press Association to report the effects of the peace in South Africa after the ending of the Boer War. His wanderlust revived, and with it, his adolescent hope that freedom lay in leaving home. He immediately accepted the offer, and his parting with Anna at the railroad station was painful. As he sailed off to see the coronation of King Edward VII in England on August 9, 1902, he answered an "ink-beteared" letter from Anna. The Sahib loved her, he wrote.[7]

Absence does not make the heart grow fonder; it makes the heart forget. When Jack's assignment to South Africa was canceled and he continued to stay away, disappearing into the London slums, Anna came to her senses and ended the affair. Her letter of rejection does not survive; his angry reply does. He wrote that he had a mad, blind reaction to the blow from her, like a prizefighter's. He should take the knockout clean and put up no defense. In future, he would dream romances for other people and transmute them into bread and butter. The publication of *The Kempton-Wace Letters* must be the filtered record of their passion. He had closed certain volumes of his life for ever. "These volumes will remain closed. In them I shall read no more."[8]

His flight from the toils of unexpected—and rejected—love

Jack dressed as a tramp for his research on *The People of the Abyss*.

led him into the slums of the East End of London. After seeing the coronation procession with its mighty display of imperial force, from the shining Horse Guards to the coolies swinging along under the weight of their machine guns, Jack vanished into the East End, buying some old clothes for 10 shillings and pretending to be an American sailor who had lost his ship.

Before leaving New York, he had discussed a book on the London slums with George Brett and he knew what he wanted to find there. He meant to expose the underside of imperialism, the degradation of the workers who made and sent off the goods in the ships that dominated the seven seas. As an evolutionary Socialist, he had already preconceived his vision of the East End as the Black Hole of capitalism, the slough of human hope. Before the boat had reached England, he had announced to Anna that he meant to take "the standpoint of the London beasts. That's all they are—beasts— if they are anything like the slum people of New York—beasts, shot through with stray flashes of divinity."9

Only among the muggers, thieves, and tarts of the Commercial Road did Jack find his bestial savages of the city jungle. These snarled and fought and killed in a tooth-and-claw struggle for existence. But he saw no Darwinian conflict among the working masses of the East End; rather, a sluggish tide of general misery in which some families felt a dull animal happiness, the content of a full belly. A deadly inertia inhibited any progress. There was no sense of ambition, no working-class aristocracy striving to better itself. The color of life was gray and drab. Everything seemed helpless, hopeless, unrelieved, and dirty.10

This vision of a City of Dreadful Monotony was made darker by Jack's own revulsion from urban life. His move from Oakland to the Piedmont Hills had made him recant his early love of the stimulus of the streets. "The city life is too unnatural and monstrous for us folks of the West," he told Cloudesley Johns. "To hell with it. There's more in life than what the social shambles offers."11 When the workers from the East End of London did escape briefly to pick hops in Kent in the summer, they were so degraded that they desecrated the sweetness and purity of nature. They should stay in their own festering slums and ghettoes, where they would certainly die. The Abyss of London was a huge man-killing machine.

Jack found his desired apocalypse by deliberately hunting for the worst areas of poverty in the East End. He was taken by guides to a sweatshop and to the tramps' dosshouse on the benches of Spitalfields Garden under the shadow of the church spire. When he saw the down-and-outs rotting there, he wrote: "A lung of London? Nay, an abscess, a great putrescent sore." He then managed to spend two nights in the casual ward of the Whitechapel workhouse. To pay for his hard bread and gruel, he was sent as a scavenger into the Whitechapel Infirmary to dispose of the refuse from the sick wards. His comments on this dangerous task were characteristically harsh and Darwinian. Perhaps there was a wise mercy in the scavengers dying of germs from the refuse. "These men of the spike, the peg, and the street, are encumbrances. They are of no good or use to anyone, nor to themselves. They clutter the earth with their presence, and are better out of the way."

Two nights in the workhouse were enough for Jack, and he fled to a Turkish bath to cleanse himself. After that and a good meal, he was ready to try the mercy of the Salvation Army. To earn a Sunday breakfast in the Blackfriars Road, he had to stand with 700 men for four hours, and then endure a sermon with a text about the feasts awaiting the poor in Paradise when they had finished starving upon earth. Such an effort at soul-snatching among the homeless seemed to him misplaced, particularly when they had to suffer being herded like swine and treated like curs for their breakfast.

Dipping briefly into newspaper accounts of crime and into the statistics collected by Charles Booth in twenty years of research, Jack completed his book, *The People of the Abyss,* seven weeks after landing in England. His conclusions were prejudged. To him, the London Abyss was another Social Pit. The inefficient were weeded out and flung downwards. The efficient emigrated, taking the best qualities of the stock with them. The British race was enfeebling itself and dividing itself into two classes, a master race and a ghetto race. A short and stunted people was being created—a breed strikingly different from their rulers. Mismanagement by the government had condemned the working masses to this fate. If this was the best that civilization could do for the human being, then savagery was preferable. "Far better to be a people of the wilderness and desert, of the cave and the squatting-place, than to be a people of the machine and the Abyss."[12]

Jack was later to say that *The People of the Abyss* was the book he loved the most, for no other book had taken so much of his young heart and tears. Yet his compulsion to condemn the nightmare of his surroundings had prevented him from seeing many of the truths about the East End. To cooler observers, the place seemed to be a group of working urban villages with a strong sense of tradition and community. Jack even admitted to George Sterling that his work was rather hysterical in "the country God has forgotten that he forgot."[13] His prose and point of view were overwrought, more propaganda than philosophy, more passion than description.

Yet *The People of the Abyss* still has the power to move and to shock. It has all the merit of the urgent first impression, none of the saving grace of the judicious survey. There is some truth in an unfavorable contemporary review of the book, which said that the author described the East End as Dante might have described the Inferno if he had been a yellow journalist.[14] Yet there is another truth in Jack's own defense. "Is the picture overdrawn? It all depends. For one who sees and thinks life in terms of shares and coupons, it is certainly overdrawn. But for one who sees and thinks life in terms of manhood and womanhood, it cannot be overdrawn."[15]

If the book is not finally a masterpiece of indignation, it is because of a flaw in Jack's method and intensity of feeling. His experience as a Road Kid and Klondiker had been prolonged. He had lived those lives as a participant, not as a mere reporter. His brief descent into the London Abyss was planned and artificial. He found a clean study in the home of a police detective where he could write, he took a camera with him to distance himself from the people, he chose guides to take him into the worst of the slums. He was setting up the situations of his wrath, not living in them.

The Abyss was also opening within himself. It was the gap he had to bridge between his doing and his words, between his logic and his emotion. His appetites and fears and lusts were breaking loose. He confused the fury of his disappointed love for Anna with his hatred of an unjust industrial system that had ruined his youth. His rushing words masked the failure of his integrity as an observer who had hurried through his research and writing. He had begun, not to gild the lily, but to flick red paint on his own wounds.

After his slumming, Jack set out to enjoy himself in Paris and Spezia and Rome. He discovered with excitement the revolutionary feeling among the comrades of the French and Italian cities. He drank with them, he roistered with them, he was once again the free adventurer and radical. "Oh, it was glorious," he wrote back to Anna. "The Revolution looms large but the bourgeoisie will not see it. How I curse them sometimes these days when I see all this worse than useless misery. I think I understand anarchy better by far than I did before."[16]

Yet this brief escape into free wandering ended soon enough. Jack felt bound to return to the United States to take up his duties as a father and a writer. He made an effort to patch up his marriage and to hide the sickness within himself, the strain between his domestic life and his violent urge to be his own master. In a letter to Anna, he excused his apparent weakness and denial of his nature. If she wanted to pursue her wrestling with angels, she might do so and call him a coward for leaving the fight. "So be it. I am so made, as you are otherwise made. I prefer least to nothing. You prefer nothing or all to less."[17]

Yet Jack was only pretending to himself that he had settled for the least of all possible worlds. He was also forced to sit down and write for money. His first novel, which had been commissioned by *McClure's,* was a failure; they would not issue it but sold it off to another firm of publishers. They also stopped their monthly payments to Jack and insisted he repay his debt by sending them future stories for their magazine. Even he admitted that *A Daughter of the*

Snows did not work. Although it was full of the sight and sound and terror of the Alaskan wasteland, its heroine was, as one critic declared, as much a monster, a thing contrary to nature, as the phenomenon constructed by the philosopher Frankenstein. She remained incredible and inconceivable; she never lived as a human being.[18]

She was meant to represent Jack's perfect biological and intellectual mate, capable of quoting Spencer and following the huskies for 20 miles at a temperature of 70 degrees below zero, but her motives were as unlikely as her skills. She defended her Anglo-Saxon faith as if debating in Berkeley rather than having a conversation with a hopeful lover. "We are a race of doers and fighters," she declared, "of globe-encirclers and zone-conquerors. We toil and struggle, and stand by the toil and struggle no matter how hopeless it may be." Yet she was no feminist. She despised the propaganda for women's rights. She did not stand for the new woman, but for the new womanhood.[19] She was the companion and the mate whom Jack did not meet on the Klondike trail. And finally, she was as unreal as Michelangelo's sculpture of Morning—a hard-limbed youth with breasts tacked on as an afterthought.

George Brett at Macmillan's did not agree to publish this failed novel, but he did agree to save Jack's finances. He provided him with $150 a month for two years in return for the right to publish all his books, including *The People of the Abyss* and *The Kempton-Wace Letters*. Jack promised for his part to try to write his best work, and to stop spending most of his time on magazine articles and potboilers. That winter in his home in Piedmont, he did take the time to write his masterpiece, *The Call of the Wild*. The novel is not so much the story of a dog that becomes a wolf as a myth about life and death and nature. It is a saga of the unconscious, written without self-criticism in an age before Jung was known in America.[20] Jack claimed later that he wrote it without any thought about its deeper significance as a human allegory. "I was unconscious of it at the time. I did not mean to do it."[21]

The achievement of the book lies in Jack's fusion of his own suppressed nature with that of a beast. His hero Buck begins as a

children's pet, sloppy in the lap of Californian luxury. A kidnapping
and a beating by a human demon in a red sweater break Buck's trust
in men. As Jack was clubbed into fortune through overwork, Buck
is clubbed into the terrible toil of service as a sled-dog in the
northern wastes. He transcends his role as a servant of the greed
of mankind by reverting to his archetype, the wolf from which he
derives. In a fight to the death, he kills the leader of the sled-dogs
and becomes the chief of the work-beasts; but his new human
masters, as careless of their labor force as any tycoon, make him toil
to the edge of extinction. When the love of his saviour John Thornton briefly reclaims Buck, it is only an interlude in his descent to
the primitive. With Thornton's death at the hands of human savages, Buck becomes the leader of the wolfpack and an avenger
upon men, a master of the wilderness.

Psychologists can recognize the significance of the symbol of
the wolf in Jack's life. After 1903, he signed his intimate letters
"Wolf." He named the house he was to build Wolf House. He kept
a husky called Brown Wolf. His bookplate was a wolf's head. He
became more and more aware of his correspondence with the wolf
—the destroyer and preserver of Norse mythology, the dark force
of destruction to the Greeks, and the life-giving inspiration of the
Romans who believed that Romulus and Remus were suckled by
a she-wolf. Both aspects of the wolf appealed to Jack's split nature:
the lone wolf which went about its business in solitude, and the
leader of the wolfpack which survived by its coherence.[22]

As Jack called up his unconscious to write his best book, the
nightmares of his childhood began again to haunt his life and his
work. His dog hero, Buck, had bad dreams, harking back to the life
of his forebears. Buck forgot domestication, he lifted his nose to the
stars and howled like a wolf at the mystery of the world and the dark
and the unknown ages of his inheritance. He dreamed of hairy
apish men, his first masters, and he dreamed back to a time of great
beasts of prey and total savagery. He also heard the call from the
depths of the forest, which filled him with a great unrest and strange
desires. He felt a vague, sweet gladness, and yearnings and strivings
for he knew not what. His longing for raw meat and blood sent him

back to the hunt and the forest. And when his loved master died, he became a spirit of the wild, a ghost dog forever running at the head of the wolfpack, leaping and gigantic, bellowing the song of a younger world.

In Buck's bad dreams, Jack recorded his own childish fears of cold, deprivation, and solitude, as well as his compulsion always to be free and roving, on the hunt to gratify every desire, yet leading his brothers of the wild in the quest of eternal youth. Of course, these were myths—the myth of the birth from nothingness and darkness, the myth of the death of the father in Buck's loved master, and in the pulling down of the bull moose by the pack, the myth of the innocent savage in the wilderness, the myth of the ghost leader forever calling on the young. But Jack believed that people respond to the literature of fear and nightmare, because fear is deep in the roots of the race. However civilized men think they are, fear remains their deepest emotion. In the same period, he had written an essay praising Edgar Allan Poe for his grasp of the terrible and the tragic. He thought the public would respond to his private terror as it did to Poe's own.[23]

In another book created during the three years of his "long sickness," *Before Adam,* Jack relied even more on his dream consciousness. The narrator said what was true of the author, who slept so little because he was scared of sleep: "My nights marked the reign of fear—and such fear!"[24] Like Jack, the dreamer in *Before Adam* suffered a procession of nightmares, full of forests and horrors without end, great serpents and prowling monsters; he had lost his true primeval father, and his alien stepfather pushed him out of the treehouse where he lived with his suspicious and unprogressive mother into the tooth-and-claw world of prehistory. As an atavistic projection of Jack's distorted vision of his deprived childhood, the opening of *Before Adam* can serve as a document in Jungian analysis.

Yet in his life, Jack managed to keep up the façade of domesticity, although early in 1903 Cloudesley Johns visited the house in Piedmont and noticed Jack's forced exuberance and the strain on the marriage. Later, Johns claimed that Bess had already persuaded her husband to play a terrible game of "Let's pretend" for the sake of his career and the children.[25] At any rate, Jack sought his old pattern of escape. He bought an aged sloop with the money from the outright sale of *The Call of the Wild* and called it the *Spray* after that other aged sloop in which Joshua Slocum had sailed single-handed round the world.

Jack was an exceptional small-boat sailor and a daring one. The *Spray* was small and fast, with a roomy cabin, where he could cook and bunk down with a guest. He was thinking of writing a novel about his sealing voyage on the *Sophia Sutherland,* to emulate Conrad as he had emulated Kipling. He also wanted to write out of himself the violent war between his appetites and his acquired courtesies. The working title of this book was *The Mercy of the Sea,* and he felt he needed the immediate taste of the salt air to stimulate him. Despite the demands of his family, his friends, and the Crowd, he finished the novel in the course of 1903, mainly sitting on the hatch of his sloop as it lay at anchor.

Cloudesley Johns spent the last two months of the writing period on the boat with Jack. They crossed the tiderip through the Golden Gate and made the Sacramento River; they stood on watch in the fog in a tule swamp with its 12-foot rushes; they shot mud-hens to send as a joke to George Sterling for one of his duck dinners; they got drunk with the surviving oyster-pirates in Benicia; they played chess and argued and wrote their daily stints. Johns noticed how Jack relaxed in simple male company. He even slept six hours a night without disturbance and awoke refreshed.

Herman Scheffauer also remembered a sail on the *Spray* with some of the Crowd. To him, the scene was always his symbol of Jack, a devil-may-care sailor defying the unknown. Jack had taken them out into the path of the ferryboats plying between San Francisco and Sausalito, when a fog suddenly came down and blinded them. The little sloop was surrounded by the droning siren calls of the ferryboats and the clap-clapping of their paddlewheels. Some of the young women began to scream.

> And there stood Jack London with a rusty fog-horn in the bow of the boat, lustily blowing his warning note against the white wall of the

unknown from behind which Destruction was approaching. The next moment—white, spectral, gigantic—the ferry-boat shot past us a mere boat's length away. We heard shouts from the horrified passengers, and the next moment it vanished again as we were flung to the side by the wash.[26]

Jack not only impressed the Crowd with his daring, but he also recorded the scene in the opening of his best long novel, *The Sea-Wolf.* Two boats collide in a fog on the Bay. A weakling critic, Humphrey van Weyden, is flung overboard and then rescued by a seal hunter called the *Ghost,* captained by the savage Wolf Larsen. The creation of the character of Larsen, blended from Melville's Ahab, Milton's Lucifer, and an actual seal-poacher called Alexander McLean, was a triumph that could call forth praise even from Ambrose Bierce. Larsen also seemed to be a version of Nietzsche's Superman, although Jack had merely heard of Nietzsche from his old Socialist friend Frank Strawn-Hamilton and from stray references in magazines. Only after the book was completed did Jack begin to read the new translations of Nietzsche and to recognize an explanation for his own "long sickness," a phrase he found in the German philosopher. As he so often did, he studied and affirmed his supposed influences after he was told they had influenced him. Actually, the inspiration for Larsen's dominance seems to derive more from the giant heroes of the sagas and the frontier tradition. The conflict of Larsen and Van Weyden also appears to be based on Spencer rather than Nietzsche. Evolution rather than the ego, the survival of the fittest rather than the drive to mastery are the root ideas of *The Sea-Wolf.*

The novel itself contains three plots. The first is taken from Kipling's *Captains Courageous;* in it, the sissy Van Weyden is forced by necessity into becoming the rough sailor. The second is the fight to the death between Van Weyden and Larsen, who both repels and attracts his opponent by his animal magnetism. "His body, thanks to his Scandinavian stock, was fair as the fairest woman's," Van Weyden writes of Larsen. "I remember him putting his hand up to feel of the wound on his head and my watching the biceps move like a living thing under its white sheath. It was the biceps that had nearly crushed out my life once, that I had seen strike so many killing blows. I could not take my eyes from him."²⁷

In such terms, Jack revealed a great deal of his feelings in 1903, the summer when he was confessing to George Sterling his man's love of the poet's beauty. He also revealed his new and artificial romance with another woman in the third plot of *The Sea-Wolf,* the love story between Van Weyden and the castaway Maud Brewster—awful, in Bierce's opinion, with its absurd suppressions and impossible proprieties.²⁸

Yet Jack's new love affair with Charmian Kittredge was truly full of absurd suppressions and impossible proprieties, and he resented people who identified him only with the primordial beast in Larsen, since he saw himself equally as the delicate and respectful Van Weyden:

> The critics had expected to have my hero make love with a club and drag my heroine by the hair of her head and into a tree. Because I didn't they branded my love as sentimental bosh and nonsense—and yet I flatter myself I can make love as well as the next fellow, and not quite as ridiculously as the average critic.²⁹

Charmian Kittredge certainly thought so. When she became the object of his sentimental and excessive passion, she was quick to respond and take on his manner, just as she had been quick to fence and box with him in the Crowd. She liked to play the role of the Eternal Kid, always ready to enthuse and even gush. She appealed to the suppressed adolescent in Jack, who had never been able to pour out his romantic longings to a teen-age love, absurd as they might be. Now he could indulge himself with a woman who played the girl. She might be five years older than he, but she also refused to grow up. He could share with her the dream of perpetual youth and play, which would only become an illusion when they had to stop.

In the opinion of most of the Crowd, Charmian hunted the discontented Jack until she broke up his marriage. Yet Jack was the hunter in the beginning. He had lost Anna Strunsky, his marriage was stifling him, he had his eyes on a dozen women, looking for somebody brave enough to have a flaming affair with him.[30] This one began in the June of 1903. Jack had sent his wife and children to Wake Robin near Glen Ellen, where he had rented a summer cabin from Charmian's aunt, Ninetta Eames. He had remained behind at Piedmont to write *The Sea-Wolf* and sail on the *Spray.* Then he had an accident. Out in his buggy with George Sterling and some of the Crowd, he drove it into a ravine, took a toss, and hurt his leg. He was always morose over his illnesses because his sickness interfered with his work. He was isolated, miserable, vulnerable, and looking for love like a sick child. One visitor came to see him while he was lying in bed in Piedmont: Charmian Kittredge. She was ending a love affair, and also looking for consolation.

He made the running. She did not resist, because of her frankness and previous experience. Attracted by such emancipation, Jack soon found out that she was also full of the proprieties. She insisted on his delicacy and his discretion. He responded to her insistence, for he was in love with his new ideal of love—a noble, sensitive, and passionate relationship with another person. He even put the blame for their affair on George Sterling, for his love of the poet had revealed to him his own need to love.[31] He was no longer inhibited from declaring what he felt. To Charmian, indeed, he wrote of his dream of the great Man-Comrade:

> This man should be so much one with me that we could never misunderstand. He should love the flesh, as he should the spirit, honoring and loving each and giving each its due. . . . He should be delicate and tender, brave and game; sensitive as he pleased in the soul of him, and in the body of him unfearing and unwitting of pain. He should be warm with the glow of great adventure, unafraid of the harshnesses of life and its evils, and knowing all its harshness and evil.[32]

Charmian in her boyish vitality seemed to approach such an all-round comrade and, finally, she conquered him as a woman.

It was difficult for Charmian to personify this ideal all the time, but she always tried gamely. She was a superb horsewoman, who mastered her mounts and drove them hard; she had a strong and trim body that did not tire easily. Anything Jack did, she attempted to do as well without flinching. In the hundreds of albums of photographs of their relationship which she kept, she was always smiling, whatever the cost.

Jack's new passion was so strong that he wanted to gratify it often; but he had first to deal with his wife. He joined her and his family at Wake Robin for a time. There they lived communally and frugally, sharing a kitchen with the other families camped beneath the tall redwoods. Jack damned the stream and taught his children to swim in the little pool he had made. Then Charmian came to stay with her aunt. One night during July, she and Jack spent several hours together in a large hammock by the stream. He could not make a decision, nor could she.

One of his letters to her recalled the time:

> It makes me thrill with gladness when you tell how you hesitated and half turned back that night in the hammock. And I am more than glad that you did not turn back. Our way, our own way, the way we have come together, was the best. And yet, had you turned back, the result would not have been altered. My need for you was too great, too deep, too intrinsic, for me to have ever been contented with less than *all* of you. And, God! God! I have all of you, and I am loved as it is given to few men to be loved! I could pray, did I have aught to pray to. I have only you, and I am on my knees to you.[33]

It was still an age of discretion. Jack was married; Charmian's reputation could be ruined. He left her in the hammock and went to his wife Bess to announce that he was separating himself from her. Bess was not told the cause. She was already jealous of Anna Strunsky, although Anna was now living in New York. *The Kempton-Wace Letters* had been published anonymously, but gossip had discovered the names of the authors and the mocking references by Herbert Wace to a loveless and biological marriage had wounded Bess deeply. Remembering the intimacy between Anna and Jack during the writing of the book, she assumed that Anna was the other woman, especially as Charmian took care to remain her good friend. Bess was even to cite Anna in her eventual divorce petition, claiming that Jack had told her of his love for Anna before he went to England, and that he had said to her then: "We must part. You shall have Joan."[34]

The separation began the next morning. Jack left for Oakland, where he rented an apartment at 1216 Telegraph Avenue. He brought in his mother Flora to do the housekeeping, along with Johnny Miller. Although she grew to dislike Charmian, she was happy at last, looking after her famous writer son. She defended him from all callers and from the notoriety now falling on his head, as it had fallen on hers when she was carrying him.

Jack had always striven for publicity, believing that it would sell his books and make his name. But he shrank from scandal, fearful that the secret of his birth would come out and expose his careful lies about his origins. Punishing him for his quick success, the newspapers were turning against him for the first time. They hinted that his separation from his wife was a device to make a best-seller out of *The Kempton-Wace Letters*. "Mr. Jack London, the author," the Chicago *Record Herald* declared, "has found a new method of advertising that will undoubtedly prove a great help to him and his publishers, whether he has gone into it deliberately or otherwise." The Detroit *Journal* agreed "that the semblance of a scandal has inflated and is inflating the sale of the *Letters* far beyond their worth."[35]

It was one of the first cases in the American market of a scandal being used to push the sales of a book. Everywhere, Jack's name was linked with Anna Strunsky's. He was in despair, but he would not tell the truth. He felt he had to protect Charmian's reputation at the expense of Anna's, relying on Anna's understanding and forgiveness. "It will soon die away, I believe," he wrote to her. "And so it goes. I wander through life delivering hurts to all that know me. And so one pays for the little hour—only, it is the woman who always pays."[36]

He, too, was paying. He felt guilty about abandoning his wife and his two small daughters. When Joan fell ill of typhoid fever, he

rushed to her bedside and reconciliation seemed possible; but with
her recovery, he left again for the *Spray*. He plunged more deeply
into his sexual passion for Charmian, as if his desire and the gratification of it would convince him that he had done right: he endowed
his love with mythical proportions as he had his deprived boyhood
and his struggle to become a writer. Since nobody had ever loved
a woman as he did his Charmian, the caliber of his love excused any
choice he might have to make to satisfy it. He was no trifler, he was
in the grip of his destiny.

"Yes," he wrote to Charmian on the first day of September,
"we must have been planned for each other from the beginning—
at least you for me. You meet me on every side of me. I have met
so many ones, who had this side, or that side, or the other side; but
none had every side. Here they missed, and there they missed, just
where you hit and hit." Yet, although they were alike in so much,
she was feminine and he masculine. There was a balance between
them, in which their minds and flesh came together. "You and I,
oh, dear dear Love, we are perfect animals, and we have our measure of soul too, and we love, we perfectly love, as man and woman
were made to love."

Later that month, he wrote her a long letter about how short
and terminal life was, how it had to be caught on the wing.

> Remember, each moment I am robbed of you, each night and all
> nights I am turned away from you, turned out by you, give me pangs
> the exquisiteness of which must be measured by the knowledge that
> they are moments and nights lost, lost, lost forever. For my little
> space of life is only so long. Tomorrow or the next day I cease
> forever; and the moment I am robbed of you and the night I must
> be away from you will never, never come again. There is no compen-
> sation. It is all dead and utter loss. So I live from day to day like an
> unwilling prodigal. . . . For I know I am twenty-seven, at the high-
> tide of my life and vigor; and I know that these wasted moments are
> the brightest-minted of all my moments.

On October 12, he wrote to her from the *Spray* to say that the
happiness she had given him would always keep him from the

suicidal thoughts which came to him in his nightmares and his insomnia. She had taught him that his life was worth living. "I thought of you as I had you and knew you mine on Saturday. Blessed day! And over and over I lived every moment of it, from the three bells to the parting. God! You do love me! I never needed any proof of it, yet each new proof is sweet, so sweet. And this last proof is not alone sweet; it is heroic. You *are* brave, my own Mate Woman." For she had risked her reputation in traveling to see him openly. "So long as you are alive I could never hit out on the Long Trail into the West without you. Did you die, and did I not die, too, I could NEVER, NEVER hit that same *Long Trail.* It would be impossible."

As his letters show, his pursuit and desire of her were excessive and hallucinatory. He was in a delirium of joyous physical life. He took mental pictures of her to his bed, filled with the glory of her "sweet body bathed with the starlight as I saw it in our Sacred Grove."[37] Cloudesley Johns, who knew of the intensity of the affair, warned his friend not to abandon himself utterly to the insanity of sexual love. He would set a pace for himself he could not possibly keep. He would induce Charmian to expect miracles and demand miracles. All passion grew less. In the end, it would be just as damned hard on a love mate as on a woman like Bess, married for good reason.[38]

Yet Jack's pent-up emotions were flooding out of control. Manic, he completed *The Sea-Wolf,* plunged in guilt over his children and fervor for Charmian. More important, he began to feel a commitment toward Charmian for her courage in going on with the affair. They were fairly discreet, but he was enough of a gentleman in the age of the double standard to know that he was in no danger from the liaison, while she jeopardized her position in their small society.

By such self-dramatization and exaggeration, which he took as proof of the wildness of his passion, Jack fell victim to the old conventions that had led to his revolt. He promised Charmian marriage when his divorce from Bess should be granted. The mistake of his first marriage did not stop him from pledging himself to a second one. In the meantime, his true escape was to the *Spray* and to *The Sea-Wolf.*

Writers do not necessarily do their best work when suffering from the most strain. Jack was a man who had forced his talent into mining a single, almost exhausted, vein for the market. The publication in 1903 of his fourth volume of Alaskan stories, *The Faith of Men*, showed that his invention was becoming labored, his realism was being overlaid by mannerism, his myths were turning into tall tales. He was imitating his own style and subject matter until they were collapsing like huskies in harness. Only one story was remarkable as a counterpoint to *The Call of the Wild*—"Bâtard," the grim account of the fight to the death between a wolf dog and its cruel master, which played out on the heroic scale Jack's own struggle to kill off the stigma of his bastardy.

Written out and exhausted by love, he was offered another dramatic escape. A war between the Russians and the Japanese was threatening in Korea. Jack was penniless again. Four separate news agencies asked him to report the coming war for them. The Hearst press made the best offer, so he decided to head for that distant action which would allow him to forget the turmoil of self and California. He sailed from San Francisco early in 1904 on the *Siberia* bound for Yokohama without telling Bess that Charmian, not Anna, was the other woman in his life. Perhaps he evaded that important truth because of a final caution, a withdrawal from a public commitment to his excessive love.

By 1903, it was clear that his apparent anarchy was only another disguise for the neurosis which kept him working obsessively to earn money, and which made him cling to the good opinion of society for fear of being condemned to the horrors of the Social Pit. To Anna, who had begun his liberation, Jack had confessed why he could never be liberated. It was too late, he was too deformed.

> I have lived twenty-five years of repression. I learned not to be enthusiastic. It is a hard lesson to forget. I begin to forget, but it is so little. At the best, before I die, I cannot hope to forget all or most. I can exult, now that I am learning, in little things, in other things;

but of my things, and secret things doubly mine, I cannot, I cannot. Do I make myself intelligible? Do you hear my voice? I fear not. There are poseurs. I am the most successful of them all.[39]

His poses no longer convinced himself. His chosen character was disintegrating. He had begun the long sickness of self-examination. He now admitted to the passion and torment and dream within him that he had always refused to recognize. The myths of his past no longer fitted. He must find new ones to hide behind.

MATE-WOMAN AND ANCHOR

As a brain merchant I was a success. Society opened its portals to me. I entered right in on the parlor floor, and my disillusionment proceeded rapidly. I sat down to dinner with the masters of society, and with the wives and daughters of the masters of society. The women were gowned beautifully, I admit; but to my naive surprise I discovered that they were of the same clay as all the rest of the women I had known down below in the cellar. "The colonel's lady and Judy O'Grady were sisters under their skins"—and gowns. It was not this, however, so much as their materialism, that shocked me.

JACK LONDON

Jack had long cherished a cult of the perfect male body, which he sometimes confused with his own. He had pictures taken of himself in bathing costume, flexing his muscles and shadowboxing. He took snapshots of George Sterling posing on the beach, wearing nothing. Obsessive descriptions of male Anglo-Saxon strength, grace, and sexuality began to creep into his novels, particularly *The Game*, written in the summer of 1904. In that romance of prizefighting, the hero expressed Jack's vanity about his own body—his skin was fair as a woman's, his face like a Greek cameo, his stance a perfection of line and strength, yet with a deep smooth chest and "muscles under their satin sheaths—crypts of energy wherein lurked the chemistry of destruction."[1]

His confidence in his own perfect physique began to crack during the voyage to Japan. He had already survived bad attacks

Japanese military authorities check Jack's credentials as a war correspondent on his way to Korea in 1904.

of shingles and scurvy, and he had smashed both knees and his right ankle in various tumbles. Once again he crippled himself, wrenching his left ankle in a leaping game on the deck with the other war correspondents, who called themselves the Vultures. It was the beginning of a morbid worry about his physical condition, a long anxiety that would end only with his death.

His injured ankle did not stop Jack from being more daring and unorthodox than the other correspondents. They modeled themselves on the *beau idéal* and Great White Scribe of the period, the stately Richard Harding Davis, friend of generals and statesmen. Davis and the rest of his lesser breed were prepared to sit in Tokyo until they received permission to go to the front in Korea and Manchuria. Jack was determined to take that permission for granted and get there, hell or high water.

The trouble with the assignment was that the Japanese did not think war correspondents were important. Their position in the Japanese army, in Jack's own words, lay somewhere between interloper and honored guest.[2] To the Japanese military caste, the scribe was an underling, just as to the white journalist the Japanese soldier was a little yellow man who still had to prove himself against the white Russian giants. Jack himself could not disguise where his sympathies lay. When he saw his first Russian prisoners, he found himself gasping. These men were his kind. He was sharply aware that he should not be among the brown men who were peering at the Russians through the bars. He felt his place was "there inside with them in their captivity, rather than outside in freedom amongst aliens."[3]

First he had to reach Korea, so he took a train to Yokohama, pausing long enough to revisit the bars he knew from his sealing voyage. Then he went on to Kobe and Nagasaki, looking for the first steamer bound for Korea. At Moji, he took some innocent tourist photographs, only to find his camera confiscated. Moji was a military area and Richard Harding Davis had to intervene in Tokyo before the camera was restored. The delay made Jack miss his ship, and the next two steamers were both commandeered to carry Japanese troops. So he boldly chartered a junk and set sail across the February seas for Korea, navigating himself with a crew of three Koreans, poisoning his lungs with charcoal fumes from the brazier that kept them all from freezing in the nights. He was in Klondike weather again.[4]

Once he had landed and recovered from frostbite, he had to teach himself to ride. He immediately got on a horse and treated it like a boat, luffing and steering it roughly in the right direction. He would always ride like a sailor, slumping and lurching on his saddle; but he was now a man more intent on progress than perfection. He hired pack ponies and riding horses, grooms, an interpreter, and a manservant named Manyoungi. This was his first taste of power, of living like the aristocrat he felt himself to be.

Manyoungi presented himself to his new master in the unlikely dress of an English butler, wearing a white shirt, stand-up collar, tie, studs, and dark suit. He was so obedient and efficient that he was soon indispensable. Jack rapidly built up such an entourage that the other war correspondents remarked on his style. To one of them, he seemed the most inherently individualistic and unsocialistic Socialist ever met. He walked alone in aristocratic aloofness. He always went his own way, no matter where anyone else was going. He had his own separate mess and tent. "General and private of his army of one," he rode his horse in front of pack ponies and servants with an American flag flying above his baggage.⁵

Small men usually have the qualities of their defects, while greater men have the defects of their qualities. Jack's aloofness was in part a mark of his originality, even as a war correspondent. The hundreds of photographs he sent back from Korea showed his daring and his natural talent in the medium; they were some of the first pictures of the war to appear in the American press. His dispatches from Korea also proved his courage, but they reflected his frustration. He did reach further north than any other correspondent, and he did get a scoop with the only account of the first skirmish between the advancing Japanese and the Cossack scouts. But his dash was his downfall. His envious rivals in Tokyo complained about his freedom of movement to the Japanese military authorities and he was hauled back from the front and kept well behind the lines with the rest of the war correspondents.

Too active to linger, conscious that his reports for the Hearst press were not value for money, Jack continually provoked the Japanese commanders, as if he were still a Road Kid playing games with the railroad bulls. In the worst of several incidents in Korea, he knocked down an impudent and thieving groom. The oversensitive Japanese authorities threatened him with a court-martial. Only another intervention by Richard Harding Davis, who arranged a protest from Theodore Roosevelt himself, replaced the court-martial by an expulsion order from Korea. Jack was only too willing to oblige. Disgusted at seeing no action except for a long-distance view of the easy Japanese victory at the crossing of the Yalu River, he returned to San Francisco in early July. His old Californian prejudice against cheap imported Oriental labor was now buttressed by a new fear of Japanese military prowess. "In the past I have preached the Economic Yellow Peril," he wrote to Charmian; "henceforth I shall preach the Militant Yellow Peril."⁶

Such a stand was honey to Hearst and gall to most of Jack's comrades. At a Socialist meeting in Oakland, he was heard damning the Asiatic races, declaring to those who were stressing the need for class solidarity: "I am first of all a white man and only then a socialist!"[7] But his temper cooled to a rational fear. In an article on the Yellow Peril he argued that Japanese management and Chinese industry would make the two great Asiatic nations a threat to white supremacy in the Pacific.[8] Later, this fear so ruled his apocalyptic visions that he fantasized "The Unparalleled Invasion" of China in 1976, when the world would decide to remove the billion Chinese by bacteriological warfare.[9]

At that time, such racism was a part of radicalism. Eugenics was the breakaway science which would improve the human species, and although briefly the Russian uprising of 1905 made Jack believe that instant revolutionary socialism was feasible, its quick defeat made him withdraw into his usual biological pessimism. He saw himself as the realistic spokesman of an evolving process, revolutionary only when the revolution was ripe, otherwise letting things work themselves out.

On his return to California, he found his affairs in chaos. Charmian had fled to Iowa for fear of scandal. His wife was attaching his earnings from the Hearst press in conjunction with her suit for divorce, which cited Anna Strunsky and accused him of adultery abroad. Isolated and notorious, hurt and irritated, he returned to his home at Piedmont. He was so shaken that it almost seemed easier to sacrifice himself for his two small daughters, and it took all his courage not to go back to his wife for his children's sake.[10] In the end, he worked on Bess until she gave him his freedom and changed the grounds for divorce to simple desertion. He agreed to build a small house in Piedmont for the use of his family, and he himself went to a hired cabin at Wake Robin. He was short of ideas and money, because the few thousand dollars he had earned in royalties had all to go to build the home for his family. Returning to Oakland, he rented an apartment on Broadway and imported his mother and Manyoungi to run the household.

Although *The Sea-Wolf* was an instant success and made his

name familiar throughout the United States, he himself was in the trough of his long sickness. He described it later as a monstrous disillusion.

> The things I had fought for and burned my midnight oil for had failed me. Success—I despised it. Recognition—it was dead ashes. Society, men and women above the ruck and the muck of the waterfront and the forecastle—I was appalled by their unlovely mental mediocrity. Love of woman—it was like all the rest. Money—I could sleep in only one bed at a time, and of what worth was an income of a hundred porterhouses a day when I could eat only one? Art, culture—in the face of the iron facts of biology such things were ridiculous, the exponents of such things only the more ridiculous.[11]

Such was the first of successive periods of disgust. He felt that he had been born to fight, and now he found that the victory was not worth the struggle. One thing only remained for him, he later asserted in *John Barleycorn*—the People. The hope of socialism was the one thing that kept him alive. He would commit suicide if it were not for his dependents and the people. As before, when he was depressed and full of a sense of his own corruption, he clung to the idea of the brotherhood of man. When he felt strong, he preached personal supremacy.

In this mood, he plunged into a study of pessimism and egotism and their philosophers, Stirner, Schopenhauer, and Nietzsche. He began to be aware of the appetites and selfishness that were the root causes of so many of his decisions. Even when Charmian rejoined him briefly in Oakland, his passion for her quickly died. Her diaries told of his escapes on the *Spray,* his failure to write to her, his recurrent bouts of illness, and only occasional meetings to make love—called "1216" in the diaries, the number of Jack's old apartment on Telegraph Avenue.[12] "You and I are in a very trying stage right now," he did finally write to her on September 29.

> The ardor and heat and ecstasy of new-discovered love have been tempered by time, on the one hand; and on the other hand we are denied the growing comradeship which should be our right now. Instead we must wait another year before we can enter upon this

comradeship of daily intimacy—and the intervening period is bound to be full of worry and anxiety.[13]

Charmian clung to her man, making herself as useful as possible. Once, before he married Bess, Jack had joked with Cloudesley Johns, declaring that he would have to marry a typewriter girl, for he hated the job.[14] It was Charmian who had typed and corrected the manuscript of *The Sea-Wolf* during his absence in Korea. Now she typed and corrected his short prizefighting novel, *The Game,* which began a new minor genre—the American boxing story. Superficially, it was the tale of two young working-class aristocrats, Joe the boxer and his love Genevieve. They are about to mate and procreate when Joe suddenly dies in his last fight before he retires from the ring. Fundamentally, it was another indication of the author's deep pessimism of that summer. Joe is doomed to die before the eyes of his loving mate-woman at the moment of his victory. Beauty and intellect and love are useless in the face of sly chance and brute necessity. All is the game of life and death, and the loser loses all.

The real cause for Jack's disgust was more physical than philosophical. He was already rather lame and soon would virtually give up walking for the rest of his life. He also seemed to have a tumor on his rectum, which he thought was malignant. Much of the time he was in pain, and he feared a slow and horrible death. He was identifying himself less with Nietzsche's philosophy than with the screaming agony of the philosopher's dying. He also thought he was going through a mental collapse, although he was really afraid of a physical collapse. Later he would confess to a young correspondent, "I once, in the long ago, had a beautiful body and was as proud as the devil of it. I once had the Nietzsche sickness. I know all that you are suffering."[15]

His fears detached Jack from his success and his commitment to Charmian. Afraid of dying, he wanted all he could get out of living. He began another affair with a woman from the Crowd, the beautiful poet and critic Blanche Partington. She taught him to listen to music with some awareness and revived his youthful dreams of composing. Jack played another role for her, death's jester, the mocker at all passions. How did he live, he asked her, when he had lost all the commoner illusions? "By replacing them by a single illusion, by an attitude of non-seriousness." He declared that he knew his urge toward women was merely his urge to procreate, so he exhausted its force in the delights of diving or skylarking, or else he dressed it up in the illusion of romance. "When I do obey the urge of the red blood toward women, I do so dreaming of the 'deathless creature of coral and ivory'—illusion, I know it is illusion; but for the time, at least, I must cherish the illusion if I would live."16

Jack's new illusion with Blanche Partington was eagerly encouraged by the Crowd, in order to win him away from Charmian and his increasing seclusion at Glen Ellen. George Sterling was the cheerleader, writing to Blanche that he would concede her the Wolf on Saturdays and Sundays as long as they came to visit him.17 Gossip and innuendo about Charmian flooded Jack's ears. He cooled toward her. His letters to her now began "Dear Charmian." Her comment in her diary on this change was "Hell!" She fell ill with catarrh and neuralgia and an abscess in her ear. By March 8, 1905, she recognized that she was losing her man. Her diary read, "I realize Mate's sad condition, and try to get him out of it. My growing sorrow and hopelessness over him."18

Yet she fought to keep him, using the peace of the hills above Glen Ellen to counter the influence of the Crowd in Oakland. Twice she offered him his freedom; twice he refused to break their engagement—or so she told Blanche, in a remarkable letter written to her rival after her marriage to Jack. She confessed that she often felt sick at heart during that time of trial, blinded with terror and sorrow; but she stayed faithful to Jack because she felt he needed her. She knew the best solution for him was not the Crowd and the city, but the hills and herself. In the end, the Crowd's partisan attacks on her reputation acted as a boomerang. According to her, "all the trouble and the slander wrought havoc with his emotions and madness, and made him see more clearly than ever that the

Jack took this portrait of George Sterling, the poet he called "the Greek."

wonders he had found in our mateship at first, were real and good and true."[19]

It was a romanticized version of her triumph over Blanche and over Jack's despair. She had first won him when he was ill with a smashed leg; she won him again after his operation on March 25 in the Shingle Sanitorium, during which the "tumor" on Jack's rectum proved to be merely piles, while his terror of cancer or venereal infection was groundless.[20] Jack's sense of relief brought a surge of hope. His physical well-being, as always, revived his love of life. And Charmian was there every day to reap the benefit of his plans for the future. She persuaded him of their love, no longer a mad love but a more controlled one. Her diary recorded a turning point in their affair. "We are more truly learning each other, our worth to each other. Mate is secretly occupied with the Crowd concerning me, standing for *His Own* loyally."

Jack was certainly fighting to keep friendly with the Crowd and to stay with Charmian. He decided to give up her rival. On April

12, Charmian noted that she felt something wrong when she was present at a meeting between Blanche Partington and Jack, who was uncomfortable and preoccupied. On May 10, she recorded her sadness at hearing from him about the affair with Blanche and the slander of the Crowd, but the confession made her certain that she had her man again. "Honeymooning generally," she wrote in the middle of May while Jack recuperated with her in the hills. "Everything blissful with Mate."

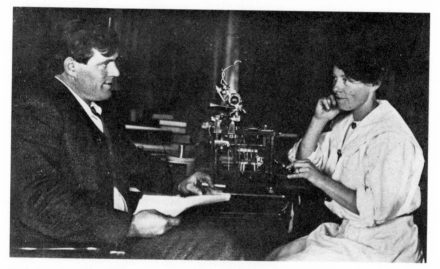

Jack London and Charmian Kittredge before their marriage. She acted as his typist and editor from the time their affair began in 1903.

Blanche, George Sterling, and the Crowd had made a concerted effort to win Jack away from Charmian. She had never been popular with them, and they rightly feared that she would do her best to cut them off from one of their leaders. Yet, by attacking Jack on his choice of her, they had incited him into playing the gentleman. "The Crowd," Charmian noted triumphantly, "trying to separate us, by fair means or foul, drove us together so that nothing on earth but death could drive us apart. And we are finding each other by day and night."[21]

Jack took a great deal of trouble to force the Crowd to accept

Charmian and to insist that she had not broken up his marriage. In two long letters to George Sterling's wife Carrie, he went through his version of his break from his wife. That he should make such an effort to explain his actions and clear Charmian's name showed the importance he put on keeping in touch with his old friends—now on the move from Piedmont to Carmel, where George Sterling was founding a new artists' colony.

The story Jack told Carrie Sterling was that he had been in a black mood when he first pursued Charmian in June, two years before, and he was ready then to have a hell of a time with any woman he could get. He was about to go on a boat trip with a married woman, but he fell for Charmian first. She had nothing to do with his rebellion. "I had made up my mind to go to pieces and get a separation. This without being in love with anybody, but from sheer disgust in life, such as I was living it." Gossip that Charmian had broken up his home was one of Bess's lies; his wife was a colossal and shameful liar.[22]

He protested his downright frankness to Carrie Sterling, but he was not being totally frank. He did not mention Blanche Partington, although Carrie knew of that affair. He may have made the running with Charmian, yet she did play her part in his separation and divorce from his wife. He had not only allowed Bess to treat Charmian as her confidante; he had remained silent long enough to ruin Anna Strunsky's reputation. He had been evasive and inconsistent, like many a man tangled in a marriage and a succession of love affairs.

These unpleasant facts he blocked out of his memory. His defense of his actions showed him at his best and his worst. When he saw himself in the role of the defender of his woman, he became a noble hypocrite, protesting too much, as if taking the blame personally for everything would excuse everything. His lifelong obsession with making a coherent pattern out of the haphazard and the inconsistent did not quite fit the facts. Yet there was a generosity in his effort to protect Charmian's reputation at the expense of his own. Raging at conventionality, Jack had behaved most conventionally. His affirmation of Charmian to the Crowd confirmed in public his commitment to her. She was most relieved. "So good to be going about publicly together—Jack and I," she confided in her diary in July 1905. "I've waited so long, so long."[23]

Jack's desertion of Piedmont for Glen Ellen and Charmian caused a separation from another of his loves. He had declared his feelings for George Sterling at much the same time as he began his affair with Charmian. When he was away in Korea, he left the manuscript of *The Sea-Wolf* to be edited by his beloved Greek. George confided in Charmian at the time that he had never loved a man a tenth as much as he did his Wolf. Charmian reported his words to Jack himself: "O, he is so noble, sweet, patient, brilliant, strong and beautiful that I cannot see how anyone can help worshipping him."[24]

Now, in the summer of 1905, Wolf rejected his worshipping Greek and the Crowd for Charmian and Glen Ellen and the hills of Sonoma. The Greek felt betrayed and complained bitterly that his dream of living beside his Wolf had been destroyed. "No, I am afraid that the dream was too bright to last," Jack wrote back to him, "—our being near each other. If you don't understand now, some day sooner or later you may come to understand. It's not through any fault of yours, nor through any fault of mine. The world and people just happen to be so made."[25]

Deeply wounded, George Sterling plucked up the courage for his own act of rejection. What the Wolf could do, he could do. He would prove his independence as well. He threw in his job with his rich uncle and moved to Carmel. There he was the unchallenged leader, escaping at one bound his recent domination by the unfaithful Jack and his old domination by the cynical Ambrose Bierce and his millionaire uncle. And there again, he could give up his petty city infidelities and return to a simple life with his wife and friends.

The artists' colony at Carmel was to be a paradise and a damnation. There was always a worm in the bud, a toxin in the abalone that was the chief diet of the colonists. For into that Eden the artists took the seeds of their own melancholy and decay. Although the writer Mary Austin considered Jack to be a founder of the colony, he only visited there twice with Charmian. It was not his place, it was his old friend's. He could make a show of his love for the Greek and he could feel it; but he could not stay in Carmel with a mate-woman who only felt safe far from the Crowd. "The direct and deplorable effect upon my life of the 'rumpus' with the Crowd," Charmian later confessed to Blanche, "was to make me feel no one liked me; and the reaction on me is that I am supersensitive and self-conscious."[26]

On the first visit of Jack and Charmian to Carmel, Mary Austin saw why Charmian stayed so close to her man. Women flung themselves at Jack and lay in wait for him, as if rubbing skins with him would give them a touch of his genius. His sexuality spilled out of him, although he seemed indolent and preferred lounging by the fire to hunting the abalone off the rocks. Mary Austin did not know about his lameness nor his operation, for Jack always pretended to be in perfect health. She put down his lethargy to a surfeit of success, and she did not admit to herself what the other colonists saw, that she wanted him just as much as the rest of the women did.[27]

Carmel was a failed utopia on the dunes, and Jack was to dissect it tellingly in his later novel, *The Valley of the Moon*. At a personal level, this book was to be a vindication of his decision to farm at Glen Ellen rather than play bohemian games in the pine-soft glades of Carmel. By that time, Jack was determined to work out the Californian dream in earnest, to escape from the city and grow a green Eden in the looted wilderness. George was creating a false Eden consistent with the idealism of his East Coast origins. He was aping Thoreau at the abalone pond, emulating Emerson in safe suburban woods. So when the hero and heroine of *The Valley of the Moon,* Billy and Saxon, leave the labor troubles of the Oakland slums, their stay at Carmel is no solution, only an enjoyable disillusionment. At first, they cultivate the body beautiful and the mind beautiful, until they discover another cult of the melancholy beautiful, which can end only in despair. As Mark Hall declares in his role as a fictionalized George Sterling, all ends at Carmel in the lies of the flesh. The wine of life is heady there, but all too quickly it turns to uric acid.[28]

Jack himself was slowly retracing his path from his long sick-

Jack and his two daughters, Becky and Joan, in 1905.

ness to an acceptance of the commonplace. He had escaped from the Oakland slums into suburban life with Bess, then on to the bohemia of the Crowd at Piedmont. He did not want another version of that bohemia at Carmel. He wanted to battle against the failure of his father figure, John London, on the land at San Mateo and Livermore. He would succeed in enriching the land again. It could bloom as in the days of those pioneers of the old American stock who, he insisted, were his ancestors. He would restore their dream of the Californian Eden, which they had spoiled by beggaring the soil. "When you think of the glorious chance," Mark Hall was made to say in the novel,

> "a new country, bounded by the oceans, situated just right in latitude, with the richest land and vastest natural resources of any country in the world, settled by immigrants who had thrown off all the leading strings of the Old World and were in the humor for

democracy. There was only one thing to stop them from perfecting the democracy they started, and that thing was greediness. They started gobbling everything in sight like a lot of swine, and while they gobbled democracy went to smash. Gobbling became gambling. It was a nation of tin-horns. Whenever a man lost his stake, all he had to do was to chase the frontier west a few miles and get another stake. They moved over the face of the land like so many locusts. They destroyed everything—the Indians, the soil, the forests, just as they destroyed the buffalo and the passenger pigeon. . . . So they gobbled and gambled from the Atlantic to the Pacific, until they'd swined a whole continent.[29]

Charmian was clever enough to encourage Jack's new mood. She urged him to buy, with the royalties from *The Sea-Wolf,* a little ranch near Glen Ellen where the land was cheap because the wilderness had swallowed up the abandoned farms of the pioneers. It was particularly her place; her aunt lived there. It was the place where their love had begun, and he should buy into it and build a house for both of them far from the intrusion of the Crowd. Then Jack could be the patriarch he sometimes desired to be.

Jack talking of improving the land to George Wharton James. They are on the first small ranch that Jack bought.

Jack weighed the alternatives. He might remain in the pessimism and egocentricity and failed creativity of the trough of his long sickness. Or else he might put another lien on his life by mortgaging the future, forcing himself to write, and settling for the responsibility of a long relationship with Charmian. He had long been planning to buy land in the woods and build, or so he told George Sterling. "I am really going to throw out an anchor so big and so heavy that all hell could never get it up again. In fact, it's going to be a prodigious, ponderous sort of an anchor."[30]

Yet his mind was still unsettled over the extent of his commitment. When his publisher George Brett questioned the wisdom of an author tying himself to the land and pledging his future to the difficult task of becoming a rancher, Jack excused himself by replying that his 130 acres of redwoods and firs, white oaks and maples, madrono and manzanita groves had no need to be profitable. They were an investment for the future—a base and a retreat, not a prison. "I shall always be free to come and go, even to the ends of the earth. Also, I was very careful to buy a place out of which no profit could possibly be made. On the land or absent, I'll never be bothered by a profit or loss account so far as the place is concerned."[31] It would look after itself, he assumed.

He assumed too much. The little wilderness ranch near Glen Ellen was never to be a self-sufficient hideaway. It could not be that, given his obsession for professionalism, for pushing everything to excess in the pursuit of mastery. He could never be content with being a small rancher and improving the land slowly. He had to become a large rancher and improve the land at speed. It was in his nature to run full tilt at a challenge. If he did not have a fight on his hands, he tended to provoke or imagine one. It fired his enthusiasm. And he had the fatal facility for trying to turn his dreams into instant facts, whatever the cost.

Jack's psychological state was revealed in two curious stories he wrote at the time, "Planchette" and "All Gold Canyon," which appeared in an uneven collection of short stories called *Moon-Face.* In "Planchette," two lovers live in the Sonoma Hills in a summer camp among the redwoods. The orphan girl has been waiting to

Joan London blows out her father's match.

marry the man for a long time, to the despair of her other suitors
and her relations. He wants to marry her but says he cannot—he
has some secret fear which he cannot confess, and which the story
does not reveal. Riding with her through the redwoods on a horse
called Washoe Ban—the same name as Jack's own horse—he is
thrown inexplicably and the horse breaks its back. A planchette
board reveals that the girl's dead father is trying to kill her lover
—and the spirit finally succeeds, plunging the lover and his second
horse over a ravine.

Evidently Jack had not wholly outgrown his mother's belief in
evil spirits. The story also makes clear that he had recognized his
charisma, and that he knew how to use it. His description of himself
through the girl's words might be called vanity, except that it was
true. However much other people might criticize the hero in his
absence, the girl told him, as soon as their eyes rested on him,
"affection and love come bubbling up. You are so made. Every
animal likes you. All people like you. They can't help it. You can't

help it. You are universally lovable, and the best of it is that you don't know it."[32]

Of course, Jack knew it, and he relied on it more and more. He knew that his power of persuasion was so great that he could convince nearly anyone who met him or read his work of anything he wanted to say about himself. It was a dangerous gift for a man who liked to exaggerate and saw himself as something of a hero. Rightly used, it presented an accurate picture of a man who certainly was larger than life. Wrongly used, it still convinced, it still seemed to be truthful in the way that Aaron Burr defined the truth, as something which is boldly asserted and plausibly maintained.

In the other important story written at the time, "All Gold Canyon," nature smiled on a small Eden in a hidden canyon in the foothills of the Sierras. A pocket miner invaded it, scarred its slope to dig out his pocket of gold, fought an interloper to the death, and left the canyon looted. His progress was like a slug's—he fouled

Some of the crowd on the beach of the artists' colony at Carmel. From left to right, George Sterling, Mary Austin, Jack London, and James Hopper.

beauty with his monstrous trail. Yet once he was gone with his booty, the peace of the place returned to heal the torn hillside. So Jack himself intended to return to the earth to heal the scars left by the forty-niners and the bonanza farmers. Yet he knew enough of his own divided nature to recognize that he would try to dig a fortune out of the soil as well as restore it to its beauty.

More important than the two stories he wrote in his time of confusion was the novel he completed after his time of decision. He wanted to create the reverse image of *The Call of the Wild,* the writing of which had signaled the beginning of his long sickness—his break from the bonds of his marriage, his morality, and his pattern of work. Now he began to write *White Fang* in Charmian's company. Mockingly, he referred to it as "The Call of the Tamed."

Charmian had ended his wildness and despair by persuading him to enjoy little things again. In *John Barleycorn,* he was to write that he climbed back to mental health by deciding to pursue truth less relentlessly, to refuse to take the big things too seriously.[33] In notes for his unwritten autobiography, he declared that he would describe "all of the compromise of life and living, and the healthful compromise—no more seek truth in man or woman or love or life, lust or battle."[34] The story of *White Fang* reflected his mood, a determined effort to tame his appetites and settle. "Instead of the devolution or decivilization of a dog," he told George Brett, "I'm going to give the evolution, the civilization of a dog—development of domesticity, faithfulness, love, morality, and all the amenities and virtues."[35]

He stuck to his deliberate and rational intention. *White Fang* does not have the feel of the unconscious that is so powerful in *The Call of the Wild.* It is written from no Jungian depth, no atavistic dream. Only the opening paragraph conjures up the northern wilderness and the white silence of despair. There, two men and six dogs are pulling a dead man on a sled, trying to escape a following wolfpack; one of the men succeeds in surviving. The story then deals with the rearing of a wolf cub from the pack; it is one-quarter dog and capable of civilization. Jack took care to get his natural history correct, writing to a friendly librarian to ask when wolves mate, how long they carry their young, and at what time of year they litter.[36] His attention to detail hides a moral fable of man's inhumanity to animals, redeemed by one man's care for one animal.

In this allegory of solitary brutishness saved by human love, two episodes reach beneath the surface of the story. The first is in the chapter called "The Clinging Death" when White Fang fights with the stumpy and tenacious bulldog which pursues him, bloody and unbowed, grips him by the throat, and will not let go. The bulldog incarnates the power and endurance of the civilized breed, even when matched against the ferocity of the wild. The second episode is set in California and represents White Fang's last fight against a human beast, an escaped convict who has been brutalized by the San Francisco slums. White Fang kills him, surviving three bullets through his ribs to play with his puppies and drowse in the sun.

At the end of the book, however, White Fang remains a wolf —the family calls him "the Blessed Wolf," a name George Sterling used for Jack himself, but he is still a wolf by nature, an individualist who will not join the community of mankind. Jack explained at length how White Fang, as the leader, harnessed to the sled in the northern snows, is driven by his master's whip and by the teeth of all the dogs snapping behind him and wanting to kill him. He is supreme among them only because he is the fastest on his legs and with his jaws. To that extent he represents his creator, who saw himself as solitary and voracious, the leader of the pack by fighting skill, not by social instinct.

There is always a remove between a hero, particularly an animal hero, and his creator; but Jack did his best to blur the distinction between animal and human. As far as he was concerned, evolution largely determined the actions of both. He left notes for two human stories to parallel his two major dog and wolf stories. One was to be the history of the bestial convict killed by White Fang. "Begin with childhood, boyhood, give nature its potencies, the potencies that were realized by pestilential environment—work up the whole thing, in detail, from infancy to frightful, wild-beast climax." This call of the human wild was also to be counterpointed by the white fang of the struggle for redemption. "Trace life of a slum and jungle beast . . . to the power of love and changing and elevating—a new force in environment."[37]

These books on the human beast would never be written, for Jack had already lived their courses. He had clawed his way out of the slums to reach suburban married life. Then he had reverted to the solitary wolf in the woods and on the *Spray*. Now he was emerging from the wild back to domesticity through his love of Charmian. Within the four years of his revolt and reassessment of himself, he had written three of his major books—the reversion to solitude of *The Call of the Wild*, the struggle between the brute ego and social sentiment in *The Sea-Wolf*, and the dubious acceptance of domesticity in *White Fang*. He had survived his time of despair to reach for the Californian dream of a small home in the Sonoma Woods, as if Emerson had always been right about men being able to renew their natures in the wild west.

EARTHQUAKE AND ESCAPE

Nor did I fare better with the masters themselves. I had expected to find men who were clean, noble, and alive, whose ideals were clean, noble, and alive. I went about amongst the men who sat in the high places —the preachers, the politicians, the business men, the professors, and the editors. . . . Where they were not alive with rottenness, quick with unclean life, they were merely the unburied dead—clean and noble, like well-preserved mummies, but not alive.

JACK LONDON

For Jack, it was the time of all the possibilities. His many contradictions could be satisfied simultaneously. His pessimism could briefly flare with the failed hope of the first Russian Revolution. He could shock society politically, yet marry Charmian conventionally. He could preach confiscation of the property of the rich, yet become a landowner himself. He could commit himself to a cause and a place, yet set up his usual escape from the pressure of his commitments. Among all his other projects, he decided to build a boat and sail it for seven years round the seven seas. "These days, we're full of the proposed trip round the world," Charmian wrote on August 19, 1905. "Jack is enthusiastic—full of ambition, and laughs when I ask him if he's lost *all* his ambition."[1]

The goal was to experience all, and not to count the conflicts. To satisfy the appetites, and not to worry about appearances. To be individual in practice, Socialist in speech. Why not travel in a Pullman railroad car, served by a Korean manservant, and denounce the other rich passengers as parasites and plutocrats? Jack knew he had earned his ticket. He had also earned the right to speak.

For the Socialist cause, Jack was a figurehead. He was an impresario and a popularizer in the eyes of the rigid Marxists, neither a good party member nor sound on doctrine, but his heretical opinions were pardonable because he was so personable. He was used by members of the party for his name and his charisma. He could lecture and attract an audience in places where other Socialists could not go.² He ran again for mayor of Oakland, increasing his vote four times, but still coming in third behind John L. Davie and the Republican winner. He was also made president of the new Intercollegiate Socialist Society, so that he could preach the coming revolution in the ivory towers of privilege.

Although some of the Socialists were guilty of using Jack, he was also guilty of using the cause to suit his personal life. "This lecture trip," he confided to Charmian, "will masque my Eastern trip beautifully. And we must have our little pre-nuptial honeymoon."³ Charmian was delighted to go with him for the beginning of the lecture tour. She wrote in her diary, "He *loves* me—talks about it ceaselessly—marveling that such things can be—after 27 months of intimacy." She soon left, however, for discretion's sake to stay with relatives until his divorce was completed. He traveled on to speak for revolutionary socialism, with the newspapers beginning to attack him for his radical views.

His notoriety grew when he decided to flout convention by marrying Charmian in Chicago on November 19, 1905, the day after his divorce had set him free. The young man in him wanted the drama, the child in him wanted the instant gratification. But the haste of the remarriage put its legality in question, and he was besieged by reporters at the Hotel Victoria. He declared angrily that if his Chicago marriage proved to be invalid, he would remarry in every state in the Union. One newspaper wondered if he would remarry the same lady each time. The gossip over *The Kempton-Wace Letters* and Anna Strunsky was resurrected, especially as she was delivering lectures on revolutionary socialism in California and was about to leave for Russia. Jack seemed to be seeking any publicity he could get at the expense of his cause and of the women in his life. The newspapers were full of his supposed love affairs and his violent speeches. He himself admitted later that, even if the journalists had often misrepresented him, the bad publicity was fine advertising for his books.[4] Charmian found the notoriety a hideous nightmare, but "Jack adorable—my perfect bridegroom and lover, at last."[5]

The scandal was due to his own carelessness and his insistence on having his own way. He did not plan a personal publicity campaign. His promotion of himself was willful, not rational. The newspapers, indeed, by trying to damn him, excited the curiosity of his audiences. He filled the halls at Harvard and Yale, in Boston and in New York, and wherever else he chose to speak. He came on stage dressed casually in a black baggy suit, a white flannel or silk shirt, and a loose tie, looking bohemian rather than proletarian. His low and vibrant voice held his listeners without inciting them. His usual speech was carefully balanced between prophecy, menace, and harrowing statistics.

He would begin by saying that there were 7 million Socialists in the industrial nations of the world, and that all were comrades. The cry of this army to the managers of capitalism was: "No quarter! We want all that you possess. We will be content with nothing less than all that you possess. We want in our hands the reins of power and the destiny of mankind." If that power could be taken by the ballot box, it would be. If not, it would be taken by violence. In Russia, for instance, legal violence had properly been countered by assassination. "I am a revolutionist," Jack would declare at this point. "Yet I am a fairly sane and normal individual. I speak, and I *think,* of these assassins in Russia as 'my comrades.' "

At this moment of shock for his audience, Jack emphasized the inevitability of the coming revolution. Socialism had arrived with the machine. It was another product of industry. Its victory was certain as machines spread across the world. The capitalist classes had failed to manage the machines well enough to feed and clothe mankind. Their inefficiency would lead to their inevitable downfall. They had misjudged so badly in America alone that 10 million

Americans were short of food and living in worse conditions than
the cave man.

Case histories and statistics proved the degradation of the
working classes. Capitalism offered nothing which was clean, alive,
and noble. "The revolution is a fact. It is here now. Seven million
revolutionists, organized, working day and night, are preaching the
revolution—that passionate gospel, the Brotherhood of Man. Not
only is it a cold-blooded economic propaganda, but it is in essence
a religious propaganda with a fervor in it of Paul and Christ."[6]

This was the substance of Jack's written speech. It showed him
more of an evangelist than an economist. Occasionally he reminded
his listeners of the American Revolution for liberty, and he declared that the Russian Revolution was for the same cause. He
would sometimes quote the rabid phrase, "To hell with the Constitution!", attributing it to a military commander of strikebreaking
troops, in order to prove that lawlessness was also a weapon of the
bosses. Of course, the newspapers quoted the phrase as if it were
Jack's own. He found himself accused of being an anarchist, which
he was not. His college audiences, indeed, were often disappointed
at his gentle voice and reasoned words—he was not vehement, he
liked the facts.

Only once did he burst out, when he was addressing a gathering of wealthy New Yorkers, in the same way as Ernest Everhard
was to burst out at the Philomath Club in *The Iron Heel.* The
silk-stocking audience went purple as he attacked them to their
faces, telling them that they were incompetent and weak. They
would have to surrender one day to the vital people in society, to
men like himself. "We are the strong, and in that day we shall give
you an exhibition of power such as your feeble brains never
dreamed the world contained!"[7]

Above the bedrock of his faith in evolution, the roots of Jack's
socialism were emotional—a cry for justice, a fear of degradation,
a loathing of the waste of human potential. This was the note he
struck in his generous praise of Upton Sinclair's novel, *The Jungle*
—so dependent on his own views in *The People of the Abyss,* which
Sinclair echoed in writing of Chicago's "wild-beast tangle [where]

human beings writhed and fought and fell upon each other like
wolves in a pit."[8] Jack called Sinclair's book the *Uncle Tom's Cabin*
of wage slavery, brutal with life.[9] It reminded him of how barely
he had escaped the jungle of the slums in Oakland, and so he raised
his voice against the human waste and low wages of the sweatshops
in Chicago, against the slow starvation of the millions of the unemployed and their families. This emotional side of his nature even
welcomed the criticism of the aesthetes at the Ruskin Club in Oakland, where Fabian idealism ruled the roost. To his loyal friend
Frederick Bamford, he showed the remnants of his humility and
willingness to learn from others. "I am self-educated," he wrote,
"and never have any time any more to educate myself further. But
criticisms like yours *do educate* me further and therefore I am eager
for them."[10]

This was the last time he would eagerly accept the criticism of
his old comrades. He soon resigned from the Ruskin Club because
of his commitment to his new ranch at Glen Ellen. And he rejected
the criticism of the more rigorous Socialists, both the militant
"Wobblies" who were setting up the Industrial Workers of the
World, and the doctrinaire members of the official Socialist and
Socialist Labor Parties. His own militancy was highly individualistic, founded on his paranoia and his uncanny sense of prophecy,
which were the reverse of his rational and hopeful socialism.

One particular story, "The Minions of Midas," revealed Jack's
powers of prophecy. He told of a group of intellectual proletarians
who decide to blackmail the very wealthy. They can kill at random,
shop girls and workers, children and policemen. Their price to stop
their terror campaign is tens of millions of dollars to serve as their
working capital to set themselves up in industry. Their creed is a
crude form of Social Darwinism:

> We are the inevitable. We are the culmination of industrial and
> social wrong. We turn upon the society that has created us. We are
> the successful failures of the age, the scourges of a degraded civiliza-
> tion. We are the creatures of a perverse social selection. We meet
> force with force. Only the strong shall endure. We believe in the

survival of the fittest. . . . *Under the present social environment, which of us shall survive?* We believe we are the fittest. You believe you are the fittest. We leave the eventuality to time and law.[11]

The Minions of Midas kill at will and without risk. They are totally efficient and destructive. Society is shaken. Instead of the masses against the classes, it is a new class displacing an old class. Assassination, indeed, in the future or the past never seemed to Jack to be an intolerable weapon. It was largely irrelevant, given the law of necessity. "The President is dead," he once wrote to a friend after McKinley's assassination. "What of it? We have another President in his place, and so we will continue to have like Presidents until society, economically ripe, compasses the inexorable change which is coming."[12]

Jack's prophetic gift was also evident in his disturbing Socialist novel *The Iron Heel,* written in 1906. It is written in the form of a revolutionary text, discovered centuries after socialism rules the earth, and it predicts in detail the rise of fascism through its various stages. The free press becomes the suppressor. Para-military groups and *agents provocateurs* break up labor resistance. An artificial collapse of the stock market wipes out property values and the middle classes. Even the Hearst press is destroyed by the withdrawal of advertising. Those who opt out of society to live by barter on the land are assessed for taxes they cannot pay, and then evicted. The union movement is split in favor of the powerful unions at the expense of the smaller ones, so that an aristocratic caste of workers emerges.

The Oligarchy creates a vast Metropolis (a society imitated in Fritz Lang's later film of that name), where an aristocracy of management rules from a beautiful urban height with the help of a favored labor caste which oversees the People of the Abyss in the bowels of the city. This power is achieved by a false bomb plot which, like the Reichstag fire to come, is a pretext for putting all the Socialist leaders in jail. The United States controls North America, while Japan has risen to dominate the Far East and the British Empire has collapsed. Elsewhere, economic depressions have led to Socialist governments.

Inside America, now the country of the Iron Heel of totalitarianism, the deprived workers go underground and use the methods of modern subversion. Their blond superman of a leader, Ernest Everhard, creates terrorist fighting groups. The identity of the leaders is hidden by plastic surgery. The insurgent cause takes on the character of avenging religious cells. The revolt culminates in a final apocalypse, in which the "roaring abysmal beast" of the Chicago mob is slaughtered by mercenaries in "that modern jungle, a great city."

As a vision of the rise of totalitarian power, *The Iron Heel* still is more disturbing than either Aldous Huxley's *Brave New World* or George Orwell's *1984.* Its pessimism about the immediate future shook the democratic Socialist leaders in 1906.[13] It shakes the modern reader, especially as the first assault of fascism has come and gone—and like the hydra, grows its heads again in South America and Africa. It is more than a blueprint for class war, it is a dark glimpse of the *Gotterdämmerung* of human society. In it, Jack conjured up from his nightmares his inner conviction that the struggle must be long and murderous before the rule of the best.

In a footnote to *The Iron Heel,* the author paid tribute to the third important influence on his writing after Kipling and Poe: H. G. Wells, "a sociological seer, sane and normal as well as warm human."[14] Although many critics believe that *The Iron Heel* is derived from an obscure contemporary work, *Our Benevolent Feudalism,* its mood and vision of the future are particularly reminiscent of the Wells of "When the Sleeper Wakes" and "A Story of the Days to Come." Again, in his dreamlike account of prehistoric life in *Before Adam,* Jack derived his style and ideas more from Wells's "A Story of the Stone Age" than from the source he admitted to plundering, Stanley Waterloo's *The Story of Ab.* It was as if he could confess more readily to inspiration from a writer of talent than from one of genius like himself.

Nietzsche once asserted that a genius has the right to use the minds of his friends. Jack certainly thought that he had the right to use other people's plots in the same way as he used other people's political ideas. "Expression with me," he wrote to an early correspondent, "is far easier than invention. It is with the latter I have the greatest trouble, and work the hardest."¹⁵ That hard work consisted in the voracious reading and filing of newspapers and magazines and books for themes. He did not light out after inspiration any more with a club, but with a folder.

In an attack in the *New York World,* sentences and paragraphs from one of Jack's supreme Alaskan stories, "Love of Life," were printed parallel with a story written by two collaborators four years before his, called "Lost in the Land of the Midnight Sun."¹⁶ Eighteen cases of plagiarism were evident. Jack's reply to the charges was graceful. He claimed that he and the other authors had taken the story from a newspaper account of the wanderings of Charles Bunn in the Arctic Barren Grounds. Yet he had added material from his own Alaskan experience. He had even taken the final episode from Greely's account of his polar expedition. There was simply nothing new under the sun, even under the midnight sun. There was no real plagiarism, as his style transformed journalism into literature.¹⁷

Shakespeare had occasionally used the same method, and Jack got away with it. Most of the newspapers were flattered to serve as the source for literature. One of them even pointed out that Poe often used newspaper stories as his sources. Some of the press, however, considered Jack little better than a burglar, who justified "the theft of a silver bucket on the ground that he converted it into a tea service before selling it."¹⁸ More serious was President Theodore Roosevelt's later charge that Jack was a "nature-faker," because in *White Fang* a bulldog and a lynx both beat a wolf dog. In fact, the wolf dog killed the lynx in the book, as Jack pointed out to the President, while it was a matter of opinion whether a bulldog could whip a wolf dog or not. It was evidence of Jack's unawareness of the mythical quality in his writing that he bothered to defend its naturalism so insistently.

Other authorities also attacked him on biological grounds. They claimed that animals could not reason, but worked solely by instinct. This seemed like medieval thinking to Jack, and contrary to the lessons of evolution. It was also untrue of two of the dogs he had owned himself, Rollo as a boy and Glen as a man. "Let us be very humble," he concluded in his defense of himself. "We who are so very human are very animal. . . . You must not deny your relatives, the other animals. Their history is your history, and if you kick them to the bottom of the abyss, to the bottom of the abyss you go yourself."[19]

If he were more paranoid, Jack would suppose the assaults on his originality and veracity to be disguised attacks on his popularity and socialism; fear or envy of his influence did seem to lie at the back of many of them. Certainly, his notoriety and fiery lectures in 1905 did lead to an eventual fall in his book sales. His works were even banned from the library shelves of Derby Neck, Connecticut, and some other small towns. Yet he persisted in his defiant role. Ignoring the warning of his friends that he would add to his notoriety, he published a series of newspaper sketches about his time as a tramp. They were later collected into a short book, *The Road.* His new wish to shock the bourgeoisie was shown in the change in his plans about the use of the material. In his respectable days with Bess, he had wanted to make Frank Strawn-Hamilton the hobo hero under the alias of Leith Clay-Randolph. Now he chose to make himself a sort of knowing Huckleberry Finn, the hero of a new type of folk novel that was to inspire Dos Passos, Orwell, and Kerouac to imitate his example.

Actually, Jack did not have the courage to present himself as a roving radical in *The Road.* He wrote the sketches as an adventure story, only hinting at the discontent of the dispossessed. "In fact, it's all written in a light, facetious vein," he told the unenthusiastic George Brett. "Only once in a while have I skated on the edge of things serious."[20] He wanted to be nostalgic about the delinquency of his youth, to make a drama of liberation from his days of deprivation. He was reckless now about the opinion of society, as long as a few people loved him for his private and secret self. "That I tramped or begged or festered in jail or slum meant nothing by the telling," he once wrote to Charmian at the beginning of their affair. "But over the lips of my inner self I had long since put a seal."[21]

That was true of a man determined to wall off the sensitivity and fears and conflicts within him. It was also true of a man beginning to flaunt some of the facts of his biography to create a public image. Already, he was beginning to exaggerate the record without actually falsifying it much. Comparing his tramp diary with *The Road* is like comparing a penny whistle with a theater organ. If both seem to play the same tune, the piping of the bold and scared youth becomes the grandiose thunder of the successful national performer.

There was also an assumption, in Jack's apparent frankness about his past, that the mass of the American people were curious about him and his adventures. By making myths out of what he had done, by presenting his new decisions as episodes in the continuing saga of his life, he was trying to create an interest in his actions that he could turn into money. And he needed the money badly, for he had overspent his income to satisfy his various desires. As well as paying for his ranch and his growing tribe of dependents, he was beginning to squander a fortune on building a boat called the *Snark* for his seven years' voyage. He was in debt even before the keel was laid. "I am not only sailing close into the wind," he confessed to Cloudesley Johns. "I am dead into it and my sails flapping."[22]

He wrote continuously for himself and for his causes, for the market and for his spirit. He returned to panning out a living from Alaska in the stories collected in a volume with "Love of Life." His confidence in his own tenacity was shown in that extraordinary story of man's will to survive at all costs. Yet the instability of his long sickness also appeared in "The Sun-dog Trail." In that underestimated story of a man and woman bent on vengeance against another man, the reason for action is hidden, and the white silence of the north is as ambiguous as it is murderous. The couple pursue their prey ferociously to the frozen wastes of the end of the world, but they remain as impalpable and implacable as the sun-dogs which pack about the brief Arctic sun until there are three suns in the sky. Reality and appearance, willpower and dream, are all confused in a last reckoning.

He also wrote a play, *Scorn of Women,* adapted from an Alaskan short story, but he was unable to translate his strong paragraphs about the confrontation between nature and mankind into stage dialogue. Even actresses who were his friends, Blanche Bates and Minnie Maddern Fiske, turned it down. And he found the time to write his most haunting and hidden self-justification, "The Apostate." In that story of a sweated millworker who becomes so exhausted that he gives up his job as a work-beast to become a hobo and do nothing at all, Jack was excusing himself for giving up his role in the rise of socialism. He had worked hard for the cause and had earned his long loaf round the world on the *Snark.*

Before he could finish building his boat, earthquake and fire struck San Francisco on Wednesday morning, April 18, 1906. Jack was upcountry at Glen Ellen, and the shock toppled his new barn, revealing a fraud. The builder had filled the walls, supposedly of solid stone, with gravel. The catastrophe became a turning point for people in the Bay area. They would date their lives from "before the earthquake" or "after the earthquake." For San Franciscans, it would be "before the fire" or "after the fire."[23]

Although Jack was no longer living on the Bay, the two disasters were also a turning point for him. He hoped that they had destroyed the evidence of his past life. He could be born again in the image of himself that he was creating. If City Hall were burned down, there would be no birth certificate of John Chaney, a child without a father born unwanted in a slum thirty years before. He hurried along to watch the devastation of San Francisco. He found that one twitch of the earth's crust and the following fire were leveling all the social barriers of the city. "Not in history has a modern imperial city been so completely destroyed," he recorded.

> San Francisco is gone. Nothing remains of it but memories and a fringe of dwelling houses on its outskirts. Its industrial section is wiped out. Its business section is wiped out. Its social and residential section is wiped out. The factories and warehouses, the great stores and newspaper buildings, the hotels and the palaces of the nabobs, are all gone.

The city burned for three days and nights. There was no opposing the flames at first. To limit their spread, the firefighters at last began to demolish whole blocks. For the first time, Jack watched the effects of explosives on a modern city. "Wednesday night saw the destruction of the very heart of the city. Dynamite was lavishly used, and many of San Francisco's proudest structures were crumbled by man himself into ruins, but there was no withstanding the onrush of the flames."

Yet he saw no mob terror. Among the refugees, there was courtesy, not the tooth-and-claw struggle of his predictions. As he walked through the streets, he found them deserted and littered with abandoned trunks and possessions. The newspaper buildings were burning; so were the good hotels, the symbols of power and opulence. By Thursday morning, he was sitting on Nob Hill with some blacks and Chinese and Italians and Japanese, the despised workers of the city. "All about were the palaces of the Nabob pioneers of forty-nine. To the east and south, at right angles, were advancing two mighty walls of flames." What the flames did not devour, the dynamite crumbled. The smoke pall rose above the watchers, mauve and yellow and dun.

City Hall and its records did burn, and Jack photographed the ruins with his camera. He met only a few people on his wanderings, for the rest had pulled out to camp on the surrounding hills. Those who remained were like "the handful of survivors after the day of the end of the world." The city now seemed like the crater of a volcano. Yet already the bankers and businessmen were denying that the disaster was total and were preparing to rebuild.[24]

So he recorded the earthquake and the fire. He wrote of the obliteration of urban society without drawing revolutionary lessons from it. He observed the wiping out of his past without public comment. He did, however, use the fire for the end of *The Iron Heel,* when the Chicago ghetto is razed by dynamite and flame. Yet that was merely prophecy, and the actual devastation of San Francisco seemed to produce in him a withdrawal from his inflammatory speechmaking. At the end of the fire, he wrote to Gaylord Wilshire, "I am afraid so enormous a destruction of capital will somewhat retard the Socialist movement here, especially in San Francisco. If an equal destruction of property had occurred all over the United States, I doubt not that Socialism would have been retarded a generation."[25]

The earthquake also provoked Jack into writing two of his finer Socialist stories, "The Dream of Debs" and "South of the Slot." In the first, San Francisco is destroyed by another form of catastrophe, a nationwide general strike. The wealthy narrator wakes up with the premonition of an earthquake to come. Yet there is only silence, the silence of nobody going to work. Slowly, the city breaks down. Violence flares between the slum people and the upper classes. The militia and the workers' brigades keep some sort of order, but the starving people riot and loot and flee. Finally, the general strike breaks the resistance of the capitalists. "It was worse than a war," the narrator concludes. "A general strike is a cruel and immoral thing, and the brain of man should be capable of running industry in a more rational way."[26]

The earthquake also loosened a block in Jack's mind, so that he could deal with the problem of his divided loyalties and slum inheritance. "South of the Slot" is more interesting as a psychological study of the author than as a story. Its events take place in old San Francisco before the earthquake, when the Slot divided the city —the iron crack down Market Street, which ran the cable cars and separated the rich from the poor. North of the Slot were the theaters and banks and shops; south of the Slot were the factories and laundries and slums.

Jack's surrogate hero is a professor of sociology at the University of California, who lives a double life. North of the Slot, he is an academic; south of the Slot, he is a labor leader. In the end, after a fantastic fight on a coal wagon against the police and the strikebreakers, the hero stays south of the Slot for ever, renouncing a good marriage and bourgeois manners. He has finished his time of study, he would rather fight for his own. Such was Jack's dream at the time. He even mocked at his old god Kipling in a third story, a prehistoric parable, "The Strength of the Strong," in which primitive men choose brotherhood rather than early capitalism and reject the lies of "Lip-King."

The earthquake also brought him closer to ruin because he persisted in pushing ahead with the building of the *Snark*. Labor and materials soared sky high after the disaster, since the city had to be rebuilt; instead of the $7,000 of his estimate, the final cost of the *Snark* approached $30,000—and even then it was many months behind schedule.

The saga of the building and manning of the 45-foot ketch emphasized Jack's qualities and defects. His generosity to his dependents, relations, and workmen reached the point of dangerous folly. He chose his wife's uncle, the aging Roscoe Eames, to navigate the *Snark* with him. There was a comic row between them as to who was the captain, but neither of them learned to navigate the boat. Charmian was coming, but she knew nothing about sailing. Manyoungi was horrified that the boat was so small, and he had to be replaced after insolently asking Jack, "Will God have some beer?"[27] A Stanford engineering student was given a berth to service an expensive engine that did not work, wrenched itself loose in its trials, and had to be used as ballast. Finally, an adventurous youth from Kansas, Martin Johnson, was signed on as a cook before he had learned to cook at all. It was a comedy of errors that looked like becoming a tragic farce, thanks to Jack's belief that anyone could do anything well with good will and hard work.

There were dozens of seaworthy schooners Jack could have bought in the Pacific ports. Yet he had to build his own boat, asserting that it was the strongest boat ever built in San Francisco with a garboard strake 3 inches thick and planking 2 inches thick, brought from Puget Sound. Its strengthened bow was designed to punch storms, its watertight bulkheads to resist typhoons and shipwreck.[28] So Jack wrote of the *Snark* as if his will and desire could actually be translated into seaworthy wood.

Work on the craft dawdled on until the end of April 1907, and Jack's frustration mounted at delay after delay. He had to deal with 47 kinds of union men and 115 firms, none of which delivered the goods on time. He fretted and waited and raged, his desire rising with each difficulty, his appetite whetted by his disappointment and the jeers of his friends and his enemies. "I won't be happy until I get away," he wrote to the editor of the *Woman's Home Companion* , one of the magazines which had contracted to take his articles about the voyage. "And I'm going to get away as fast as God, earthquakes, and organized labor will let me."[29]

Organized labor, indeed, seemed determined to keep him in America. Many of the Socialists were up in arms about the desertion of their chief propagandist. A letter from one of the comrades announced: "When you swallow the last mouthful of salt chuck you can hold before sinking, remember that we at least protested."[30] He should have protested himself at making commitments for years of hackwork in the magazines to pay for his debts in building the boat. He had to mortgage his Oakland house, pledge his future earnings. Every day he was forced to scribble under the pressure of his borrowings.

He would not be thwarted, but he nearly went bankrupt. On the Saturday of his sailing, he was served a writ by an Oakland grocer and had to spend the weekend unsnarling the legal process. Three days later, on April 23, the *Snark* did finally sail through the Golden Gate on a choppy sea. Everyone was immediately sick except for Jack, who stayed at the wheel. The decking and the lifeboat and the stores of kerosene leaked, the fresh vegetables were spoiled, and the wave-breaking bow swung round on the sea anchor and became the stern. Yet Jack sailed on toward the west in the wake of Melville and Mark Twain and Robert Louis Stevenson. Wisely, he had left his stepsister Eliza Shepard to look after his legal affairs, for she was the only woman in his whole life who was always devoted to him. Unwisely, he had left the bulk of his ranch and literary business in the hands of Charmian's aunt and Roscoe's wife, Ninetta Eames, who was manipulative, mercenary, and incompetent.

In his recklessness in going to sea in a sieve, hazarding his own life and the lives of his crew to satisfy an image of himself as master of his own ketch and dream, Jack seemed ready to jettison the ambition that had driven him from the cellar of society onto a pinnacle as the most famous writer in the United States. It was as if the earthquake and the fire in San Francisco had burned the chip on his shoulder by destroying the evidence of his deprived boyhood. Now, as careless as any aristocrat, he could indulge himself at the expense of his career. At last, he could admit to the force of his own desires.

The foreword to his account of the voyage, *The Cruise of the Snark,* was very revealing. "The ultimate word is I LIKE," he confessed. "It is I LIKE that makes the drunkard drink and the martyr wear a hair shirt; that makes one man a reveler and another man an anchorite; that makes one man pursue fame, another gold, another love, and another God. Philosophy is very often a man's way of explaining his own I LIKE." Yet what of a man who wanted drink and revolution, revelry and intense study, fame, gold, love, and faith in mankind all at once, as Jack did? He could only try to do everything simultaneously, at the waste of his energy, at the eventual cost of his life. I LIKE is the cry of the child, not the voice of the grown man, which is I ACCEPT.

He gave a second reason for sailing away on the *Snark.* "Personal achievement, with me, must be concrete. I'd rather win a water-fight in the swimming pool, or remain astride a horse that is trying to get out from under me, than write the great American novel. . . . I am so made. I like, that is all." His cult of his body, his thrill in physical mastery was still his image of himself, the Californian dream of eternal youth.

Finally, Jack wanted to scale up his myth of himself on the *Snark.* He had cast himself in the role of the poor boy forcing himself to the rich man's table and women. He had set himself to struggle against the necessities of the frozen northland. He had tilted at the windmills of social ethics and government. Now he wanted to match himself physically against the greatest force of nature, the anger of the ocean. "Fallible and frail, a bit of pulsating, jelly-like life—it is all I am. About me are the great natural forces —colossal menaces, Titans of destruction, unsentimental monsters that have less concern for me than I have for the grain of sand I crush under my foot."

Through these cyclones and tornadoes, lightning flashes and cloudbursts, tiderips and tidal waves, undertows and waterspouts, great whirls and sucks and eddies and surfs, Jack saw himself steering his little *Snark* on its precarious way. "It is good to ride the tempest and feel godlike. I dare to assert that for a finite speck of pulsating jelly to feel godlike is a far more glorious feeling than for a god to feel godlike."[31]

Jack sails back to San Francisco on the *Mariposa* in the middle of the voyage of the *Snark.*

Before he set sail in pursuit of his own dream and divinity, he had gone on a beer bust with some students. Manic and outgoing, he could persuade them that he was as exceptional as he believed himself to be, with his power of suggesting to others the grandeur of the human spirit in one smallish man. To one of the students, his personality seemed that of a Kitchener, a von Hindenburg, a Stanley with the full force of command over circumstances. His eyes appeared to change color with his speech, sometimes filled "with the anguish of sins impossible to commit," sometimes "all steel and dew, all sweetness and hidden ferocity." His only fault in the student's eyes was his insistence on applying scientific principles to everything under the sun.[32] It was as though he were trying to deny his own myth by insisting it was a mere matter of fact.

He did not recognize two elements in his urge to escape. The first was that the pressures of his life had built up to an intolerable point. He could not stand the monthly problem of paying all his bills, and his appetites were raging out of control. Even Charmian had noticed his ravenous greed before his departure. He was consuming whole flights of underdone wild duck—canvasback, mallard, and teal—washed down with his favorite Liebfraumilch. "For he, who 'bothered' so little what he put in his stomach, was devoted to this type of game, excessively rare."[33]

His mother was the second unadmitted reason for Jack's escape. Even his success had gained her approval only briefly, since Charmian had now displaced her just as Bess once had. In revenge, she had made up her longstanding quarrel with Bess and was taking Jack's place with his two little girls. Although he had left a large pistol in Bess's house as the symbol of his continuing authority, Flora was on the spot.[34] With her son away, she came into her own.

She tried to correct his version of himself as a male Cinderella. She asserted to a visiting reporter that he had not grown up like Topsy, homeless and rudderless. It was his fantasy that his mother was a washerwoman and that he was raised in Tar Flat. She had, in fact, been a music teacher in Oakland for thirty-three years and had raised him well. He was not totally self-made, as he claimed. He had got his brains, his love of education, and even his height and the curl in his hair from her. She might now look like a singed chicken with her curved spine and short hair, but her looks deceived because she had been stunted by an early illness. The truth was that everything in Jack came from her and her side of the family. Even the reporter wondered at her complete silence about the father's contribution to his son. But now Flora saw herself like Mrs. Dickens. "Many a time I weep bitter tears. He belongs to the public."35

He did, indeed, and it was useless for his mother to try to correct his public image. Jack was the ultimate source of his own myth, and autobiography was much on his mind as he sailed off on the *Snark*. He wanted to write a fictional version of his own struggle to fame without the benefit of anyone's help at all.

10

THE ILLUSION OF THE *SNARK*

Here are the seas, the winds, and the waves of all the world. Here is ferocious environment. And here is difficult adjustment, the achievement of which is delight to the small quivering vanity that is I.

JACK LONDON

The cruise of the *Snark* was a sad illusion. It was begun to show off Jack's physical dominance, yet it ended in his physical collapse. It was meant as an escape from worry for seven years. In fact, it was all over in two years of financial disaster and growing obligations at home. These disillusionments changed Jack's presentation of himself, so that his autobiographical novel, *Martin Eden,* would become more a reflection of his mood at the time than any true version of his past. In the end, Martin commits suicide, while Jack just managed to remain alive.

The voyage to Hawaii was a matter of pluck, skill, and chance. All the crew proved useless except for Charmian, who was game for anything. She and Jack spent most of their time steering the ketch, while the only accomplishment of Roscoe Eames was to mark their course on the chart. According to his reading of the sextant, the *Snark* progressed by leaps and lulls, making its bounds on windless days. His incompetence led Jack to learn the art of navigation in a week, proving his theory that he could do anything he chose to do. He became full of the sense of power, feeling that he had solved mathematically the mystery of the heavens and could

144

plot their way across the deep. "I was a worker of miracles. I forgot how easily I had taught myself from the printed page."[1]

There were storms and alarms aboard the leaky boat, which lumbered through gales and lay becalmed in the doldrums. Because the fresh food was spoiled, the inadequate diet brought down both Roscoe and Jack, so that Charmian was forced to steer as often as not. She proved herself increasingly a "blowed-in-the-glass, A Number One, crackerjack,"[2] as Jack wrote back to Eliza; she fulfilled his ideal of a male comrade. Although he hardly mentioned his sickness or her strength during his cheerful account of the cruise, he was both physically and emotionally dependent on her. She exulted in having him all to herself and sometimes in her hands.

In the periods of calm, Jack worked at writing *Martin Eden,* which began with the sailor hero lurching into the genteel *bric-à-brac* of Ruth Morse's drawing room. The best part of the novel was the opening, in which Martin's feeling of social inadequacy developed into his adoration of Ruth, a caricature of Jack's first love, Mabel Applegarth. Although Martin was meant to be the author, Jack was again cleaning up his past—with some of the worst teeth in the world, he gave Martin white and regular teeth that had never known or needed a dentist's care. He also paraded his sexual attractions, for Ruth was always longing to fondle Martin, who admired himself in the mirror for his balance of strength and sensuousness —his steel-gray eyes, his mouth like an ascetic cherub's, his mop of brown hair that women wanted to caress.

Martin then overworked frenetically to become a writer, a process which Jack always exaggerated in his version of his struggle for literary success. Yet Martin was not dependent on his mother but on a Portuguese landlady, whom he rewarded generously when he was in the money. The working title of the book was "Success"; its secondary title "Star-dust," as though these were the true lures that could pull the aspirant to ultimate victory.

In the event, *Martin Eden* was a broken-backed book. While most of it dealt with the rise of the hero to fame and disillusionment with middle-class values, the end was despair, disgust, and abrupt suicide. First, a decadent poet modeled on George Sterling killed himself, then the hero deliberately died by drowning. The break occurred in November, when Jack had nearly completed the book on the third leg of his journey to Tahiti. At that point, he seemed to have had other plans for the ending, including Martin Eden's adventures in the South Seas. But finding himself forced to return to California because of his financial problems, he killed off Martin as he set out across the Pacific, pushing his hero through the port-hole of the very boat that was taking him and Charmian home, the *Mariposa*.

The problem was that Martin Eden's despair and self-destruction were not explained, so that his suicide appeared childish and willful. Of course, Jack could not explain such urges in himself. He knew he had them from time to time, but he would not examine his inheritance of instability, his violent appetites, his nightmares and occasional loss of control, his anxiety about his bodily decline. He was always to claim that Martin Eden died because he did not believe in anything, while his creator believed in socialism and the brotherhood of man, and so he lived. It was not the only reason. Charmian's diary revealed that, while he was finishing the book on the *Mariposa*, "Jack is sick sometimes, mentally, or he wouldn't do as he does. This reflection helps me through some hopeless, love-less times—seldom, thank God."[3]

On the arrival of the *Snark* in Hawaii, Jack had shown himself both disgusted with the ketch and nothing much of a Socialist. He neglected the boat, leaving its refitting and engine repairs to the lazy Roscoe, while he and Charmian led the life of the leisured. They were invited everywhere, for it was an island society and they were celebrities. They were entertained in a round of dinners and poker parties and invited to a reception given by the native queen of Hawaii. A prince of the blood royal took Jack fishing, while the von Tempski family invited him and Charmian to a cattle drive on their huge ranch. Jack rode all over his horse, like a sailor, then was bucked off it and landed on the back of his neck. Charmian thought he had brain fever for a day, but it was only concussion. It did not stop him from learning to surf from the last Hawaiians who prac-ticed the sport. So he became one of the first Americans to experiment in that national pastime of the future. He called it the royal sport of the natural kings of the earth, and he himself tried to become "a sun-burned, skin-peeling Mercury" on the crests of the breakers.

His accumulation of disgust with the world and people at this point caused the worst rage that Charmian had ever seen.[4] The engine of the *Snark* seemed irreparable, and he threatened to sell the ketch and go home. Roscoe had allowed the sails, ropes, and decking to rot in the sun. He was sent back in disgrace and the rest of the crew paid off except for Martin Johnson. The newspapers reported that the men had all had to leave, because Jack had beaten them to a pulp like Wolf Larsen. He shrugged off these lies, but he knew that the ketch and the trip were a failure. Yet he could not return home to meet the mockery of the press. He had left in such a blaze of publicity that he would be roasted alive if he gave up too soon. The trouble with setting himself up as a public image was that he risked an *auto-da-fé*. So he hired a new captain and a new crew and a new servant. He would sail on.

His problem was to find the money for the repairs to the *Snark*. He was penniless. He begged George Brett for another $5,000 on account of royalties and unpublished books. The long-suffering Brett sent him the money, which was enough for him to refit his boat and continue his voyage. He did not know yet that Ninetta Eames was squandering his earnings as fast as she could cash the checks. She did not pay his debts, but increased her salary and lavished his royalties from Macmillan's as much on her own house and dependents as on his. She even attempted to replace his mother in his life, and he responded by addressing her as "Mother-mine" in his letters and chortling with joy at her spiteful gossip about Flora's rejection of her son. "You have not seen one thousandth part," Jack wrote of his mother, "of the real devil that she is."[5]

While the *Snark* was refitted and the engine repaired, Jack and Charmian visited the other islands, including the leper colony on Molokai. There Jack's compassion for the outcasts of society was revived. He found no horrors in their company and risked their contagion by shooting off their rifles with them. He pictured the colony of 800 lepers as cheerful, productive people, who accepted their segregation for the good of society. He found the conditions on Molokai better than in the slums, declaring that he would rather live among the lepers there than in the East End of London, the East Side of New York, or the stockyards of Chicago. To be a leper was better than to be a work-beast. That was the worst degradation of all.

To be a sailor risking death was the best of all. When he left in October on the 2,000 miles of the Pacific Traverse to the Marquesas, he found out that no sailing boat was known to have made the journey. His engine, as usual, failed. It took two months of beating in variable winds and lying in the doldrums and roaring before the trades to reach the islands where Gauguin had come to find his own disillusion and death. It was a voyage of vast solitude, for no other ships were sighted. Jack was in his element, the entertainer of his little world as he read them Melville, Stevenson, and Conrad in the evenings, the lord of the sea as he pitted his pride and skill against the sudden squalls. As usual, he saw the struggle for existence about the ship, particularly among the flying fish, which tried to elude the gunys in the air and the bonitos in the sea, only to leap against the mainsail of the *Snark* and be devoured by its crew. He caught dolphins, too, and, like Byron, he admired their change into all the colors of the rainbow before they died, as mutable and doomed as he himself. He found it hard to sleep after catching one, so he wrote to the Greek. "The leaping, blazing beauty of it gets on my brain."[6]

At Nuku Hiva in the Marquesas, Jack rented the clubhouse where his boyhood idol Robert Louis Stevenson had lived. And on the second day, he and his party rode out to Melville's paradise of Typee, the valley of Hapaa. Tuberculosis, leprosy, and elephantiasis had decimated Melville's perfect warriors and had made the survivors into freaks and monsters. The noble savage was now the ignoble sufferer from the white man's plagues. Jack was almost driven to the conclusion that the white race flourished on impurity and corruption, but he discarded the idea. The white race had built up an immunity through natural selection, and the Polynesians must go through the same bath of organic poison before they could lay the foundations of a new race.

After sailing on to Papeete in Tahiti, Jack found a noble white savage, one of the first of the pioneers in organic living, whom he called "The Nature Man." This city child from Oregon had been dying of pneumonia, when he cured himself by vegetarianism and by living in the sun and the woods. Hounded out of America and Hawaii by various authorities because of his insanity, he had cleared a plantation in Tahiti and lived like a prophet of the simple life, doing handsprings rather than shaking hands, preaching the cooperative commonwealth and the flesh-free diet. Jack admired him and rejected his advice. He was too bound to the reward system and raw meat.

In Tahiti, too, the mail told of disasters at home. There was a financial panic in the United States. One bank had foreclosed its mortgage on the Oakland house where Jack's mother lived because the newspapers had reported the *Snark* lost at sea with all hands. Checks which he had issued in Hawaii had been returned by his Oakland bank for lack of funds. Bess and his children were not receiving their support payments, and Bess herself was on the point of marrying again and escaping his dominance over her life.

Jealous and possessive about his children, angry at the attacks on his reputation, fearful that he might lose his ranch, Jack booked his and Charmian's passage on the *Mariposa,* bound on a round trip to San Francisco. He would not give up the cruise of the *Snark,* but he would interrupt the voyage to put his affairs in order and reassert his grip on his own. In a vile mood, he returned to face up to the responsibilities he had tried to escape.

His brief stay in California was successful enough. Claiming that *Martin Eden* was finished, he raised another $5,000 as an advance from George Brett, paid some of his debts, and saved the Oakland house from the bank. He also did his best to stop Bess's remarriage. Using as a weapon his ownership of the Piedmont house she lived in with his daughters, he discouraged her attempt to break free of his influence. It was a sad story of bullying.

Jack had had so little as a boy that he could never get his giving into proportion. Either he wasted a small fortune on his indulgences like the *Snark* and his exploiters like his new "Mothermine," or he grudged the pennies he gave Flora and his children out of fear of losing them if he did not keep them on a financial leash. Both spendthrift and mean, Jack was always his mother's son, lavishing his earnings to buy the love of the disloyal, skimping on his own people as if to test their ties to him.

The disgust he felt on his voyage back to Tahiti on the *Mariposa* was alleviated by having his bad and painful teeth fixed in Papeete and by good news from California. Ninetta Eames had had her first stroke of luck, selling the serial rights of *Martin Eden* for $7,000. The money would make Jack solvent, but Ninetta advised him to buy the adjoining ranch, which was up for sale. A down payment of $3,000 would secure it. Jack agreed to pay that sum, doubling his acres and his debts. He was full of manic confidence again, happy in his escape from toothache, heading to the freedom of Bora Bora, Samoa, and the Fiji Islands.

Yet there was no escape from the defects of his body. An old complaint arose to afflict him like Job. His piles returned, and worse. A new ulcer swelled and opened inside his rectum. It hurt him so much that he had to give up the fiction of his perfect body and allow Charmian to treat it with olive oil and other remedies. She could not cure it, however, and Jack was left to put up with his agonies.

As his illness increased, so did his pride and temper. In Fiji he discharged the third of the temporary captains of the *Snark*. He claimed that the first had been lazy, the second angry, and the third crooked.[7] The truth was that he himself wanted to command the ketch. He could endure no rival. Even if he was only an amateur navigator, the poison of power was swelling in his veins as much as the poison of disease.

He steered the *Snark* onward to the savagery of the New Hebrides and the Solomon Islands. There, his logbook noted, the islanders wore "small gee-strings—women and maidens nothing at all. The real goods."[8] There, too, the people were still headhunters, and white pirates cruised, ready to kidnap primitive men to work as slave labor for three-year terms on the Australian copra plantations. Jack and Charmian joined a recruiting expedition among the cannibal tribes with the captain of the black-birder *Minota*. They carried revolvers in their belts, they fished with dynamite, they heard stories of villages burned in revenge for the killing of the previous captain of the ship. Soon the *Minota's* deck was packed with recruits for the plantations, many of them with sores and blood poisoning and ringworm. The ship ran aground on a reef and was surrounded by war canoes, but luckily another black-birder arrived, rescued the *Minota,* and took off Jack and Charmian. Both of them had come down with new tropical diseases.

Two of these new diseases were malaria and yellow fever; their victims were reduced to sweating and raving. Jack, Charmian, and the crew of the *Snark* all fell ill of the fevers time after time. They had remissions, but were never cured. Then they all caught the worst of the local diseases, "Solomon sores" or yaws, which were horrible versions of the supposedly malignant "tumor" that had terrified Jack during his long sickness. Yaws were caught from a mere cut or spread by flies, but their effect was like an attack of syphilis. "Oh, we came pretty near having some very bad blues," Charmian confessed to her aunt Ninetta from the Solomons. "Poor Jack was in despair. . . . It wasn't a nice thing to think of living a perfectly clean and moral life and then get something like that."9

Sometimes Jack had up to eight yaws at a time. He treated himself and the crew with blue vitriol and iodoform, lime juice and hydrogen peroxide, boracic acid and lysol. He could only stop the spread of the yaws, he could not cure them. Unfortunately, he got as addicted to home medicine and dentistry as he had to amateur navigation. He felt he could treat everybody from his medicine chest and his reference library. Expertise was merely a matter of opening the right bottle and the right book.

The *Snark* by now had become a hospital ship. Jack's last newspaper article on the cruise was called "The Amateur M.D.," and it read like a medical bulletin. The diseases of the crew had become worse. One of them caught blackwater fever, which Jack could not treat. Two of them went off their heads from their suffer-

ings. Jack himself attracted more illnesses. The first was nervous in
origin and made him faint regularly; he lost control over himself
and had to stay below. The second appeared to be leprosy of the
hands. The disease may have been pellagra, aggravated by his
heavy drinking to deaden his rectal pain; but more likely he was
suffering from psoriasis. His palms and fingers began to swell, his
skin flaked off, his nails thickened. He was in such agony that he
could not hold the wheel. There was no diagnosis in the books for
his disease; he was in a torment of suffering and fear.

The voyage was now not so much into the heart of darkness
as into the horror of light. The burning rays and the treacherous
islands were destroying him. He ordered the *Snark* back to Pen-
duffryn, the largest plantation in Guadalcanal, where the steamers
called on their way to Australia. His elbows were becoming silvery
like a leper's, and his hands were swelling to the size of boxing
gloves as their skin fell away, layer after layer. It was a tribute to
his courage that he managed to start a new novel, *Adventure,* while
he was waiting for the steamer to take him and Charmian and
Martin Johnson to hospital in Sydney.

Adventure is his worst novel, written at the time of his greatest
physical agony and public humiliation. Underlying a romance of
the Solomon Islands between an English plantation owner and an
American girl was a dark story of disease and sadism, a horror of
the flesh and its torments. The book begins with a very sick white
man, riding pickaback on a savage with pierced ears, going the
rounds of his 200 cannibal plantation workers, dosing them for
dysentery. As he rides through the festering shambles of the large
hut where they lie, he does not know whether they will rise like
wolves to tear him to pieces on his errand of mercy. Only his
revolver and his rifle defend him from a mass revolt. He orders a
runaway worker to be whipped side by side with a rebel black man,
until they scream and howl as the blood oozes down their backs.
His partner returns on a slaving schooner, dying of blackwater
fever, and as the hero buries his friend, he wonders why he too does
not let go of life. "He was a fool to hang on. He had died a score
of deaths already, and what was the use of prolonging it to two-
score deaths before he really died. Not only was he not afraid to

die, but he desired to die. His weary flesh and weary spirit desired it, and why should the flame of him not go utterly out?"

Soon a shipwrecked girl appears, wearing sea boots and a Baden-Powell hat, with a long-barreled Colt in her belt, escorted by tall and noble Hawaiians, a different breed from the bushmen on the plantation. She nurses the planter back to health and becomes his partner, excelling him in daring and do, grit and go. "We whites have been land robbers and sea robbers from remotest time," she is made to say. "It is in our blood, I guess, and we can't get away from it."[10]

Jack's rage at the useless tortures of his flesh also showed through the *South Sea Tales,* which he was writing at this time. In the most sadistic of these, "Mauki," an insane brute of a German torments the savage Mauki by burning him with the lighted end of his cigar, ripping open his pierced nose, and skinning patches off his neck with a rough mitten made from the hide of a sting ray. Mauki waits until the German is stricken with blackwater fever, skins him alive with the mitten, then beheads him. And in "The Inevitable White Man" and "Yah! Yah! Yah!", Jack's delight in the slaughter of the cannibals rises to an orgiastic frenzy. Only in "The Seed of McCoy" did he present a descendant of the savage mutineers of the *Bounty* holding together the scared crew of a burning schooner by his seductive and compelling presence, a mysterious emanation of the spirit. In that tale of humble certainty mastering brute terror, Jack set down his rare hope for his own future as well as that of the white race.

During the voyage to Sydney, he remained a very sick man. The doctors there put him into hospital, then kept him as an outpatient for five months. His rectal disease turned out to be a double fistula, which an operation corrected. His malaria responded to quinine. His silver skin and psoriasis baffled the physicians—then slowly healed over the long voyage home and in the Californian climate. It was no wonder that he now went about in the sun wearing a broad-brimmed Baden-Powell hat. He was not playing the *ranchero,* he was merely keeping his vulnerable skin from the hard light.

More terribly, the Australian hospital treated his yaws with an arsenic compound which left a trough in Jack's skin.[11] Experiments in using arsenic were already being made in Europe and Australia, particularly for the treatment of syphilis and yaws. Jack might have undergone a previous mercury treatment for the gonorrhea which Bess had cited in her divorce petition. He certainly did undergo an arsenic treatment for his yaws. The effect of both mercury and arsenic was to attack the rectum, the kidneys, the brain, and the nerves. On the voyage home in 1909, he was already beginning to have trouble with his bladder. With his usual confidence that he could doctor himself, he wrote ahead to Ninetta Eames, asking her to order for him the *Uric Acid Monthly*.[12] Unfortunately for Jack, in that same year a Dr. Ehrlich was putting on the market something touted as the wonder cure for syphilis, an arsenic compound called salvarsan. It had not been properly tested, and its wide use before World War I would harm as many millions of people as it cured, the guinea pigs of their generation. Later Dr. Ehrlich would have to modify salvarsan to make it less toxic.

Of course, Jack had to admit defeat and abandon the voyage of the *Snark*. He sent a round robin to his friends, telling them that he had five diseases without specifying what these were, and claiming that his collapse was more nervous than physical. He was still clinging to the myth that his body would not let him down for long. "Somewhere, somehow, and God knows how," he wrote, "in the past year and a half in the tropics, I have had my nervous equilibrium thrown."[13] He would not make the obvious connection between his health and his mental state, even though a mere toothache had contributed to that sense of disgust on the *Mariposa* which had made him push Martin Eden out of the porthole to drown.

When his friend Jimmy Hopper heard the sad news, he wrote to George Sterling that he was sure Jack would come out of it, because there was still so much mental vigor in the man. There was a physical cause for the nervous collapse, Hopper thought after talking with some physicians. Perhaps Jack had a syphilitic taint—*"everyone* is liable to have that." He only needed the new treatment.[14]

Charmian was the rebel when Jack ordered Martin Johnson to

Jack convalescing with Charmian in Australia in 1909.

rejoin the *Snark* in the Solomon Islands and sail her back to Sydney, where the ketch would eventually be sold for only $3,000 and end her days ingloriously as a black-birder. Charmian wanted the cruise to continue. It was the first and only time that Jack had been wholly hers, wholly dependent upon her capabilities. On the *Snark,* she had played the man-comrade and true mate of his desires, and she could not credit the extent of his physical and nervous collapse because he had made her believe in his cult of the body without end, and daring before all. Because of her melancholy and his nerves, their quarrels became so fierce that the newspapers talked of a rift. She denied this to her aunt, pointing out that "a man with an ulcer for four months is not in a very happy shape." Then she loosed her cry of anguish, "Dear Christ! how terrible it would be to be widowed!"[15]

Even when he was ill, Jack could still project his magnetism, as if he also were the Seed of McCoy. To a suspicious Socialist interviewer in Sydney, who had heard of his bluster and conceit, he presented a chastened version of himself in a torrent of "uninterruptable, well-phrased, clear-cut, aggressive eloquence." The talk was seldom about him, and when it was, there was no glorification of self. There was also no air of the great author about him; he looked and dressed like a straightforward American worker. His power and persuasiveness lay in his directness. "On every subject that appeals to man, London has made up his mind, and can give you reasons for having done so, and is eager to show you where his views are right and everybody else's views are wrong."[16]

A measure of Jack's illness was, indeed, his revived interest in socialism. Physical weakness always reminded him of his duty to his neglected comrades. So he wrote an article on strikes in Australia, pointing out that these were orderly, although in America where industrialism had developed more fully they were more like a civil war. In the end, there would be no strikes, because capital would own labor, or labor would own capital. Jack thought it would be the second solution. Chattel slavery was already finished for the white worker, whatever might be the situation in the Solomon Islands. The future belonged to labor.[17]

Yet not the present, which Jack still believed to belong to capitalism and imperialism. He knew how to defend himself to the Australian comrades for his seeming neglect of the cause:

> Because I can tell stories about dogs and wolves and gold miners and ships and cannibals—all of which are unrelated to the tactics, strategy and philosophy of Socialism—I can get a whacking big crowd to listen when I turn loose and talk on Socialism. If I accepted . . . subordination of literary art to the incorporation in all my fiction of Socialistic tenets and methods, I wouldn't sell any stories at all.[18]

So Jack defended his last illusion. He could go on writing racist pulp fiction such as *Adventure* and *South Sea Tales,* as long as he sold an occasional Socialist story or delivered an occasional Socialist lecture. The first created the audience for the second. Yet that mass audience had become an incubus at the end of the voyage of the *Snark,* when the myth of his physical strength and unbreakable will was shown to be a false one. He could not continue acting and writing about the blond beasts of biology in their triumph over nature and lesser breeds. He must develop another myth of himself at home, on his ranch—the struggle for the mastery of land and of self. He must return home and turn inward.

11

THE BEAUTY RANCH

I do believe that we are just in the infancy of the science of psychology,
and that in the next few years we are going to learn tremendous things.

JACK LONDON

Jack and Charmian lingered on the way home. They did not want
to face up to the bad publicity of abandoning the voyage of the
Snark. In fact, there was little resentment except in their own
minds, even if many of the critics thought that Jack was almost
finished as a writer. If anything, the press and Jack's friends were
glad to see him as frail and human as other people. Yet he took his
time to return, going with Charmian to Ecuador before sailing to
New Orleans through the Panama Canal. They needed to recuper-
ate from their illnesses as well as plan a new life.

In Ecuador they saw a bullfight, which offended Jack. With his
own flesh tormented, he could not stand the goring of the picadors'
horses, the endless pricking of the fighting bull until its final death.
The sight inspired him later to write one of his best short stories,
"The Madness of John Harned." Harned acts out Jack's fantasy of
protest. Jack had himself jumped up in Ecuador to cheer the bull
in the tense silence while it was menacing the matador, and John
Harned leaps up to show with his fists his outrage against the
cowardice of the audience watching the torture of the horses and
the bull. "You came for a bull-fight," Harned shouts, "and by God
I'll show you a man-fight!"[1] He knocks down dozens of Latins and

kills seven of them before he falls dead, a sieve of bullet holes. No longer did Jack accept man's cruelty to animals as a biological necessity; his old doctrine of mastery had turned to protest.

When he and Charmian returned to the ranch in July 1909, he found that Ninetta Eames had nearly beggared him with her self-serving incompetence. He pensioned her off and gave her $500 when she divorced the lazy Roscoe and married a Unitarian minister, Edward Payne; he appointed a competent literary agent to handle his affairs and recalled all the second-rate material which Ninetta had been trying to peddle to the magazines. For three months the editors were thankful to receive no more of his torrential output. He moved into an annex at Wake Robin Lodge, and settled down to write competent, saleable stories, in an effort to regain his popular reputation. Charmian guarded him from all intrusion, while he was coddled by Nakata, who had been hired during the voyage of the *Snark* as the third of his Oriental servants.

The reception of *Martin Eden* showed how low his prestige had sunk. The reviewers all condemned it, misreading the story as an attack on his past socialism and with an unbelievable ending. In fact, Jack protested that it was an attack on individualism; Martin committed suicide because he had no faith outside his own hollow success. To one critic, he pointed out the fallacy in saying that, if Martin had lived, he would have forgotten his brief despair. "The case is exactly parallel with that of a beautiful young man, with the body of an Adonis, who can not swim, who is thrown into deep water, and who drowns."[2] Disgust might not last long, but it was enough to kill a man while it lasted.

If *Martin Eden* failed with the critics, it succeeded by word of mouth. To a whole generation of young American writers, all suffering from the mild paranoia produced by a series of rejection slips, Martin's struggle against all the odds matched their own fantasies of persecution. The book was to sell a quarter of a million copies in its hardcover American edition—a vindication of Jack's belief that he could make a national mythology out of his own biography. Even Narcissus had a public image.

The competent writing of the first year of his return was a

matter of paying for his ranch, and nothing else. He was frank enough about that to a reader of his books who complained that his writing was going to pieces. "I'm living so damned happily that I don't mind if I do go to pieces. I prefer living to writing."[3] He broke back into the *Saturday Evening Post* with a boxing story, "A Piece of Steak." He sold his South Sea tales to the Californian magazines. He finished *Adventure* and began on *Burning Daylight,* the novel of transition from his Klondike myth to his Californian dream. His hero, Elam Harnish, is the last of the blond supermen in his major novels, but he finishes not as a triumphant and ruthless millionaire in the northland, but as a small rancher in Sonoma, a chastened man who has undergone a spiritual change.

At first, there is no morality in Harnish's scramble for fortune in Alaska and Oakland, for he sees humanity divided into suckers and robbers, with luck dealing the stacked deck of cards. "Society, as organized, was a vast bunco game."[4] He is not saved from the bunco game by socialism, but by love. He falls for his secretary, Dede Mason, an idealized version of Charmian, candid and self-sufficient and hard-riding. She will not marry Harnish until he has renounced the moral corruption of his whole business empire. Then she takes him to a little ranch in the Sonoma Hills, where he gives up the cocktails that have made him flabby and becomes fit again by breaking in horses. In that final fantasy of regeneration, Jack's hero discovers gold and covers it up again with eucalyptus trees. Harnish would rather grow woods than make another fortune.

It was a romantic and incredible plot, but it fairly represented Jack's reconstruction of the myth of his past and his future. "When I tell you that Dede is my wife," he wrote to one fan, "and that many of the love-experiences were hers and mine, and that the ranch they came to live on is the ranch we are living on, you will appreciate our joy in your joy in Dede and Elam."[5] The essence of Jack's myth was that he had not failed, he had never failed, despite his defeat in Alaska, despite the fiasco of the *Snark,* despite his financial worries. It was Harnish's choice to leave Alaska as a multi-millionaire, it was another choice to give up a financial empire for love and a small ranch. The wilderness and big business did not defeat him. He wanted rebirth as a good man in the country.

So Jack accepted necessity and called it choice. It was the beginning of his maturity. He certainly settled on his Beauty Ranch of 260 acres as if he intended to lead a rural life of virtue forever. He referred to himself as quite a farmer and became quite a horse-breaker. Accidents followed his steps. "Talk of Devils of a *Snark* voyage!" he complained in one letter—"was bucked off one colt and kicked by another before was back one week."[6] In December 1909 a buggy wheel smashed his ankle again. Yet soon he was as good at horsebreaking as the regenerated Harnish, dominating the colts without ever riding them well. Charmian, who had been worried by his series of accidents, told him that she had ceased to worry. Instead of being proud of it, he looked like an abandoned child.[7] He wanted her to worry over him. It was her role.

Yet she must not give way to illness herself. When she came down with one of her frequent bouts of malaria, he pretended to take it well, but actually plunged into despair. He relied on her to be permanently cheerful, the Eternal Kid of her pretense. When she could not laugh him out of his melancholies, entertain his guests, type his daily manuscripts, and tidy up his life, he felt deserted. Only when she became pregnant did Jack cosset her. He longed for a son to carry on his work on the land, and he was so inspired that he started to plan a large new house for Charmian and her infant. It must be stone-built to withstand any earthquake—the final security of his wandering life. He would call it Wolf House, the symbol of his nature.

With Charmian pregnant, he could not run his own affairs and write enough to earn the money for Wolf House. Wisely, he invited Eliza Shepard to become his ranch manager on salary, if she would live near him at Glen Ellen. She was willing to separate herself from her elderly husband and devote herself wholly to Jack's business. He had always been the passion of her life, as she had been the support of his. He could do no wrong in her eyes, however inconsistent he might be. So he acquired a third loyal helper to add to Charmian and Nakata. Moreover, he had bullied

Bess enough over the Piedmont house to stop her from marrying again, so he was still the only man in the lives of his daughters. He felt secure enough to indulge his dreams of the future to the point of folly.

His next act was madness. Although the building of Wolf House would cost at least $70,000, he contracted to buy the 500 acres of the neighboring Kohler vineyards for another $30,000. The ruin of the *Snark* seemed to have taught him nothing. Although he was now earning over $70,000 a year from his stories and novels, the expenses of the ranch he already had, the demands of his dependents, and the cost of Wolf House were taking everything he earned. He was again willfully mortgaging his future as an author, condemning himself to write the commercial at the expense of the good.

And yet he persuaded himself that his compulsion to buy land was also a vision of the future of America. It was not the hunger of the unwanted child that could never be appeased. It was not the appetite of the deprived youth that demanded satiation. It was the new myth of himself and of his country's need. As always, he was determined to live out his fiction of his role in his society. He was no longer the chastened invalid of Sydney, preaching industrial militancy. Within two years, he had become the agricultural radical. His soft shirt and worker's cap had been dropped for a yellow worksuit and the Baden-Powell hat. He would not talk of how he became a famous writer, he simply said he hated writing short stories but had to do it to pay for the expenses of the ranch. He would rather write poetry or pamphlets. His enthusiasm was no longer for urban revolution, but for rural change. The strong should see that the battle had left the streets for the fields. There was no more opportunity in industry, only on the land.

"In a few years," he told one Californian reporter,

> this valley about you will prove what I have said. Men will learn that by modern methods more reward can be brought from ten acres of land than in the old days could be obtained from two or three hundred. Able men will be the farmers. Every stroke will count.

They will in time wonderfully improve what we think is the last word in intensive farming. . . . Not one single luxury of city life will be lacking, while the cash reward for the worker will be greater than he can earn in any town. As I told you, we are just now at the turning point. The movement from the cities to the country has scarcely begun.[8]

Jack played out his new role, ignoring the simple fact that no worker could make the capital he himself had earned to buy the land. He did not seem to care that his new enthusiasm was meaningless to the poor city worker, however able, any more than he seemed to care that his extensive acres had crippled his chance to write carefully and well. He borrowed money right and left, even persuading George Brett to advance him a further $5,000 by saying that another publisher had offered him double that for *Burning Daylight*. When Brett protested and sent him the money, Jack ate humble pie and swore that he would stay a Macmillan author for ever.[9] At least, Brett understood his hunger for land and sudden needs for cash.

Yet Jack was not deliberately dishonest in the frequent changing of his goals. He was always excessive, if not ecstatic, about what he believed at the moment. His error was to think that all his enthusiasms were held together by unifying, scientific laws. In fact, they were held together only by his vehemence. In the self-awareness that began to come upon him after the failure of the *Snark*, he could confess as much.

To Blanche Partington, he revealed that he knew his passion was often the enemy of his consistency:

I am, as you must have divined ere this, a fool truthseeker with a nerve of logic exposed and raw and screaming. Perhaps it is my particular form of insanity. I grope in the sand of common facts. I fight like a wolf and a hyena. And I don't mean a bit more, or less, than I say. That is, I am wholly concerned with the problem I am wildly discussing for the moment.[10]

Such was the paradox of a man who believed himself faithful to the truth as it changed for him, and who seemed more and more of a chameleon. By now, he was widely accused of being a nature faker. He had not been back to Alaska for thirteen years, but he was still panning gold from his brief stay there. Even his old supporter Richard Harding Davis wrote a story in mockery of him, called "The Nature Faker," in which the hero gives up advertising in New York to retire to his suburban home in Connecticut. He sneers at city life and makes a wilderness next door to his house, stocking his retreat with some wild bears, which turn out to be from a circus and invade the house during a party to dance waltzes with the terrified guests. What Davis attacked was the false vision of a man who lives in comfort but writes of the wild.

Jack too knew how false his visions could be. A new shock of disillusionment came when Charmian gave birth to a daughter, Joy, who died within a few days. It was more than Jack could bear. He went out drinking and collected a black eye in a fracas with an Irish saloonkeeper. Both men spent the night in jail and accused each other of assault, but the judge dismissed the case. Notorious again for brawling on the day of his baby's death, he left for Reno to report the prizefight between Johnson and Jeffries for the *New York Herald.* Among male company in the training camps, he forgot his despair about his child, although he remained hysterical about the judge who had failed to convict the saloonkeeper, pillorying him in open letters to the press and even writing a fantasy, "The Benefit of the Doubt," in which he beat up a judge who happened to be trespassing on his ranch.

Nevertheless, a new self-awareness and compassion showed even in his descriptions of boxing. Some years before, his novel *The Game* and his account of the fight between Britt and Nelson had been brutal and supremacist. But his reporting of Johnson's victories against Tommy Burns in Australia and Jeffries in Reno were infused with reluctant admiration for the black champion's grace and repartee, as well as with pity for his white victims. Jack's respect for Johnson's mastery and ease showed in his mocking exposure of the racket of the fight game, *The Abysmal Brute,* although in that story his hero was a white backwoods giant who would rather read Browning than slug his opponents. His pity was further revealed in his account of an old boxer going down before a young one in "A Piece of Steak," and in his masterpiece of the genre, "The Mexican." In that story, the underfed Mexican scrapper wins against the cheating *gringo* hero, because he has to gain the prize money to buy guns for the revolution. Jack's compassion for the fall of the old white boxer becomes a fierce cry for a whole exploited people, sending out their little last hope.

Jack claimed that the people who cringed at prizefighting were hypocrites. Those who lived off the profits of machines that mangled workers were worse than prizefighters. Those who supported the building of navies and the making of munitions were worse than prizefighters. Intellectual brutality and unkind epigrams were more cruel than a blow in the teeth. "Far better to have the front of one's face pushed in by the fist of an honest prize-fighter than to have the lining of one's stomach corroded by the embalmed beef of a dishonest manufacturer."[11]

Jack always claimed that he wrote as he spoke, straight from the shoulder. His stories did, indeed, have strength of style and speed of action like a combination of punches. However incredible the plot, he wrote with such pace and such controlled use of simple words that his readers could not put his books down, even when they did not believe what he was saying. In the collections of short stories published in 1910 and 1911, *Lost Face* and *When God Laughs,* he included some of his best stories and his worst. "Lost Face" itself and "To Build a Fire" were as memorable in their grim irony as "Semper Idem" and "The Francis Spaight" were ghoulish in their lip-licking over throat cutting. He could no longer distinguish between the sublime and the sadistic, the tragic and the sentimental, the heroic and the cruel, the myth and the posture.

He was not a precise man, but a powerful and persuasive one. The shifts he made in his beliefs were accommodated in his arguments. He had compromised his socialism by becoming a large rancher, but he put the blame on the Socialist Party, because it was beginning to temporize on the need for a revolution. "I shall stand always for keeping the socialist party rigidly revolutionary," he wrote to Anna Strunsky's husband, the millionaire radical William

English Walling. "If the socialist movement in the United States goes for opportunism, then it's Hurray for the Oligarchy and the Iron Heel."[12]

His insight foretold the future defeat of American socialism, even if he was often himself an opportunist. He had stumbled on the truth that the American proletariat was not rooted enough to become truly revolutionary. The workers would do better to stay on the small farms they were leaving than to wander from slum to slum in search of jobs as his family had. They were too footloose to organize themselves properly. Unlike the less mobile European workers, they had no tradition of radical protest over the generations.[13]

Jack himself had moved often enough to give up any group or club or union. He had personally experienced the downward social mobility of the time, the marginal existence of most of the proletariat that prevented it from sticking together. He knew that there would never be a national general strike because labor could not organize itself that well. There could only be a sudden revolution led by a band of fanatic leaders like himself. Until then, it was better to feed off the land than starve in the Social Pit of the city.

So self-justification for his style of life had its social logic, although it was far from a precise philosophy of rural socialism. Jack still confused his own necessary myth with the need of the national proletariat to return to the soil. In point of fact, he knew perfectly well that industrialism and urbanism must take their course. The flight from the land must become a migration, before there could be a return to it. Only a long economic depression could halt the drift to the cities.

He even thought out a manifesto of his beliefs, trying to extend his crude faith in the biological determinism of Herbert Spencer and the dialectic of Marxism into a cosmic explanation. Although the thinkers he quoted were all moral philosophers, he still claimed that his approach to the problems of the universe was positive and scientific.

> I assert, with Hobbes, that it is impossible to separate thought from matter that thinks.

I assert, with Bacon, that all human understanding arises from the world of sensations.

I assert, with Locke, that all human ideas are due to the functions of the senses.

I assert, with Kant, the mechanical origin of the universe, and that creation is a natural and historical process.

I assert, with Laplace, that there is no need of the hypothesis of a Creator.[14]

These assertions made slogans out of complicated philosophies; they confused ethics with science. Yet it was the necessary illusion of Jack's life, the only way he could reconcile his furious appetites and divided loyalties. He could justify his actions if they were part of a vast scientific process outside his personal control. He could evade the moral problems of his choices if he could believe his choices were unreal.

His ailing body urged him to try to take things easily, to enjoy life as it came. "You'll find me more of a kid than in Piedmont," he told a friend—"less serious, less prone to argument save in Jesuitical ways for the fun of it, laughing more than I used to, and laughing at more things."[15] He went on long cruises with his friends in his new small boats, the rented *Phyllis,* and the *Roamer,* which he bought and loved. George Sterling once sailed along with his wife but he was as out of his element on Jack's boat as Jack was among the bohemians playing in the false wilderness of George's colony of artists. "It's useless to deny we are Carmel-hungry," George wrote from the *Phyllis,* "and I, for *my* part, will never go on one of these long trips again. Hell! Better twenty days of Carmel than a gale on a yacht. And yet, we have had an interesting trip, the Wolf has been most generous and entertaining, and it's up to us to be grateful and appreciative. Nevertheless, no more long cruises for *me!"*[16]

It was the same for Jack and Charmian. They only visited Carmel once more. There they were grateful and appreciative, but they did not enjoy themselves. The fact that they arrived with two Japanese servants was enough to annoy the advocates of the simple life, and during the two weeks of their stay, Jack hardly budged, preferring to play bridge, talk, or read. He introduced "three minute" wild duck to the cuisine, which was usually dominated by mussel soup or abalone steak. The young and hopeful writer, Sinclair Lewis, happened to be there and was disappointed in Jack, finding him too much the country gentleman, and all at sea with the sliding, slithering, glittering prose of Henry James.[17]

Yet Lewis was a hustler and took advantage of his opportunity when he heard Jack complaining that he had run out of plots for his short stories. Lewis pulled out the hundreds of plots which he kept in a trunk beneath his bed, and sold Jack fourteen of them at $5 each. They were bad on the whole, and Jack only used three of them to write three inferior pieces of fiction. Perhaps, as Mary Austin commented, it was disguised charity. When Jack bought plots from Lewis or later from George Sterling, it was due more to the poverty of his friends than of his imagination.

Out of nostalgia for his gregarious Piedmont days and a hidden wish for approval by his peers, Jack did go to the annual High Jinks of the smart San Francisco artists in the Bohemian Grove. He even managed to keep his new control over his habits. He drank little, yet he bought more drinks than ever. This, as he told Charmian, was the paradox of moderation. In the old days, everybody bought him drinks for the pleasure of his company. Now he had to buy them drinks to hide the fact that he was hardly drinking at all.[18] Even George Sterling on a quick visit to the ranch recognized Jack's restraint. "That was surely a moist evening!" Sterling wrote. "I wished, next evening, that I'd been under your 'three drinks' regime. Such a headache!"[19]

Jack's deteriorating health dictated this self-control. He wished to preserve himself because of his long commitment to the land, and from this time on, he became more of a hypochondriac. When he had been coughing badly after his fight with the saloonkeeper, he thought he had tuberculosis; in fact, the cough was caused by his incessant smoking. Although there was an old scar on one lung, his chest was in good condition.[20] But his worries about his skin diseases, his teeth, his kidneys, and his bladder were real. He was morbidly interested in medical articles and added to his reference library on diseases. His usual public lecture was no longer on socialism, but on his methods as an amateur doctor aboard the *Snark*.

One interesting series of notes on "Psoriasis" survives in Jack's handwriting, reflecting his concern over his skin condition. Quoting a book which said that syphilis most resembled psoriasis, he added the comment: "Have never had syphilis. Does my disease resemble syphilis?" As he noted, arsenical poisoning could cause severe rashes, and his skin condition had become much better when he had stopped taking arsenic in 1909. Moreover, having cut down on the alcohol which he had swilled in the tropics to deaden the pain of his fistula and to still his twitching nerves, he could conclude his notes on "Psoriasis" with the remark, "I am not a toper nor a large meat-eater, nor am I gouty or rheumatic."[21] He would be all of these within a year, due to a new course of arsenic treatments.

The first twenty months on the Beauty Ranch were Jack's last period of happiness, when his myth of himself coincided with his style of life, when his dreams of the future seemed attainable, when his health allowed him a relaxed self-discipline. He had become a large landowner, he was building a large house, he was secure in the love of his family and friends. Even the loss of his child with Charmian showed that she was fertile, that she might yet bear him a son. His ambition was spent, yet his vision was clear. He saw himself as a man who had made his compromise with life and found it good. He put down some notes for the memoirs that he intended to write:

> My memoirs.
> The Philosophy, no desire for fame; next, no fear to retire to ranch and grow chickens and potatoes.
> The Philosophy, no fear of death, yet loving life. Develop it. Then no fear of sickness—leprosy. No fear of injury, except for dislike of pain.
> Then oncoming of age—decay of body, first weakening. . . . Always philosophical.[22]

12

CONFESSIONAL

Thou Wolf!
  You sure have your list of troubles—"the cost," my son, "the cost." The gods *do* love a shining mark. When a head sticks a few inches higher from the muck, they lams it.

GEORGE STERLING

In 1911, Jack was turned down for the first time as a bad health risk by an insurance company. No reason was given for his failure to pass.[1] He never took a medical examination for insurance again. And however cheerful he seemed to Charmian about the loss of her child, he brooded over a possible taint in his system that prevented him from having an heir. He believed that his yaws had not been cured properly in Australia. He became a subscriber to *The American Journal of Urology and Sexology,* and collected a small library on venereal diseases. One of the books was heavily underlined, particularly the passages about the transmission of syphilis in the conception of children, the three stages of the disease, and its old cures. Another was a pamphlet called *The Treatment of Syphilis with Salvarsan or 606.*[2]

The pamphlet asserted that salvarsan was one of the most important drugs ever discovered, and the first capable of curing yaws and tertiary syphilis. Although it mentioned the dangerous effects on the central nervous system of other arsenical compounds then in use, such as atoxyl and arsacetin, it claimed that salvarsan had bad side effects only in a few cases. It did, however, list these symptoms, specifying that the new drug could attack the kidneys, causing transient symptoms of nephritis, and could lead to diarrhea and bladder disturbances which made urination difficult. Salvarsan could also attack the nerves and produce an illusion of manic good health, followed by severe depression. Finally, in many cases, injections might cause an increase in body weight. From this time forward, Jack had continual trouble with his kidneys, his bowels, and his bladder. His state of mind after 1911 was one of alternate elation and melancholy. He gained weight and also began to suffer from the swollen ankles and rheumatism, the sciatic pains and pyorrhea listed as possible side effects of a course of salvarsan.

Most probably the loss of Charmian's child led Jack to begin his course of salvarsan. Her diary for December 2, 1910, reads: "We are talking a great deal about these new medical discoveries and *wondering* some! But the knowledge makes a man more than ever appreciate a monogamous existence—with the right one."[3] The likelihood was that he started on injections of salvarsan during the year of 1911. His nerves worsened. He became more of a manic-depressive, afraid that he was going mad like Maupassant or Nietzsche, both of whom died of tertiary syphilis. Because of persistent headaches and eyestrain, he had to wear a green eyeshade. He wrongly believed that he was suffering from a tumor on the brain, the result of the yaws or an earlier infection, and he consulted a medical text on diseases of the brain, paying particular attention to the pages dealing with his supposed condition. On the pages he marked, the book stated that syphilitic growths in the brain occurred "chiefly during the period of active adult life, from twenty-five to fifty." Jack was in the middle of that period, and he was suffering from symptoms similar to those he underlined, "severe and persistent headache, vomiting, and optic neuritis."[4]

All the symptoms of the latter years of Jack's life point to arsenic poisoning. He became more and more concerned about the crack-up of his body. In notes for *John Barleycorn* scribbled in the back of Josiah Flynt's autobiography, he set down his fears:

World-sickness—my disintegrating body, that has been dying since
I was born. I am aware that I carry a skeleton inside this flesh, a
grinning, noseless, death's head. . . . My smashed knees and ankles
—ruptured tendons of my thumbs, scars and mars. Arsenic slough on
cheek from Australian hospital—broken bone, never set, in hand
from hitting horse—my missing teeth, dropped from me, the jewels
of youth. . . .[5]

He was concerned that an ill-treated disease of his waterfront days,
perhaps the gonorrhea contracted in 1902, might have worsened
the effect of the yaws caught during the voyage of the *Snark*. The
cure for gonorrhea before arsenic compounds was based on mercury, itself a poison and bad for the kidneys. As the old saying went,
one night under Venus meant a lifetime under Mercury.

Another book in Jack's library was *Active-Principle Therapeutics*.
He particularly marked a section on how to inject oneself with a
hypodermic syringe. A silver traveling pocket case still exists at the
Glen Ellen ranch. In it are a silver hypodermic needle and syringe
with six vials containing the stimulants, strychnine sulphate and
atropine sulphate, drugs which were thought to help a patient get
rid of the toxins produced by damaged kidneys. Jack did know how
to give himself injections of salvarsan without even going to a
doctor. What he did not know was the effect of the salvarsan on
him.[6] He was a victim of the age before antibiotics. Like Byron at
Missolonghi, he was slowly killed by the mistakes of the doctors.
Also, as a believer in the American faith in home medicine, he was
slowly killed by his own mistakes.

The writing of his confessional book, *John Barleycorn*, bore
witness to the fear behind Jack's renewed and excessive drinking
at this time, as well as revealing one reason for his exaggerated
preaching of the virtues of the clean Anglo-Saxon race. The prohi-
bitionists had cleverly used the universal terror of syphilis to urge
the crusade against the saloon. Only after a man had too much to
drink—the propaganda said—would he pick up a woman and a
disease to blight the home.[7] With his secret fears about contamina-
tion by disease or alcohol, Jack provided in *John Barleycorn* the best
ammunition that the drys had ever been handed by a major writer.

He felt so guilty, because of what he claimed the drink had made him do, that he even supported female suffrage in California in 1911. He was no feminist, but he wanted women to vote for prohibition and the preservation of the white race—men were too weak to vote dry, even when they knew alcohol was poisoning them. He took the way out offered by the dry spokesmen: that only the availability of liquor caused him to misuse it. If it were taken from him on long ocean voyages or in a dry California, he could do without it perfectly well.

John Barleycorn was sensational as the history of a man who drank too much, yet who claimed to hold his liquor. Its author only hinted at the psychological and physical fears that made him a heavy drinker, and while the book overstated the deprivation of his youth, it understated the internal disturbances and agony in his kidneys which drove him to the stupor of the bottle. "The only trouble, I may say, about JOHN BARLEYCORN," he wrote in 1913, "is that I did not put in the whole truth. . . . I did not dare put in the whole truth."[8] The truths he omitted were the apparent truths of dry propaganda, the connection between his drinking and early whoring on the waterfront, his horror that Charmian's loss of her child might have resulted from a taint in his blood due to the mixed poison of alcohol and residual disease. In *Martin Eden,* he had put a similar fear in the mouth of Mrs. Morse, who advised her daughter Ruth not to marry the young ex-sailor. "It is that, the children, that makes Mr. Eden impossible. Their heritage must be clean, and he is, I am afraid, not clean. Your father has told me of sailors' lives and . . . and you understand."[9]

There is an important work to be written on the destruction caused by bad medication at the opening of this century. At least one-tenth of the American and European peoples were estimated to be suffering from venereal diseases, and in many cases the medical history of the radicals and artists before World War I is more interesting than their psychoanalytic history. To understand the wilder aberrations and extravagances of the period, Dr. Ehrlich may be a better key than Dr. Freud, fear of venereal disease more relevant than an Oedipus complex. Chronic arsenical poisoning caused more crack-ups than parental mistakes or bad whiskey.

When Jack's first daughter Joan was born after a difficult labor, her head distorted by the forceps, he had shouted to the doctor to let her die.[10] When Charmian's baby did not survive, he set off on a long debauch. Throughout his heavy drinking of 1911 and 1912, his old nightmares and insomnia came back to him. In the opening chapters of *John Barleycorn,* the book he wrote to exorcise his shame, he recalled the delirium of his wine-drunk at the age of seven, when he had hunted his lost father through the cellars and dens of Chinatown. His new abuse of alcohol to kill the pain of his rotting kidneys and blocked bladder led to another form of nightmare, which he called the White Logic. It was as deadly and sterile as the White Silence of his northern myth, not so much logical as schizoid. In the dawns of no sleep, he found himself split into two personalities. One was the death's jester of his long sickness, who jeered at every action as a sick joke and an illusion. The other was his regenerate self, who clung to the commonplaces of love and the land. The White Logic was his name for the dialogue between the two extremes of his personality. When he did anything, he sneered silently at it. When he made a decision, he asked himself the use of any action. He knew this bleak clarity was the result of drink, but he could not give up the drug that stimulated his mind and soothed his physical ills. For, as he had confessed in the notes for his Memoirs, he could not be philosophical about pain. He used the nearest remedy to put an end to it.

Now suffering from severe colds, sties on his eyes, and pyorrhea, he was also sickening from an inflamed appendix. The toxins in his system became worse. He knew that he must flush the poisons out of his body, so he drank at least three bottles of water, grapejuice, or buttermilk every night. He told Charmian that he needed the fluid to sweat because he was so sedentary; in fact, he needed it in order to pass water often, which also added to his disturbances in the night.[11] He slept apart from Charmian in the annex at Wake Robin, and later in the sleeping porch of the old cottage, which they adapted for their use in the 12 acres of the ruined winery that had been bought to round off the Beauty Ranch. He still disguised his state of health to her because he could not admit even to himself just how bad his physical condition was.

This was the beginning of the time of courage and maturity in Jack's life. A prisoner of his public image as the strongest and most life-loving American of his time, he felt bound to go on playing the role. In the solitudes of the night, he might recognize the White Logic of despair, yet in the writing routine of the morning, in the running of the ranch, in his play with his many guests, he wore the brave face of good health and enthusiasm for living. Much of the time, his composure was admirable. On the few occasions when it slipped, the agony of his body and mind flared into unbalanced rages that ruined his reputation. His final tragedy was ironical. While applying himself to the land and to those he loved, the last years of his courageous endurance of his pain were obscured by the reports of his rare outbreaks. The heroic myths, under which he hid the failures and hungers of his youth, only became true when he seemed corrupt and spoilt by success.

His uncontrollable changes of mood showed in his treatment of his divided families. On the ranch his generosity was proverbial. He insisted on hiring and entertaining freed and paroled convicts. He allowed them to exploit him and did not complain at their behavior. He was a model employer to the thirty workers engaged on building Wolf House. The Italian stonemason in charge of setting up the hand-scoured walls of local volcanic rock thought Jack the best man he had ever met, kind and considerate and fair, a true democrat. In the three years of the building of the house, Jack never lost his temper nor complained about the slow pace of the work.

Yet to Bess and his two daughters, he could be an object of terror. The little girls saw him so rarely that they became hysterical at his visits. When they started romping with him, he set the rules for the romps: there should be no tears, however much the children might be hurt by mistake. Everything went well, however roughly they played, until one day in 1911, when he slipped while playing with Becky and pushed her through the glass of a closed window before pulling her back to safety. It was a traumatic incident for

Becky and her mother, but Jack apologized for his brief loss of balance, saying that he was like a tiger playing with his cubs. Indeed, Joan, the elder, wrote to him proudly that she was his tiger cub.[12]

During that year of depression and irritation he was fighting tooth-and-nail with Bess, and showing himself at his most suspicious and ungenerous. She refused to let his two girls visit him at the ranch, claiming that Charmian was unfit to look after them. Jack lashed back, accusing Bess of being an unmotherly sexual beast. Such bitter remarks were made on both sides that he lost his sense of decency and wrote a mean will, which effectively left everything to Charmian and cut Bess and the two children out of his estate except for such charity as Charmian might choose to dole out. It was an act of self-destruction, for after the death of Charmian's baby, Jack yearned to have his children with him on the ranch. "Don't forget this danger," he warned Bess. "The less I am acquainted with my children, the less I shall know my children, the less I shall be interested in my children."[13] The act of exclusion from his will was his revenge for Bess's exclusion of his children from the ranch. If Bess kept them away, they should not inherit.

Flora and Johnny Miller were also absent from Jack's new country life. Neither of them ever visited the ranch. Flora's crime was to side with Bess and her grandchildren. Johnny Miller's crime was the old one of displacing Jack in his mother's affections. Ninetta Eames had already increased the misunderstanding between mother and son, writing to Jack: "It makes my blood boil to hear her slander you all the time and you giving her such a home and so fine a support. I see no good in standing it. I would make her stop it—the slandering—or let her starve. She is utterly without decent gratitude, and has no more love for you than a viper has."[14]

This new slander, written by Ninetta in an effort to take Flora's place and get her income, fed Jack's sense of betrayal and desertion. When Mammy Jennie, too, went to live with Flora, he took this as a further betrayal. Notes on his mother and wet-nurse in his proposed autobiography, *Jack Liverpool,* read: "How, after second marriage, both were treacherous and side with Bessie."[15] He was not overgenerous to either of them; each had to live on $60 a month, and Flora even took to baking bread and selling it on the streets in an effort to shame her son. He managed to stop her exhibitionism, but with both mother and son convinced of the other's neglect, the misunderstanding was now too wide to bridge. It was, in Eliza's opinion, a seething pot that was constantly boiling when there was no need for it to boil at all.

Nevertheless, Jack's attacks of nerves and irritation were usually contained by Charmian and Eliza on the ranch and by the pattern which he imposed on his days. His routine in his study and sleeping porch was immutable. It was the lifeline which kept him from sinking into lethargy and despair. Every night, Nakata arranged his bedside table with the galleys of his most recent book, with sharp pencils and scratch pads for any ideas he might have, with manuscripts from other authors for his comments, and with the magazines and pamphlets he had ordered. He worked on and off through the night, never sleeping more than five hours unless he drugged himself. Nakata woke him again at dawn, bringing coffee and a light breakfast. He read through the manuscript Charmian had typed the previous day, then he went to his desk to do his daily stint of writing—1,000 words, more or less. By eleven o'clock the draft was ready for Charmian to type, along with the various answers he dictated to some 100 letters a day. His correspondence reached about 10,000 letters a year, so that he took to signing his replies with a rubber stamp; but he was courteous enough always to respond to any crank or reader. Just before lunch he finished the day's mail, and then he was ready to join the guests staying at the ranch.

The second half of his day began with Jack's inquiries into his guests' work and nature, knowledge and limitations. There was something both teasing and relentless in his manner, as though he wanted to amuse himself, but also to gut his guests for all they had to give him. The afternoons were for riding or swimming or wrestling or boxing, the rough sports he still loved and inflicted on all his friends. Then, in the evening, cocktails and conversation at dinner. Usually his moods, exalted or attentive, boyish or dominant, set the pace for the gathering at the long table that he kept open for all comers in the style he had learned from the Strunskys. Then came the horseplay and the practical jokes, or card playing and reading aloud until the time of his retiring to begin his nightly routine.

The months passed. When he could not stand the monotony of it all, he had the horses harnessed to the buggy and drove the 2 miles to Glen Ellen or the 16 miles to Santa Rosa. Once there, he drank in the saloons, arguing on every subject under the sun, the only Socialist among the farmers and storekeepers. If he sometimes drank a quart of whiskey, it never seemed to affect him on the drive home. His control over himself was a habit—and had something to do with his mother's early training. "Jack is always punctilious about his bowels—" Charmian once wrote to her aunt, "his morning and evening passages are holy rites, in which he must not be disturbed."[16] He was a regular man.

The books and stories poured out, despite his many illnesses. He was in touch with the market again, and he needed his income of $70,000 a year to meet his commitments. His professionalism was overwhelming, his output prodigious: six books were written in quick succession. There was a humanity and a relaxation in his Smoke Bellew stories and they sold well in book form. Gone was the myth of Alaska, the sense of a superman pitting himself against necessity and the unknown. The deeds of daring of the hero from Harvard were often tongue-in-cheek, more Twain than Melville. Particularly mocking was the tale of the confidence trick that founded the town of Tra-Lee, the "most popular solitude on the Yukon."

His light mastery of his material extended over the collection of Hawaiian stories, *The House of Pride*. His prejudices had mellowed. His Chinamen were courageous and wise and sometimes wealthy, while miscegenation could produce admirable and beautiful people who made Anglo-Saxon bias look foolish. Many of the stories conveyed a pleasant nostalgia for a way of life that he liked. Only in the tales about the lepers was his calm broken by his compassion and his horror of diseased flesh. There but for the grace of luck went he, and his terror of becoming a virtual leper was transferred to the superman sheriff of Kona and to the beautiful singer Lucy Mokunui. The understanding he showed for the natives' last stand in his Alaskan story, "The League of Old Men," was joined to terror and pity in "Koolau the Leper," the tale of an old man who fought off the white policemen and soldiers who had come to arrest him. They were the ones, after all, who had taken the land and had brought in the Chinamen who carried leprosy with them, and Koolau would not yield to such injustice.

These were stories of Polynesia, where the people were half-children and half-gods in Jack's eyes. His Melanesian stories were of half-devils and all beasts. They were good yarns for boys, without the ghoulishness of *South Sea Tales.* Jack's good humor and his commercial sense made him present that loathsome paradise of his memories as if David Grief in *A Son of the Sun* were Smoke Bellew under sail. Only once did his neurosis about the tortures of the flesh obtrude. In "Jokers of New Gibbon," a cannibal chieftain who lived in a world of pain inflicted yet more pain on others. The description of his making the meat on his wives tender for the pot by breaking their bones and hanging them up alive was sadistic, and Jack reverted back to the gallows humor of his White Logic in the gruesome moral—"set your face sternly against any joking with the niggers."

A third uneven collection of short stories, *The Night-Born,* and two fantasies came from this productive period. The first fantasy was *The Assassination Bureau Ltd.,* from a plot by Sinclair Lewis, a complex tale of an international band of murderers who were set to kill their leader before he killed them. The death of Charmian's baby interrupted the writing, and he never completed it—it was his only abandoned work, and rightly so. *The Scarlet Plague,* however, was a haunting futurist novel about the end of the world, with San Francisco reduced to an archeological site beside which an old man tells a group of young savages about the breakdown of society after the attack of an incurable plague. In one graceful reference, Jack acknowledged his debt to Poe, saying that some called the plague "The Red Death," although its result was not a final orgy but a bloodthirsty tribalism in the cosmic flux of the rise and fall of civilizations. Almost casually, *The Scarlet Plague* ends in a hope of horses, with a beautiful stallion and a small herd standing on the wild beach in the sunset.

That love of horses as the redemption from the urban wasteland became the theme of the only good novel he wrote in these years. *The Valley of the Moon* was the reverse image of *John Barleycorn,* a confession of his suppressed romantic nature. Trying to sell it in advance to George Brett and the magazine editors, Jack misjudged its quality as usual, calling it "a big story, a true story, and offensive to none."[17] In fact, it is on the small scale, still a fantasy, and offensive to some. Yet it has an innocence and wonder that cannot be found in his other writing. His two lovers, Billy and Saxon Roberts, are frail and human. Jack himself appears three times in the book as their guide on their pilgrimage to the Valley of the Moon, an old Indian name for the Sonoma Valley. First, Jack is the boy in his little boat in the Bay, who tells the abandoned and despairing Saxon that Oakland is just a place to start from, he guesses. Then Jack twice appears as a successful writer, to point the route to Billy and Saxon, until they do reach their final haven.

By taking Billy Roberts for his hero, Jack seemed to be answering critics of his propaganda for the return of poor whites to the land. Billy is Jack without education. He has only his fists and his decency and his knowledge of horses to take him back to the farm. He need not follow the example of the Portuguese and the Dalmatians, the Chinese and the Japanese, who have made fortunes out of the intensive cultivation of the worn-out soil. He can lease a farm and loot it and abandon it, while making enough to buy a few acres of his own. In the end, however, Billy makes his capital in two prizefights and by dealing in draft horses. He then starts his fortune by becoming a teamster boss and discovering a claypit for a brickyard. It is the old story, that in America riches are gained not by stooping to till the earth, but by ripping out the treasures that lie beneath it.

If Billy is Jack without brains, Saxon is Charmian without polish. At one point where Jack appears in his own person, he compares his wife to Saxon and declares that they both came out of the same mold before it was broken. Like Charmian, Saxon is older than her husband, and she treats him as a great man-boy. She also loses her child—after a battle between workers and scabs in Oakland. Billy then turns into an alcoholic brute, liable to sullenness or mad rages; but with the beginning of their pilgrimage through the Californian countryside to the Valley of the Moon, he is restored to the gentle lover she has always known. The moral is clear. The mess of the cities corrupts and destroys lovers and workers. Only back on the road or the land can they find space and harmony.

Jack seems here to be dealing again with modern preoccupations—wandering along the byways for years with a tent and a Hawaiian ukelele, finding the end of the quest in organic living and a bit of business. Only George Borrow's *Lavengro* captures such a sweetness of love on the road, yet, as in *Lavengro,* fists rather than naked bodies provide the moments of excitement. Although Jack wrote to the editor of *Cosmopolitan* that he was glad to be serialized in an adult magazine which would allow him to "handle sex frankly and cleanly in the Anglo-Saxon way," he never got beyond the bedroom door or under the blanket in the woods.[18] Even with Saxon, the only scene with sexual implications is one in which Billy shows her the dirty tricks of fighting, so that she is dizzy with pain before she ends the battle with a kiss.

It would be easy to say that Jack avoided sexual scenes because of his fear of women, his immaturity, his aggressive nature, or whatever. It would not be true. When he gloated over violence, as in *South Sea Tales,* his disgust was at the world, not at women. His horror was of his own flesh, not female bodies. He did not put explicit sex into his writing because the magazines would not buy it, and he depended on his income from them. Nearly every novel he wrote was meant for serialization, and he could not offend his major source of cash. The censors were the editors, not his own suppressed lusts. "I have for years specialized on sex," he wrote to the author of *The Intermediate Sex,* and his library proved his point.[19]

The Valley of the Moon fails to be a great novel because it is too personal. It loses its poignant sense of quest and regeneration in the trivial descriptions of how to make money out of the land, and its propaganda destroys its art. Its major flaw, for many readers, is that it seems to deal with blood, race, and soil. Billy and Saxon are forever saying that their birthright is the land, and that foreigners have pushed their families off the soil into the slums. "We're the losers. We've ben robbed," one character says. "We're the white folks that failed." Yet finally, Billy and Saxon come to admire the labor of the recent arrivals in America, which does enrich the soil. Those of old American stock were robbed by their own kind. They were not pushed off the land, they gave it up because they did not want to work it. "We wasn't wised up to farming. We played at it."[20]

Jack was not playing at it now. He was studying it and sinking all his money into it. That was why he worked to crank out saleable stories. That was why *The Valley of the Moon* was weakened by agricultural homilies. His enthusiasm for saving the earth sometimes overcame his good sense. He fell under the spell of the promoters of eucalyptus trees, and he planted 60,000 of them over the years. They did not make him a fortune in hardwood, but they did stop the erosion of the soil. He was so keen on the commercial possibilities of growing trees for furniture and veneer that he uprooted many of the vines in the 500 acres of the Kohler winery, so that he could plant more eucalyptus. He wanted trees and fodder for his livestock rather than bad grapes. So he planted vetch and Canadian peas, and he plowed the crops under for three years, enduring the mockery of his neighbors in order to restore the earth. But the improvements in the ranch brought in nothing; they gobbled more than he earned. "My head is bloody," he complained to an old friend, "but the ranch is still uncowed."[21]

He did, however, build and furnish quarters for himself and his guests. The ruined cottage near the winery became a comfortable ranchhouse, informal and attractive, with nine additional bedrooms in cabins nearby. There were so many visitors that he had to have a circular printed to warn people of his routine and of the way to Glen Ellen. "Our life here is something as follows: We rise early, and work in the forenoon. Therefore, we do not see our guests until afternoons and evenings." His pleasure was to mix the most disparate of people, philosophers and convicts, rich men and tramps, businessmen and poets. He did what he had once prophesied to Anna Strunsky: "Some day I shall build an establishment, invite them all, and turn them loose upon each other. Such a mingling of castes and creeds and characters could not be duplicated. The destruction would be great."[22]

Ed Morrell, a convict pardoned from San Quentin, was a special guest. He remembered Jack on the ranch as a boyish man with a mind like a time machine or a rapid-fire gun. His sentences leapt from the commonplace to the cryptic. Pathos made him weep openly, injustice fueled his passion. He was both personal and universal, so that he only bullied a man in order to reach an abstract conclusion. However much he might offend by his keenness in argument, he was always forgiven. People loved him, bias and all.

Morrell particularly enjoyed entering into Jack's fantasies and conspiring with him to steal the state of Arizona by setting up a secret political machine which would capture the state government. The laws that Jack wanted to have passed were illuminating. He wanted to prevent crime by stopping the wrong sort of children from being born. Marriage should not be allowed until a doctor's certificate of health had been obtained. Immigration should be rigidly controlled to prevent the unfit from entering the state. When children were born, they should be sent to schools where psychiatrists could eradicate any criminal tendencies. Only by controlling the genetic material and the environment could Arizona become the cooperative commonwealth of his utopian dreams.[23]

When he was not conspiring with his guests or enjoying their company, Jack was often testing them. He did it through practical jokes. He had hundreds of these—glasses that poured water on shy guests, exploding cigars for smokers and detonating books for anarchists, snake stew and frog soup, mock earthquakes and mud puddles. A guest might find himself swallowing a live goldfish or pushing a peanut along with his nose. It was all good clean sport with an edge to it. Jack hated gentility, and he liked to separate the goats from the sheep by putting them to the ordeal by fun. His hobo friend, Frank Strawn-Hamilton, thought that he laughed off his fears by his horseplay, and that his burlesques masked his inadequacy.[24]

There was a simpler explanation. Jack was a new Californian. He wanted to point out his sense of difference, his victory over his origins. He did not hide his light; he used it to set fire to the bushel. His brash behavior did not come from inadequacy so much as from a need to flaunt his achievements. His natural delicacy prevented vulgarity, yet it did not stop his buffoonery. He enjoyed games of all sorts at all times. As Anna Strunsky said, he did not want to become rich for the sake of the money, but for the sake of playing the game.[25] Outwitting publishers and public, the establishment and the gullible, was itself a game. "I've had the goat of New York all the way from California for fourteen years," he once boasted to Eliza, "and I think I shall continue to keep my hand on the goat of New York."[26]

If he did occasionally show off what he had won for himself, he was explicit about the roots of this failing in *John Barleycorn.* He remembered his first mutiny against his mother: she had just given him his first store-bought undershirt, and he insisted on wearing it without a shirt to prove to the other little boys that all his clothes were not made by his mother. So he would now trace his uncontrollable generosity, his avid appetites, to a reaction from his deprived boyhood. "Only a man who has undergone famine can properly value food; only sailors and desert-dwellers know the meaning of fresh water. And only a child, with a child's imagination, can come to know the meaning of things it has been long denied."[27]

He knew that his lavishing of his hospitality and his earnings was a neurosis, that it could not appease his hunger for love in general. This knowledge led to his rare outbursts of bad temper and disgust at his sycophants, whose affection he suddenly feared might be bought. He was alternately too generous with such flatterers as the envious Oakland journalist Joseph Noel, and then too violent in his reaction from them. Noel was dangerous both as friend and enemy. He managed to wheedle some $4,000 from Jack to back a lithographic process called the Millergraph, and he left for New York to make both their fortunes on the invention. When it went wrong and he abandoned Jack to save his own skin, he was struck off Jack's roster as a Judas and a liar. So he became the destroyer of Jack's reputation, spreading the poisonous stories of Jack's occasional sprees and aberrations in the final years of his intense pain.

Fame and notoriety were fed not only by the gossip of the journalists but by the lies of doubles. Jack's public image as a drunken and brawling ladies' man was so exaggerated that many a fellow, caught in a bar fight or in the wrong woman's bed, gave his name as Jack London. His doubles were dope fiends in Guthrie, Oklahoma; poisoners in Mexico; drunkards in Sioux City; and adulterous art salesmen driving Stutzes in St. Louis. The scandals provoked a spate of aggrieved letters from Jack, proving that he had never been near the places where his name had been used. "I have been pestered for a long time with a 'double,' " Jack wrote to one friend, "who cashes bad paper on banks, in my name; in my name makes love to married women, spinsters, virgins, and widows with large families; and does a few-score other things that are embarrassing to me."[28] He might occasionally use the fiction of a double to conceal some of his sprees, but he certainly was not guilty of one in a hundred of the offenses the yellow press claimed for him. "Whenever you meet a 'double' of mine," Jack pleaded from the ranch, "knock his block off for me, will you please?"[29]

The daily demands of his writing, his guests, and his land were so great that Jack still sought relief in long escapes. He sailed off for weeks on the *Roamer,* "waiting, always waiting, for the skiff to come alongside, for the lighting of the fire in the galley-stove, for the pulling off of gaskets, the swinging up of the mainsail, and the rat-tat-tat of the reef-points, for the heaving short and the breaking out, and for the twirling of the wheel as she fills away and heads up Bay or down."[30] He also broke four horses to harness, put them in the traces of a light Studebaker trap, and set off for three months with Charmian and Nakata through the mountains of northern California. He hardly walked any more and exercised as little as he could because of the weakness in his legs and his stomach, relying instead on the strength in his arms and chest to move with the wind and the horses.

Jack doing his four-in-hand on the trails of Northern California.

He studied Californian history, and decided to emulate the voyage of the old pioneers on a clipper round the Horn. He had business in New York with the Millergraph investment, and he took Charmian there in the winter of 1911. It was the worst time of her marriage. He abandoned her most of the time in an apartment on Morningside Heights, while he roistered night and day round the city with Joseph Noel and a pack of friends. He stopped writing and drank heavily, unable to resist the lure of being a literary lion. He went to boxing matches, he spent the nights on Broadway in smart saloons or with chorus girls. "Rome in its wildest days," he told a reporter with typical exaggeration, "could not compare with this city. Here, making an impression is more important than making good."[31]

He was trying both to make an impression and to do better for himself. Sinclair Lewis deliberately fed him information that his magazine rates and publisher's royalties were less than Rudyard Kipling's, Conan Doyle's, Edith Wharton's, and Theodore Roosevelt's. When Jack asked George Brett for a 20 percent royalty on his books instead of 15 percent, Brett refused. Jack then made a bad error of judgment and left Macmillan's to sign up with the Century Company for *Smoke Bellew, The Night-Born, The Abysmal Brute,* and *John Barleycorn.* In fact, he found that Century had none of the patience or understanding of Macmillan's, and he soon had to beg George Brett to take him back. But in the "wild maelstrom" of that winter in New York, Jack's heavy drinking developed his suspiciousness and his sense of superiority to a pitch of folly.

He was not a good businessman. In the Millergraph dealings, he tried to behave like Elam Harnish, and he ended by being squeezed out of control of the process by Wall Street manipulators. He had generously granted Joseph Noel the right to do a dramatic version of *The Sea-Wolf,* and now he was forced to pay Noel's financial angel nearly $4,000 to buy back the motion picture rights on his own novel. He contracted to supply twelve short stories to the *Sunday Magazine* for the highest price he had yet received, $1,000 a story, and then spoiled the market by supplying old and rejected stories with the dust still on their pages. He was both too aggressive and too contemptuous in the big city, like a provincial visitor who despised the sophistication which had lured him there. He even compared New York to the state institution for the feeble-minded down the valley from his ranch, a place he had described in his strange "Told from the Drooling Ward." The Manhattan citizens' feeling of superiority over the rest of their countrymen seemed to make them as witless as the inmates of the asylum.[32]

To justify all his nights on the town, Jack revived an earlier project for a New York version of *The People of the Abyss.* In his previous notes on this, "The American Abyss," he planned a chapter on a prostitute and a street boy and an old man reduced to the gutter. He wanted to attack the college settlement worker's approach to the slum problem and dwell upon the ferment of life. He even intended to repeat his worst experience. "Find out some hell-hole of a prison, and have myself arrested and sent to it," the notes read. "A splendid chapter, to say nothing of newspaper articles I might write."³³ But in truth, he would no longer take the risks of his younger days. His spirit was unwilling now, and his flesh too weak. He would not try to gather material which gave him a bad time of it. So he changed his project to an autobiographical account of what he was finding out about Broadway. The stars now interested him more than the slums.

His stomach problems had made him acutely sick, and he saved himself from a physical collapse just in time when he and Charmian set sail on the clipper *Dirigo* from Baltimore in early March 1912. His last acts on shore were to have himself shaved completely bald, and to be photographed standing by the grave of another literary debauchee, Edgar Allan Poe. On the second night of the voyage, Charmian's suppressed fears emerged in a terrible dream of Jack having syphilis which turned into leprosy. "It's no dream," Jack said in her dream before she woke.³⁴ Yet the nightmares soon left them both, there was no drink on the clipper, the trip round the Horn was five months' long, and Jack had the time to get into shape again. When the alcohol passed from his system, he was triumphant and claimed that he did not need it at all. "I have learned, to my absolute satisfaction," he declared, "that *I am not an alcoholic* in any sense of the word."³⁵ Charmian did not believe him, knowing that he would take to drinking again when the pain in his bowels became intolerable. But during the voyage, it was the captain who slowly died of stomach cancer, while Jack's health improved, now that his system was free of both alcohol and the arsenic in salvarsan. During this time of detachment, he rediscovered the sense of innocence and wonder which were to infuse *The Valley of the Moon* with its particular charm. He completed the novel and Charmian became pregnant again. There might yet be a future for his hopes.

13

DISGUST

All my life has been marked by what, in lack of any other term, I must call "disgust." When I grow tired or disinterested in anything, I experience a disgust which settles for me the thing forever. I turn the page down there and then. . . . Please believe me—I am not stating to you my strength, but my weakness. These colossal disgusts that compel me to turn down pages are weaknesses of mine, and I know them; but they are there. They are part of me. I am so made.

JACK LONDON

The beginning of the new time of disgust was Charmian's miscarriage soon after her return to California. It confirmed Jack's fear that he would never have a son and heir for his ranch. He seemed to take it well, writing to Charmian in hospital: "I am so sorry; yet my gladness is vastly greater, in that you are all right."[1] But long ago he had confessed to Cloudesley Johns what he felt about a barren woman or a defective child. "Barrenness is a terrible thing for a woman; but the paternal instinct is so strong in me that it would almost kill me to be the father of a child not physically or mentally sound."[2] After this second mischance, he no longer believed that he and Charmian would ever have a child. When she had recovered, he told her that he had turned that page down for ever. His disgust was such that he wanted no more children. When she fell ill at the news, he relented and said that, of course, they would try again.[3] Yet these were words said out of kindness, and he did not believe them.

189

The knowledge that she could not bear a child affected Charmian. As she watched Jack getting sicker each day and withdrawing from her, she withdrew from him, afraid of his dying. "I have no baby to make me know this fear of death," she wrote to Anna Strunsky Walling, "but I feel it with sharp keenness with reference to Jack. I am not a physical coward, but I shrink unspeakably from danger, because any accident that would break up the combination that is ours seems so utterly disastrous. I am shadowed by this fear all the time, and often realize that I must shake it off."[4]

Knowing that Joan should now be the eventual heir to the ranch, Jack tried to make her leave her mother and choose him. He treated her like an adult capable of responding to his desperation, forgetting that she was only a child of twelve who could not understand his need. The battle between father and mother tore the girl apart.

Jack began writing to her in the summer of 1913 about his sickness and his misery. He wanted her to remember that he was her father, who had fed her, clothed her, housed her, and loved her ever since she was born. Was he just a meal ticket? Was he a creature whose whim or fantasy compelled him to take care of her because he was a fool who gave much and received nothing? The world belonged to the honest ones, and he wanted Joan to break her silence and say that she loved him and would come to see him on the ranch. She would if she was great and true. It did not matter that she was only twelve years old, for truth was no respecter of age or youth.[5]

Joan was forbidden by her mother to go to the ranch, but she managed to persuade Jack to come to a meeting with Bess in Oakland. She hoped that their quarrels could be settled for her sake. Instead, Bess could not forgive Charmian, and Jack became angry at having to defend his second wife from his first one. He quoted the Bible at Joan: "To everything there is a season, and a time to every purpose under the heaven . . . a time to get, and a time to lose; a time to keep, and a time to cast away." He was in such anguish that he even burst out with the confession that he had never known his own father, had never seen his own father, had never heard a word of good about his own father. So Joan at the age of twelve learned the truth about Chaney and also learned that her father did not want to do to her what his father had done to him.[6]

Yet Joan delayed her answer, unable to defy the mother who had cared for her every day of her life. Jack sent her another letter, saying that he knew Nakata ten thousand times better than his daughters. How should he feel about them? Joan then replied with a mixture of childishness and stiffness, saying that she resented his opinions about Bess, who had always been a good mother to her, and that she had made up her mind to stay with Bess until she was old enough to support herself. She begged her father not to make her write any more such awful letters to him, because they hurt her so much.[7]

Her answer from Jack took four months to arrive. It was written at the same time that he had turned down the page on having another child by Charmian, and it was unbalanced and untrue on the subject of his feelings for Joan. He said that all his life had been ruled by moods of uncontrollable disgust, during which he became tired or uninterested in anything. He had warned Bess that, if he could not see his daughters, he would become uninterested in them. That had happened. He would continue to support his daughters, but he did not care to see them any more. He had a father's strongest love and hope for Joan, but she had been ruined by her mother's stupidity. It was nobody's fault, except God's, if Joan believed in God. Disgust had finished his love of her. "Unless I should accidentally meet you on the street, I doubt if I shall ever see you again. If you should be dying, and should ask for me at your bedside, I should surely come; on the other hand, if I were dying I should not care to have you at my bedside. A ruined colt is a ruined colt, and I do not like ruined colts."[8]

This savage letter was written after an attack of appendicitis in the summer of 1913. An Oakland doctor called Porter operated on him and took him as one of his patients, warning Jack that he would die of kidney failure if he did not stop drinking, give up raw fish and meat, and start exercising and losing weight. Jack ignored the advice and went on drinking, gobbling underdone duck, and avoiding exercise. To him, the chief merit of his new doctor was that he could now get increasing supplies of the opiates he had first begun taking in the Solomon Islands to ease the pain of his double fistula and psoriasis. From this time forward, morphine and heroin began to replace alcohol as analgesics for his white nights.

Although he still liked to keep up the pretense of undamaged health to all the world, he would admit ironically that his body was no longer a perfect mechanism. In one curious letter to a reader, who complained that his writing had lost its vigor, he replied: "You are right. I am all in. The fires of my youth are out. I lie on a mattress grave, in a hospital, spitting out the entrails of my youth night and day. The one last adventure remains to me—the making of my will."9 If his entrails were not giving him hell, his teeth were. He spent much of 1913 visiting the dentist, finally having all his upper teeth pulled in mid-November to halt the pyorrhea raging in his gums. There was little that was physically right with him by now, and only his courage kept him on his feet.

There were more catastrophes in store before the bad year of 1913 ended. A fortnight before its completion, Wolf House burned down. Jack thought he had built a fireproof house of twenty-three rooms; but the redwood beams and floors created a firestorm that totally destroyed the interior, leaving only the stone walls standing and blackened. The wood of the house had been cleaned with turpentine to remove any stains, so that the whole place burned with a mysterious blue flame. Beyond some trees near the walls, a stand of redwood planking had also caught fire, although the trees were untouched. The two simultaneous fires made spontaneous combustion unlikely, and suspicion pointed to Eliza's husband, whom she was divorcing; he had quarreled with Jack that day over taking Eliza away to manage the ranch. There was also talk of a workman who had been fired, or of a disgruntled Socialist envious of Jack's wealth. No one could discover whose hand actually set the match, but it seemed to be the act of man, not God. "I would rather be the man whose house was burned," Jack said during the fire, "than the man who burned it."10

His disgust was increased by his ruin. Only the mortgage on

Wolf House was insured. He now owed about $100,000, two-thirds of it wasted on Wolf House. His other extravagance had been the purchase of the 436 acres of the neighboring Freund ranch, which brought his holdings up to 1,400 acres. He did not seem able to stop buying land, and his income was mortgaged for eighteen months ahead.

Very little on the ranch gave him pleasure except for his live-stock. He bought a pedigree bull and a prize dam, and he laid the foundation for a small herd of Jersey cows and fine bulls for sale. His pride was a great Shire stallion called Neuadd Hillside and four pedigree Shire mares—the five animals cost him over $5,000. He thought that draft horses still had a future, although the first tractors were already being used on the farms of California. His lifelong fanaticism about improving the quality of human stock was now transferred to animals. He even wanted prize pigs and prize goats. "I believe," he wrote to the *Medical Review of Reviews*, "that the future human world belongs to eugenics, and will be determined by the practice of eugenics. . . . Humans breed in ways quite similar to those of animals; and if humans misbreed, the results are mis-breds."[11]

So his new interest and his despair made him revert to the bleak consistency of his beliefs before his long sickness, when evo-lution seemed the basis of everything to the young writer. Once again, he asserted that the individual had no free will, that he was the victim of bad heredity. "I breed too many horses, cows, pigs, sheep and goats, on my ranch here," he told one Christian, "to accept for a moment your baseless assertion that evolution is wrong and is not."[12] As his faith in humankind and his hope for a male heir vanished, he was left with nothing else except his youthful arrogance in pursuit of other goals. "I am trying to master this soil and the crops and animals that spring from it, as I strove to master the sea, and men, and women, and the books, and all the face of life that I could stamp with my 'will to do.' "[13]

The condition of that mastery was the huge income from his writing. A five-year contract with *Cosmopolitan* magazine in Novem-ber 1912 enabled him to stop pouring out short stories, because

Cosmopolitan agreed to pay him $2,000 a month to have exclusive rights on serializing all his fiction, whether long or short. He told the magazine that he had already written thirty-nine books in thirteen years, at the rate of three books a year, and he would continue to produce and produce. When George Brett accepted him back after his flirtation with the Century Company, he wrote to Brett that he expected to finish ten novels in the next five years and two autobiographies, one about his writing and another about his farming.[14] He was still sure that the American public was vastly interested in all he did.

Free of the need to turn out short stories, Jack wrote the three novels of his disgust in the eighteen months after the end of the voyage of the *Dirigo.* The two earlier ones, *The Mutiny of the Elsinore* and *The Little Lady of the Big House,* were full of hatred, artificiality, and contempt for human beings. They were the writing of a sick man, who could not control his attacks of nausea. The third novel of that period, *The Star Rover,* praised the triumph of the spirit over the torments of the body, and it signaled Jack's escape from his physical pain through drugs.

At first sight, *The Mutiny of the Elsinore* appears to be even more racist and sadistic than *Adventure.* A world-weary, wealthy playwright ships on a steel-built clipper to sail round Cape Horn. Captain West and his daughter, the two mates, and the Asiatic servants are the master races on the poop. The crew down below are a diseased mess of degenerates and idiots, the nightmare of the Social Pit which Jack once saw in the jail in Buffalo. The captain dies off the Horn, the two mates fight each other to the death, the crew mutiny and attack the poop under their gangster leaders, the playwright reverts to his Anglo-Saxon ancestry and becomes the master of the ship with his .22 Winchester repeating rifle. It all seems good nasty racist adventure, which the Hearst press duly serialized under the title of *The Sea Gangsters.*

This was not Jack's intention. He was trying to write an allegory of the whole of imperial history, based on the extraordinary theory of Major Woodruff's *Effects of Tropical Light on White Men.* That book claimed that the blond Aryan race, born to command

and govern the world, must perish before the brunettes of lesser breeds, because its fair skin became diseased in the tropical sun. Jack's own plague of psoriasis, which he thought was leprosy, made him associate his failure on the *Snark* with the inevitable failure of the Aryan race in the heat. It was not his fault, it was the doom of his kind. So comforted, he constructed his poor allegory of Anglo-Saxon imperialism on the voyage of the *Elsinore,* specifically named after the murderous castle in *Hamlet,* "a ship of souls, the world in miniature."

The Little Lady of the Big House, written in the bad year of 1913, was meant to exalt the splendor of Wolf House and scientific farming and sex. "It is all sex, from start to finish—" he wrote to the editor of *Cosmopolitan,* "in which no sexual adventure is actually achieved or comes within a million miles of being achieved, and in which, nevertheless, is all the guts of sex, coupled with strength." His sexual triangle was composed of people who were "cultured, modern, and at the same time powerfully primitive."[15] In fact, the relationships of the three lovers were as cold and sterile as the barren marriage of the hero and heroine.

As in *The Sea-Wolf,* Jack split his own role between the two male protagonists, the ranch owner Dick Forrest and the romantic adventurer Evan Graham. Forrest is Jack's ideal of the rich commercial rancher of the future, the owner of 250,000 acres worked on strict scientific principles. Evan Graham is another version of Dick Forrest, but he has chosen to remain a writer and a wanderer—the escapist ideal of Jack himself. Both men look the same, blond, bronzed, and gray-eyed, and both compete for the love of Dick's wife, Paula—a vision of Charmian as the elegant hostess, the athletic horsewoman, and the Eternal Kid of Jack's fantasies. She is torn between her love for her husband's scientific principles and her guest's wayward passion. She kills herself to solve her dilemma the day before Dick has decided to do the same thing. "She beat me to it," he thinks.

The end of Paula is, indeed, sinister. Having shot herself, she is revived by the use of a stimulant, then given a large dose of morphine by Dr. Robinson to allow her to slip away without pain.

Robinson, receiving the eye permission from Dick, easily and quickly thrust the needle through the stretched skin, with steady hand sank the piston home, and with the ball of the finger soothingly rubbed the morphine into circulation.

"Sleepy, sleepy, boo'ful sleepy," she murmured drowsily. . . . After a long time, she sighed faintly, and began so easily to go that she was gone before they guessed.[16]

The closing lines suggest Jack's own reliance on drugs to kill the unceasing pain of his kidneys and his bladder. Dr. Porter was prescribing mixtures of morphine and belladonna, and also heroin and strychnine, to allay the pain and to stimulate his bladder so that he could get rid of the toxins his kidneys could not handle. The effect of the morphine and the heroin was initially beneficial. Jack gave up his excessive drinking, and he wrote *The Star Rover.* The White Logic of alcohol was replaced by the beatitudes of morphine. "I love to dream," he told Charmian. "It seems to me that my life is doubled by the amount of dreaming I do every night."[17]

The Star Rover was not presented as a personal story, but was based on the experiences of his friend, Ed Morrell, who had served five years in solitary in Folsom and San Quentin prisons, along with Jake Oppenheimer, who had also spent several years in solitary and was hanged for murdering another inmate. Jack was meticulous enough to make Morrell sign a sworn affidavit of his ordeals in jail. In the novel, Morrell and Oppenheimer appear as themselves, serving their time in solitary alongside the hero, a professor of agronomy called Darrell Standing who has killed another professor in a blaze of atavistic wrath. He is an incorrigible prisoner and spends most of his days in a straitjacket; but he keeps on taunting his warders to pull the jacket even tighter, to increase the torment. He uses the agony to induce a trance, during which his spirit seems to leave his body and travel back through time to its previous existences. This metaphysical device enabled Jack to make use of the chapters and plots of many other books he had been planning, particularly the story of Saxon Roberts's pioneer ancestors in the massacre of Mountain Meadow, and the tale of the Crucifixion told by a Viking mercenary called Ragnar Lodbrog.

It was an ambitious novel, and a return to the mythological underlayer of Jack's best work. In it, he tried to use the faiths of all the ages of men to explain their survival, from the shipwrecked sailor going about his business on his rocky solitude to the Elizabethan pirate waiting out his long revenge among the aliens of Korea, and then back to prehistory as the Rice Eaters defend themselves from the Snub Noses. The false primitivism of the *Elsinore* and *The Little Lady* became a genuine quest for the myths of the unconscious, which changed men through their dreams and their religions. "I have been a Son of the Plow, a Son of the Fish, a Son of the Tree," Standing declares. "All religions from the beginnings of man's religious time abide in me. And when the Dominie, in the chapel, here in Folsom of a Sunday, worships God in his own good modern way, I know that in him, the Dominie, still abide the worships of the Plow, the Fish, the Tree—ay, and also all worships of Astarte and the Night."18

Through his dreams and his drugs, Jack began to regain his power over the mysteries of the unconscious that transfigured his best writing. As always, he did not understand what he was doing and insisted that he was merely writing for the market. Darrell Standing still uses the terms of the stockbreeder to argue that men are like savage colts, and that the morality which distinguishes them from Neanderthals is only a result of their training and breaking. Jack also wrote to the editor of *Cosmopolitan* that he had concocted the novel to appeal to the pseudo-scientific and the pseudo-philosophic, "good accessible stuff to the Christian Science folks, and for all the New Thought folks, and the millions who are interested in such subjects in the United States today."19 Thus he disclaimed his achievement, apparently unaware of his true power.

One other project of the time showed the questing range of his mind under the influence of morphine. He planned to write a book called *Farthest Distant: The Last Novel of All,* the first sentence of which would read: "Far beyond the farthest star, once revolved the earth." Three men would be talking to each other by telepathy, preparing to play the Record of the human race through a machine. The brain of man would have developed incredibly leaving his body far behind. The Record, however, would be a child's history of the origins of the human race—the vitalized Slime that had raised Heaven and made God, and then, recoiling from the lie it had made, was smashed back into the Slime by the immensity of the Unknown. Then would come the era of depression and pessimism, that would end in self-destruction, after which the optimists would rise, the lovers of life who kept the face of truth veiled. After them would come the storers of energy, who managed to capture it from radium and the sun, and then the space travelers, who set off on their great journeys through the universe. This would be the Record.

These three men talking by telepathy, the first star rovers, would leave behind them cities of steel and glass that retained heat and resisted the frozen deserts outside. All germs would be dead and human beings would live for 1,000 years. Their food would be taken directly from the elements. Their voyages through space would take them past thousands of other tenanted worlds and they would find that one immutable law ruled all the cosmos. "The great universe journey took on a sort of sacred significance," Jack's notes read. "It was something that must be carried out. The carrying out being the highest patriotic, ethical, and religious form of conduct —all for science and knowledge." When the star trekkers had crossed a few abysses of space, they would be "looked upon as barbarians, as gypsies, by the great galaxies of peopled planets. Our World was like a Gypsy Vagabond; also it was very small alongside these monster worlds."[20]

So Jack's mind and spirit began to free themselves. But he was still harassed by business and legal problems. He lost $10,000 on a Mexican land deal and a guarantee for a fidelity loan. He allowed a grapejuice company to incorporate under his name, hoping that he would be able to sell his own grapes at a high price. The company, instead, floated worthless stock, went bankrupt, and Jack found himself sued by angry stockholders for $41,000, although the case never reached court. He was only a good businessman in his fantasy of himself.

His hopes of making a fortune out of the new motion picture

industry resulted in still more harassment. A small Hollywood director and producer, Hobart Bosworth, proposed to make a film of *The Sea-Wolf.* This was made and found itself competing with two other film versions and a theatrical production. Jack was forced to institute a prolonged lawsuit against the pirate producers, in order to prove that an author retained the film rights to his magazine stories. In the course of this legal battle, he helped to found the Authors' League of America with Rex Beach, Booth Tarkington, Ellen Glasgow, and many other leading writers, all of whom combined to protect their copyrights. Jack found himself struggling alongside his fellows in the trade on the East Coast and discovered that they were in a crusade with him rather than a conspiracy against him. Their united efforts put enough pressure on Congress to change the copyright laws in favor of the authors, so that piracy by film and theater producers became more difficult. This success made Jack succumb to the usual illusion about moving pictures. "There is a pot of money that we shall get hold of yet," he wrote to Eliza, "if the lawyers don't eat it all up."[21]

The legal labyrinth took Jack to New York again in January 1914, a fitting place to work out the last of his disgust. He left Charmian behind this time and thus had no restraint on his actions. One evening he was out drinking in Harlem with a Broadway producer and some burlesque actresses when his taxi cab overturned in the rain while trying to avoid a smash. "When we turned over," Jack told Charmian, "our taxi flew to pieces as if it had been exploded by a bomb. As usual, I was under the whole pile. Four other persons were mixed with me, mostly on top of me—And broken glass! I lay and spat it out of my mouth for a very long time." By great luck, nobody identified him and he got away to count his wounds. "Both my arms are black and blue, skin off knuckles of my right hand, forehead cut with glass, nose sore, left cheek bruised, right cheek so bruised that it looks as if somebody had really kicked me there."[22] Still, he was not badly hurt, and he felt that his ill health and ill fortune might be over at last.

They continued. An anonymous telegram was sent to Charmian, saying that Jack was spending all his time with a woman at the Van Cortland Hotel. Jack denied the allegation, saying that he only used the place for late-night drinks with his Broadway friends, and that he was being maligned by stupid fools. Charmian was of superior stock to the sort of women he met in New York. "Oh, I know your thoroughbredness," he assured her,

> that is at the one time irk and the highest joy to me. No man may ride a thoroughbred mare without tenseness and irritation along with the corresponding joy that is aroused by the very tenseness and irritation. You've never seen me infatuated with cows. Ergo—my arms are around you, as they shall always have to be around you for love of you and appreciation of you—you damned thoroughbred![23]

Although Jack had written to her like a Dick Forrest, loving her both as a woman and as a mare, Charmian was frightened enough never to let him go off on his own again. She knew that he was losing control of his body away from the careful restraints of his country life. When the Mexican Revolution flared up and an American expedition was sent to Vera Cruz, Jack was asked to report the war for *Collier's* magazine; but Charmian would not allow him to go alone. He was the only war correspondent to take his wife along with him. He was not allowed to leave her behind, as he had done ten years before in Korea.

MEXICAN CONFUSION

> It is always so easy to tell another man how to play his hand at cards. Take that hand and play it yourself. Get up; wake up; kick in; do something. A man who does not do anything is usually a critic. Deliver the goods; come across; arise or be forever damned.
>
> JACK LONDON

When Jack arrived at Galveston, Texas, with Charmian and Nakata to look after him, the American commander had not cleared their application to travel with the army transport ships bound for Vera Cruz. The reason for the refusal was a pamphlet, *The Good Soldier,* which had been circulated over Jack's signature. It was a call to young men not to enlist in the army, reading in part:

> The lowest aim in your life is to become a soldier. The good soldier never tries to distinguish right from wrong. He never thinks; never reasons; he only obeys. . . . No man can fall lower than a soldier— it is a depth beneath which we cannot go. Keep the boys out of the army. It is hell. Down with the army and the navy. We don't need killing institutions. We need life-giving institutions.[1]

In view of the pamphlet, the American commander's actions were understandable. It was certainly true that Jack had written an open letter in February 1911, to the brave comrades of the Mexican Revolution, in which he had attacked the grafters and large landowners who had forced a revolution by making honest men into outlaws and chicken thieves. Jack had even signed the open letter as "a chicken thief and revolutionist." He did not deny his letter, but he did deny the authorship of *The Good Soldier*. To sympathize with revolution abroad was not the same as to encourage desertion at home, and given his articles for the Hearst press on the necessity for the American navy, *The Good Soldier* did appear to be a forgery. As in Japan, Richard Harding Davis came to the rescue and secured Jack's clearance to embark for Mexico; but Jack paid the price of having to deny the authorship of *The Good Soldier* for the rest of his life, until his denials were even used as recruiting propaganda by the United States navy.

His seven Mexican articles for *Collier's* showed a confusion of mind and purpose. The American intervention at Vera Cruz was muddled, anyway, a demonstration of gunboat diplomacy to protect American oil interests in the name of righteousness and the safeguarding of American lives. In fact, the occupation of the port endangered the lives of the American citizens whom it was meant to protect. The competing factions of the revolution, the Federal troops under Huerta, the Constitutionalists under Carranza and Obrégon in the east, the mounted *guerrilleros* of the north under Pancho Villa, and the rebel peons of the south under Zapata, all protested sooner or later against the American intervention. Mobs attacked all *gringos* on the streets. These civilian victims were the product of America's armed diplomacy, not of the Mexican war, but Jack presented them in his articles as if they were survivors of Lucknow or Mafeking, overjoyed at their relief by the bluejackets and battleships at Vera Cruz.

His attitude to the warring Mexican political factions was even more indefensible. His racism grew rampant. He explained that the confusion of the Mexican Revolution was due to the childish and predatory games of the "breeds," the one-fifth of the *mestizo* population which was neither Spanish nor Indian. The troublemakers like Carranza, Villa, and Zapata were what "the mixed breed always is—neither fish, flesh, nor fowl. They are neither white men nor Indians. Like the Eurasians, they possess all the vices of their various commingled bloods and none of the virtues." They were child-minded and ignoble-purposed, incapable of administering an anarchic people. They did not even have a decent imperial tradition to imitate. "Spain, despite her world empire, which she picked up at a lucky stroke, much as a Hottentot might pick up a Koh-i-noor, never possessed any genius for government. The descendants of the Spaniards in Mexico, interbred with the native Indians, have likewise displayed no genius for government. Facts are facts."[2] Given these facts—if facts they were—the United States should intervene like a good big brother. Vera Cruz under American military occupation—the reign of "the white-skinned fighting men who know how to rule as well as to fight"—had more order and decency than it had ever known.

When Jack took a trip to the oilfields at Tampico, he also found much to praise in the adventurous spirit of the American oilmen. The atmosphere of the city reminded him of the frontier and the Klondike. He even ran into some of his old sourdough friends from the north. One of them told him: "Jack, this ain't no Klondike. It's got Klondike faded to a fare you well and any other gold camp the world has ever seen." An oil well gushed out more wealth than the Eldorado and the Bonanza combined, without any need for labor, and there were hundreds of wells, all developed by Anglo-Saxon entrepreneurs. Now they were faced with a civil war provoked by the "breeds." "Child-minded men, incapable of government, playing with the weapons of giants! A $2,000,000,000 oil body, a world asset, if you please, at the pleasure of stupid anarchs!"

Such sentiments in the articles for *Collier's* were sad stuff for Jack's Socialist followers, who remembered his story of "The Mexican" beating the cheating *gringo* because he needed the prize money to buy arms for the revolution. Jack no longer spoke as the compassionate revolutionary but as the racist and jingoist supporter of the American oil interests—a man of property, a man used to servants, who was echoing the views of other men used to property and servants. His ranch had taught him how hard it was to develop property, and he was forgetting the men who did the work and how little was their share.

He was also cossetting himself. He hardly moved from the bars of Vera Cruz and Tampico, except for two days riding with the young rebel soldiers, wearing his Baden-Powell hat and a white Palm Beach suit. In fact, his place as a romantic revolutionary had been taken by the young John Reed, who was riding with Villa's guerrillas across Chihuahua, in daily danger of being shot by his own side as a false *gringo* like Ambrose Bierce, or by the government irregulars as a spy. Jack's authoritarian generalizations seemed heavy and flat beside Reed's loving and tragic vignettes of life in the saddle and law by the pistol.[3] So the poor boy from Oakland who had made good ceded his place to the rich boy from Harvard who had turned Marxist after the Paterson strike, and the staleness of the older man yielded place to the passion of the young one.

Yet Jack would not recognize his own decline or even his loss of faith. He could still convince himself of his consistency, whatever he wrote for the magazines or the market. The English novelist and talebearer Ford Madox Ford, who accompanied him to Tampico, found him Celtic, smaller than his legend and darker and full of movement, with eyes that glowed like topazes when something exciting was happening such as a revolver fight in a bar. To Ford, Jack was a Peter Pan who could not grow up, a man who lived his own stories with such intensity that he ended by believing them.[4]

Jack's body betrayed him again. He caught amoebic dysentry, which was then complicated by pleurisy. He nearly died in the hospital at Vera Cruz, and he began a slow convalescence on a cattle boat back to Galveston. The pain in his bowels was so bad that he exhausted the opiates in his large traveling medicine chest, and Charmian had to write to Dr. Porter for 100 opium pills and capsules in doses of 1 grain and 1/2 grain as well as more capsules of bismuth subgallate for the dysentery.[5] A flare-up of pyorrhea added to his agony, and he was given intravenous injections of a new wonder drug called emetine. Already overweight and puffy in Vera Cruz, he now began to suffer from what he called rheumatism of the legs—probably the result of arsenic poisoning and gout.

He started to brood about the treachery of the comrades who called him traitor for his Mexican articles, and the outbreak of World War I further complicated his attitude toward socialism. He found his loyalties split, and even his bedrock faith in evolution tottering. For Anglo-Saxon Britain was fighting Nordic Germany. Still, his obsessive need to trace his genealogy back to its English roots, and his admiration for the success of the British Empire, brought him down on the side of the Allies. He became an interventionist, although he was unwilling to go to France as a war correspondent because his health and troubles with military authorities might keep him from the front line. Even as a young man during the Boer War he had supported the British, because evolution had already determined their inevitable victory against the backward Boers. Fourteen years before the carnage of the trenches of 1914, he had prophesied that the bayonet and the cavalry charge were obsolete, and that economics would decide the winner of a European war. "No more open fields; no more decisive victories; but a succession of sieges. . . . At the front will be the chess-game; at home the workers feeding the players. All will depend upon the stamina of the civil population."6 It was a bleak and correct forecast of the outcome of the first of the world wars.

The failure of another prophecy in *The Iron Heel* increased his disillusion with the international Socialist movement. In that book, a general strike of the workers stopped a war between Germany and America. Now with the German Socialists supporting the Kaiser's aggression, Jack saw the most powerful Socialist Party in the world acquiesce in what he termed "a war between civilization and barbarism, between democracy and oligarchy."7 For a man who also believed that war was "a silly, non-intellectual function," the spectacle of most of the European nations at each other's throats in a prolonged and senseless massacre spelled the ruin of his vision of a future world united under one Socialist government. He did support the crusade of the Allies, he did want America to intervene and prove that it exalted honor above the fat life of neutrality; but all the same, he hated the sight of the efficient people destroying each other without purpose. It was like a civil war on the poop of the *Elsinore,* while the mangy crew below waited for the leavings. "I can only tell you," he wrote to one of his readers, "that in all my life no experience has affected me so profoundly, so vitally, as this present great war. It is with me waking and sleeping; in fact in my sleep it is a positive nightmare."[8]

He was enduring terrible dreams and insomnia. He shared Charmian's frequent sleeplessness. Her diary recorded his tolerance of her white nights and of her frequent nervous illnesses and headaches.[9] She also wrote to Anna Strunsky Walling that she did not dare mention the subject of the war. "It weighs down, down, down, all the time. We get up with it, and lie down with it, and it is our day dreams and our chamber-thoughts. And it is so ridiculous."[10]

It might seem ridiculous to Charmian because of its distance from California. Yet as it shattered Jack's faith in international socialism, so it split the American Socialist movement. The revolutionary syndicalists of the Industrial Workers of the World under Big Bill Haywood attracted Jack most; but they generally considered the war an imperialist struggle in which the workers should not participate. The other American Socialists were divided, with Eugene Debs holding out for pacifism and the future revolution, while many others supported the Allied cause.

The wide gaps in attitude between the "Wobblies" and the Socialist Party and the Socialist Labor Party in America had already contributed to Jack's disgust with the politicians and fanatics of the movement. He had little respect for the various leaders, who seemed more interested in talk than action, except for Haywood, who had been tried for his life on a bombing charge. The only reason he had remained in the Socialist Party, Jack said, was that he had not been forced to leave it like Haywood, because he had not taken an active part in its councils for many years. He was a heretic, but he was staying out of the fight.

As the outbreak of the Great War made his membership in a splintering political movement untenable, so did his style of life continue to put his socialism in disrepute. He was not the only wealthy supporter of American socialism. There were others like Gaylord Wilshire and Anna's husband, William English Walling. Jack could and did claim that his wealth was self-made, not inherited from the toil of others, and he could also claim that his income involved the exploitation of nobody and jobs for some. Yet his image was most suspect because of his Oriental servants and his style of travel. One urbane Englishman saw him pass in California, driving his four-in-hand and accompanied by his wife, his wife's maid, and Nakata. He looked for all the world like an English aristocrat, or a Vanderbilt abroad with equipage and retinue. To the Englishman, a home-made, self-propelled wheelbarrow might have suited Jack's propaganda better.[11] Even Mark Twain had a lunge at his fellow writer. "It would serve this man London right to have the working class get control of things. He would have to call out the militia to collect his royalties."[12]

Yet such remarks misunderstood Jack's position. He had always praised the self-made man and the aristocracy of the working class. If he behaved like an aristocrat on the money he had made, that was his choice and his right. He had always preached equal opportunity for all, not fair shares for all. Only when socialism did rule the world would he forgo the benefits of capitalism, just as when prohibition ruled America, he would give up the pleasures of drink. His revolutionary hope was in the future, his practice in the present. Moreover, the example he was setting on the land was a demonstration of how the cooperative commonwealth should deal with the soil.

Yet he knew he was isolated both because of his affluence and his socialism. "I am at sword's points with everybody in California," he admitted in 1914, "and am not afraid to let everybody in California know it."[13] He had left the working class for ever to become a large landowner, but he still preached the hope of proletarian revolution against the landowners. As a result, both sides suspected him and looked for the hypocrite in a man who was still loyal to his origins as well as to his myth of himself.

Under attack, Jack's first instinct was to rewrite his autobiography as a justification of his present attitudes. Like a Bismarck or a Lenin, he must change the myth of his past to fit the facts of the present. His notes at the time for a "Socialist Autobiography" are revealing. He wanted to subtitle this book: "Why I, an Utter Socialist, Ceased Being an Active Socialist." He wanted to present himself as an early fighter for the movement, who even then had been misjudged as a "red-shirted anarchist" after his arrest on a soapbox. According to his reconstruction, when his revolutionary views later became notorious, his book sales had slumped. "The middle class, with capitalist psychology, struck at me and tried to starve me and my children." Then the army officers had attacked him for the forgery of *The Good Soldier*, and the comrades had attacked him for denying the forgery. When the time came to choose the leaders of the movement, he was crowded out, although he had been the John the Baptist of it all. He had had to retire; his socialism seemed antiquated; he thought the class consciousness of Marxism was developing into hatred and sabotage. The future in America did not even presage another French Revolution, but "the reign of cat and dog fighting." He had done other men the honor of thinking they had brains as good as his, when they were boobs.

> Had I been correct, then would the Revolution have happened in my time, in one year of my time, or in centuries before my time. The reason the Revolution had not happened before my time, in the first year of my time, or in the totality of my time on earth was because these poor boobs had not had my quality of brain. They are their own enemy.

Once it had been his interest and his duty to talk to the jobless, the men in the breadline, the drabs on the street. Yet their stories were all monotonous, the stories of the beaten and the stupid and the abject and the hopeless. They were the wastage of society. Now his concern was with what he fancied to be "the ways of men and women loving on this earth."[14]

This bitter justification of his withdrawal from the Socialist movement greatly exaggerated the truth. The middle class had never tried to starve him. His books had always sold in their hundreds of thousands, and only recently—after his withdrawal from working for his cause—had his sales begun falling. He had never been pushed out of the leadership of the American Socialist parties; he had deliberately stayed away from their councils. With men like Debs and Hillquit and De Leon in the movement, he was far from being the most intelligent Socialist in a party of boobs. He had chosen to live the life of a rich man and had cut off his contacts with the poor, who could not all be so abject and monotonous if he and thousands like him had risen from their ranks. It was as well that Jack did not live to write his "Socialist Autobiography," because his mythologizing of his past would have approached perjury as well as apostasy.

The tragedy was that after 1911 Jack had lost his balance. He could not admit that he had changed his mind with his style of life. Like the child in *John Barleycorn* and the young writer in *Martin Eden,* he had to see himself as thwarted and deprived by others. Nothing was his own fault. He had forgotten the easy admission of his appetites during the building of the *Snark,* when he told the Socialists that his only reason for sailing away round the world was "I LIKE." His own cause and his own class seemed to be in a conspiracy against him. He had been loyal and consistent, so they must have betrayed him. The lifeline that had kept him going through his "long sickness" had been cut. He did not believe any more in the People.

Nevertheless, he still planned to prove his loyalty. He wanted to write a novel about himself and Anna Strunsky, who had always believed that he was a true Socialist. He would be as he was "so far as Anglo-Saxon stuff is concerned," but otherwise a lover of the sea. Anna would be married to another Jew, a splendid fellow who owned a few department stores, and she would represent the best in bourgeois culture. The interest of the story would be that two people who were so different could love each other so much. Each of them would represent the genius of their race, fatally attracted, always divided. At one point, he would ask her how it was possible for the two of them to feel so deeply for each other, when she was in Egypt, in Jerusalem, in Russia, in the New York ghetto, while he was a Viking in screaming savagery.

He also planned a new series of Socialist lectures which took a gloomy view of the prospect of reform and change. He made notes for a lecture to be called "The Persistence of the Established." Institutions might be stupid, but they lasted because they existed. They could only be moved by pressure or shocks. Sometimes it took an earthquake to overthrow the established. Another planned lecture was called "Disappearing Class," and it developed the theme forecast in *The Iron Heel:* the doom of the middle class, ground to pieces in the struggle between capital and labor. Other lectures would deal with the Strength of the Strong, the selfishness that was the driving force of socialism, the softness of the "well-balanced Radical" through the ages, and the Fine Art of Murder. The lectures would end with his ultimate heresy, that the bourgeoisie was made up of "crystallized little nothings," while only Socialists could be individualists as Nietzsche was an individualist.

Finally, Jack wanted to write a fantasy called *My Great Labor Novel.* In it, he would present the prime types of reformers, the Emotional, the Intellectual, and the Fanatic. Yet the real battle would be fought with Jack representing the Socialist superhero against a champion of capitalism. His enemy would typify the highest product of the competitive system, an individualistic aristocrat who pointed back with pride to "the steel-shod steel-clad knights of medieval Europe." Against him, Jack would stand as an experienced man, "who has passed through all the phases, and attained perspective and knowledge born of pain, and who has the deep scientific basis and grasp of the working of evolution and the growth of the social organism."[15]

His projects all remained projects, for he was worried about his declining book sales, and socialism did not sell well. He wrote wistfully to George Brett that writers like Rex Beach were riding the high tide of popularity. They had best-sellers, while he had not had a best-seller for a long time. He wondered whether their work was better than his, or whether Macmillan's were treating him as an institution. Or was it because the public had soured on him at last?[16]

In fact, it was because he had lost interest in his writing in order to devote himself to the land. He told Brett as much, begging him for advances to meet his commitments on the ranch. He admitted that it was hard to get his friends to understand what the ranch meant to him. There was no profit in it, although he hoped it would break even within seven years.

The ranch is to me what actresses, racehorses, or collecting postage stamps, are to some other men. From a utilitarian standpoint I hope to do two things with the ranch: (1) to leave the land better for my having been; (2) and to enable thirty or forty families to live happily on ground that was so impoverished that an average of three farmers went bankrupt on each of the five ranches I have run together, making a total of fifteen failures to make a living out of that particular soil.[17]

It was an excessive way of redeeming his own family's failure on the land; but he did not admit to that lingering motive. He merely told Brett that his ranch was second in his life only to his love of his wife, and that his hopes were now fixed on building a brass-tack, efficient piggery.

The piggery was, indeed, more advanced and successful than the play he was writing in praise of the earth, which he hoped would be performed by the Bohemian Club at its annual High Jinks. The piggery was a miniature of Dick Forrest's ranch, with a central feed tower acting as the hub of a surrounding circle of pigsties. Visitors were made to step into antiseptic footbaths to keep germs from Jack's prize hogs on their sterile concrete floors. His vision was a true forecast of future farming techniques, through which cows themselves would be kept in towers and centrally fed, only leaving their elevated stalls for a monthly holiday on the grass.

The play for the High Jinks would have been hard to perform. In it, Red Cloud was to appear as the Indian Adam, the Acorn Planter, while his tribe was meant to sing falsely primitive chants in all seriousness. *The Acorn Planter* had its moments of nobility as a folk operetta, when it hinted at some of the myths of the soil; but Jack was no poet, and often the highflown language descended beneath the jingles of *Hiawatha*:

> Yet the Nishinam unvanquished,
> Did not perish by the famine.
> Oh, the acorns Red Cloud gave them!
> Oh, the acorns Red Cloud taught them
> How to store in willow baskets
> 'Gainst the time and need of famine![18]

The Bohemian Club refused to put on the play of its most famous writer-member: the smart set of San Francisco wanted to be entertained, not elevated.

By the beginning of 1915, Jack was still in financial trouble. If the war in Mexico had confused him, the war in Europe had ruined him. The magazines were hard-hit and wanted material of a different sort, while the English market was dead. "The war has hit the whole writing game," he explained, "and hit it hard."[19] For eighteen months, ever since Wolf House had burned down, his own hard times had been proceeding from disaster to disaster. Instead of making a fortune out of selling film rights on his books, he was being sued right and left by film companies, and he was even beginning to transfer all his assets to Charmian, so that they could not be seized by courts or creditors. The law would ruin him, if the war did not. The only way out was through hackwork.

He decided to set off to Hawaii with Charmian, and to write two new dog stories. They had never failed for him. The market would lap them up. Dog psychologists, he asserted to George Brett, would like them as much as dog lovers.[20] And he himself would be able to escape again to the leisured world of Honolulu with its lounging days and nightly poker parties, the life of the rich man who had arrived at last.

AN APPETITE FOR AWARENESS

Personality is too vague for any of our vague personalities to grasp. There are seeming men with the personalities of women. There are plural personalities. There are two-legged human creatures that are neither fish, flesh, nor fowl. We, as personalities, float like fog-wisps through glooms and darknesses and light-flashings. It is all fog and mist, and we are all foggy and misty in the thick of the mystery.

JACK LONDON

Jack spent twelve of the next eighteen months on Hawaii. He did not pretend to be adventuring, he was merely enjoying himself. The attraction was plain. It was the same attraction which kept the rich together in times of depression, because there was no criticism of them in their own company. In three articles written in praise of Hawaii, Jack was explicit that it was a paradise for the well-to-do. He advised all American workers, skilled or unskilled, to stay away from the island; there was too much competition from the immigrant Japanese and Chinese. Hawaii was already full up, except for rich visitors.

As for Socialists on the island, they could be counted on the fingers of two hands. In his missionary days during the voyage of the *Snark,* Jack had actually delivered his lecture on "Revolution" to a small audience in Honolulu, which included all three Socialists in the city. Now he preferred the company of the leisured landlords of the huge sugar plantations, whom he praised for their charity and benevolence toward the poor, and for their hospitality toward himself and Charmian. Hawaii became the land of his love, because the sugar corporations that ran the plantations were scientific in their fight for maximum production and pest control, while the field laborers were feudal in their obedience to their white masters. "See Naples and die," he quoted, but *"see Hawaii and live."*[1]

Even the national sport of surfing had been rescued by a white entrepreneur, Alexander Ford. The native Hawaiians had just about given it up when Ford began to make a tourist attraction out of Waikiki Beach. There, in the shade of the tents of the Outrigger Club, Jack could indulge his physical lethargy and his last sport, lying on the surfboard and letting the breakers do his work for him. "I wish you could hear him tell of how we go out into the deep water beyond the biggest breakers," Charmian wrote to Anna Strunsky Walling,

> and then come in with them! He says it was an old, dear dream of his youth to swim far out, laughing and talking, for hours and hours, with a woman he loved. And at last—well, anyway, we have glorious times, facing the immense combers, laying our faces in the rushing, roaring combs of them, and coming out on the racing backs of them, laughing and exulting with our puny prowess, and singing poems of sheer joy of mad motion in the tingling sunlight. I wish you might know this particular uplift—for uplift it is, to body and spirit.[2]

The sea soothed Jack's illnesses and the easy hospitality appeased his overwhelming need for love and approval. He noticed that the local word of greeting, *"Aloha,"* meant love, I love you, my love to you. The warmth of the place was so natural, so immediate, that it blunted the hard edge of his mistrust and suspicions. The very melting pot of the races out there offered a possible solution to his dark prophecies of racial degeneration and war. Hawaii seemed to him to be a great experimental laboratory in large-scale agriculture, ethnology, and sociology. With efficiency and open arms, the many kinds of people on the island had begun to tackle insoluble problems; they were seeking for new answers with their love.

It was too sweet a picture of the many tensions on Hawaii; but

Heavy and lame by 1915, Jack still loved to sail on his small yacht, the
Roamer. The wheel was taken from the *Snark*.

Jack wished to find a last paradise there, and he did. Part of its charm was that it was a long way from his difficulties in America. The various lawsuits could be forgotten until his return. As long as he could keep the money coming in from his contract with *Cosmopolitan* and the other Hearst magazines, as long as he could write some books that sold reasonably well, then gradually his income would pay off his debts. When he was on the ranch, he was only encouraged to more extravagance, and he was unable to work as easily as in Hawaii, where he had nothing to distract him except distraction itself.

The leisured life in Honolulu did not encourage him to write well, and his two dog novels were no more than competent products for the market. *Jerry of the Islands* was the worse, with its hero a thoroughbred Irish terrier specially trained for nigger-chasing. There were flashes of Jack's old skill in the passages on the Law of the Immediate and the puppy's dreams of the wolfpack; but Jerry was not a lovable pup who could win the hearts of the world. He was too much a hater. Even his last master, obviously modeled on Jack himself, exulted: "He knows the color line. He's a white man's dog that has been trained to it."[3]

Michael, Brother of Jerry was a better book. It argued that far worse than the Social Pit for men were the cages for trained dogs and circus animals. All the foul tricks of the trade were exposed; one chapter dealt with the breaking of a Bengal tiger and the failure to tame a wild bear, scenes that scream as loudly as William Blake against man's cruelty to beasts. The bear will not give way. Each time a ring is put in its nose or ear, it tears out the ring, wrenching off parts of the nose and ear, until it is condemned to be a mere cage animal. The trainer cannot understand it. "We're beaten," he complains. "There ain't nothing left to make fast to."[4] Jack's experience of the torments of the flesh and his bitter irony nauseate and shock the reader—so effective was his indignation that hundreds of London clubs sprang up on the publication of the book, dedicated to ending the trade in performing animals.

The last long novel of his life, *Hearts of Three,* was a sorry business, a piece of romantic trash that bore no mark of Jack's style at all. It was the first time he had been asked to "novelize" a screenplay. In fact, *Hearts of Three* was a serial adventure story of fifteen episodes, written by the screenwriter of *The Perils of Pauline* and *The Exploits of Elaine.* To ask an author of Jack's quality to flesh it out was an insult and an indignity. He wrote it because the Hearst Sunday supplements bribed him with $25,000 over and above his regular contract with *Cosmopolitan.* A foreword to the book tried to explain why Jack found it an exciting one to write, but however professional he was, Jack could not even complete a competent job. He thought the book would have a large sale; it was so badly done that in fact it failed.

Yet this hackwork did keep his head above water. His finances slowly improved during 1915 and 1916. In these two years the sales of his books increased, and motion picture rights brought in more than $20,000. He delayed the rebuilding of Wolf House and concentrated on relieving his load of debts. The mortgages were lifted on the six houses he owned on behalf of his dependents and himself —two in Berkeley, two in Oakland, the Piedmont house, and the ranchhouse where he lived. He paid off the mortgages on all the land except for the Freund ranch. He kept up the life insurance, which he had taken out before his illness in 1911. And he continued to maintain Charmian in the style to which she had never been accustomed. "She sailed with me from California six months ago," he wrote from Hawaii to her aunt, "accompanied by three servants. In her present Honolulu house are four servants. The chauffeur of her car makes a fifth."[5]

There were also the outgoings on the ranch, which Eliza tried to keep to a minimum. She had to pay the wages for the thirty or forty families who were looking after Jack's 1,400 acres. Then she had to build up the herds of cattle and horses, sheep and goats and pigs—especially after cholera wiped out the first batch of pedigree hogs and the prize shorthorn bull broke its neck in the barnyard. Eliza devoted herself to her job as ranch manager, gave all the orders on the ranch, and tried to run it as scientifically as possible. She received pages of instruction from Jack about learning new methods of dairy farming and agronomy, but as she wrote back,

"there is a world of work to do—and we are just beginning to get
all we can done—but it is only a drop in the bucket."[6]

Jack did not concentrate on the Beauty Ranch. What with the
voyage on the *Dirigo* and the two extended trips to Honolulu, he
had spent as much time away from Glen Ellen as at home. The
ownership of the land was obviously a satisfaction to him, yet a long
spell of living on the ranch became monotonous and harassing. His
broad visions of the future were clogged in petty details, just as the
fetlocks of his noble Shire stallion, Neuadd Hillside, were mired
in the local clay. He liked to give Eliza orders to buy a bull or build
a silo or plan a modern dairy. Then he could escape on his travels
and return to the finished work, his dreams made solid without any
effort on his part. In the opinion of his friend, Finn Frolich the
sculptor, Eliza ran Jack with love.

He needed that love to master the continual agony of his
bowels, which persisted in spite of his growing addiction to pain-
killing drugs. The medicine chest still on display at the Jack London
Museum near Glen Ellen contains strychnine and strontium sulphate; aconite and belladonna; heroin, morphine, and opium,
among other analgesics. By the latter part of 1915, Jack was order-
ing six times the normal prescription of opium, hyoscyamine, and
camphor capsules from the Bowman Drug Company of Oakland.[7]
He was also taking regular injections of atropine and belladonna
mixed with opium and morphine to stimulate his heart and bladder
muscles and to put him to sleep. In other words, he was taking the
fatal "uppers and downers" of modern pill-pushers in an age that
regulated the sale of drugs extremely inefficiently. He had no trouble in acquiring all the medicines that he thought he needed, simply
by having half a dozen people buy them for him from different
drugstores, with or without prescriptions.[8]

He had long since become his own doctor, particularly on his
lengthy travels, and there was no check on the amounts of drugs
that he used. He took enough to stop the pain and relieve his
symptoms, rather as he used to take whiskey. His strong constitution gave him a high tolerance to alcohol, and now it gave him a
high tolerance to morphine and opium. These made his swings of

mood more controllable, although he was still liable to outbreaks of sudden disgust. Two contradictory letters at the end of 1915 indicate this. In September, he wrote to one fan that his thirty-nine years had taught him that the game of life was worth the candle. He recognized that he had been luckier than many hundreds of millions of his own generation, but he had also suffered much. As a proof of his success and happiness, he was getting stout. "That, in itself, is the advertisement of spiritual victory."9 Yet three months later, he was writing to Blanche Partington to apologize for his despair and disgust on the occasion of her last visit to him. He claimed that his bad moods had been part of his nature since his boyhood.10 If that was true, his problem now was that he could not manage them when physical pain overpowered his reason.

When at the end of 1913 a young man called Richardson had attacked him for being an atheist, Jack had refused to be provoked, even though the youth returned a letter of his as unworthy of its author. He praised Richardson for being a reasoning aristocrat and only blamed him for putting too much faith in the powers of reason itself. "Really, dear lad," he wrote in his soft answer to wrath, "you are surer of yourself and of your reasoned conclusions than I am of myself and my reasoned conclusions."11

Yet as his mind deteriorated with his body, he lost his balance under attack. He could control his pain only when he felt he was loved. If an old friend or guest offended him, he lashed out in something close to paranoia. In the past, he had entertained and fenced with a young Greek called Spiro Ophens, who was then a worshipper and acolyte. But in 1916, Spiro dared to question Jack's racial views in *The Mutiny of the Elsinore*. So Jack reverted to the depths of his prejudices and, sticking to his guns, claimed that God abhorred a mongrel, and that there was no place in nature for mixed breeds. He became gratuitously personal, because Spiro had once boasted of the pure blood of ancient Greece in his veins—just as Jack boasted of his Anglo-Saxon blood. The Greeks died out 2,000 years ago, Jack declared, when they became mongrelized. Nor would he apologize for calling Spiro a mongrel: he had been asked to hit straight from the shoulder, and he was doing so.

When Spiro tried to defend himself in his reply to this outburst, Jack's rage made him childish. He accused Spiro of staying
on the ranch for twelve weeks, pretending to fawn on his host
before turning on him. "You claim you are a glorious Greek. How
have you treated this white man me? I never sought you out. I have
given you much. You sought me out. What have you given me?
You have called me a quack and a hypocrite. You have thrown filth
upon me. At the end of it all, you have behaved toward me as any
alleged modern Greek peddler has behaved toward the superior
races." Until Spiro got down on his hams and ate out of Jack's hand,
he should depart from Jack's existence. He was the only one of
Jack's guests who had broken the law of food and blanket by attacking his host, so he must pay for it.[12]

The question of race had nagged Jack all his life because of the
scandal of his birth, Flora's heavy emphasis on good lineage, and
his own experiences in horsebreeding; but usually his sense of
justice and compassion for the outcasts of society mitigated these
dark and infantile fears. Jack always said that he had lost his boyhood, but he had never lost his primitive terror of *Them*—the
unknown people beating carpets in the yard, the Chinese gamblers
of his drunken deliria, the Greek poachers of the Bay and the Italian
scabs of the slums who had robbed him of his birthright as a pioneer
American, the true heir of the land of California.

Books had saved him from his dread of the Social Pit before,
and books saved him now. He began to read Freud and Jung, and
to make a study of his own psychology at last. The most important
text in his reading was Jung's *Psychology of the Unconscious.* In his
marked copy, he underlined two phrases in the introduction:
"Freud sees a definite incest wish toward the mother which only
lacks the quality of consciousness," and "the often quite unbearable
conflict of his weakness with his feelings of idealism."[13] Jack began
to recognize some of the unadmitted neuroses of his life, his search
for his mother's love in the many women he had called "Mother-
Girl" or "Mother-mine," his denial of his physical breakdown in
the myths of himself as a superhero in search of human brotherhood. "Mate Woman," he said to Charmian in the last months of

his life, "I tell you I am standing on the edge of a world so new, so wonderful, that I am almost afraid to look over into it."[14]

What the reading of Jung had done was to begin to separate in his mind the validity of the ancient myths that illuminated his best work from the racial prejudices that darkened his worst. One of his last projects was a story of the discovery of America by the Vikings, no longer motivated by their blood lust and urge for mastery, but by the myths from their own unconscious. He had wanted to write a sexual biography of himself, "delicately realistic, beginning low down and ending high up." Yet by early January 1916, his idea for that biography had changed. A note on his night pad read: "My Biography—The dark Abysm of Sex—rising to the glory of the Sun God. All darks and deeps and fluxes of the abysmal, opening itself in God, and basing itself on hell. Write Jung and Freud, in sex terms of fiction." He planned a novel, which he left unfinished, about a half-caste called Cherry. His worries about miscegenation were turned into fears about the insubstantiality of human personality. His notes on the love triangle of the book told of "three ghosts and wraiths of half women and part women, of half men, and of part men, who in conformity occupied their entire space in the sun, but who . . . were ghosts and wraiths, shadows and glooms of shadows —nothing distinct, nothing definite."[15]

So his own character became elusive to him as he began to recognize the terrors and contradictory desires behind his effort to project a consistent image of power and candor. He reported one recurrent nightmare to Charmian; it was a confession that he had long wanted to submit his own fierce ego to a darker power or to a mystery beyond his materialism. He saw in this dream an imperial figure, inexorable as destiny and yet strangely human, descending a cascade of staircases, while he looked up at it and waited to be vanquished. The Nemesis never reached him, but he knew that he must yield to it.[16]

Most interesting, in psychological terms, was his high praise of Frank Norris's posthumous novel *Vandover and the Brute*, which Jack hailed as twenty years ahead of its time.[17] Its plot dealt with a man who actually believed that he was a wolf because of a mental illness resulting from debauchery in San Francisco. At a certain moment, Vandover drops onto his palms and toes, then pads naked about his room, swinging his head and growling, "Wolf—wolf!" His hallucinations and his degradation make him certain that he has become the brute, and he sinks into both bestiality and the abyss of poverty. The story reads like an early case history of a hysterical reaction to a repressed Oedipal conflict. It also mirrored so clearly Jack's own obsession with his image as Wolf and his own nightmares of the social abyss, that his praise of it does seem to imply recognition of certain traits in himself.

With his new self-awareness, in the intervals of lucidity between his attacks of pain and drugging himself against those attacks, Jack planned to rewrite *John Barleycorn*. Instead of calling his projected autobiography *Jack Liverpool*, he preferred the title of *A Sailor on Horseback*. The book would be the confessions of a farmer, beginning in his boyhood and working up to the present. It would explain why he elected not to be an artist like the bohemians at Carmel but "to thrill, as much as possible, to universal life instead." Art compelled a narrowness of outlook, when he had always wanted the full extent of his desires. While other men were optimistic cowards and recoiled "from their racial history, from the veneered animal," he gloried in the violent myths and appetites that led him to fight his necessary doom. "Point out pride of being a mortal mote, and struggling, as against being a degenerate immortalist." Not for Jack the windy seriousness of the little ape men, but the sensuous battle toward human progress.[18] He even intended a novel to be called *The Pearl Man* or *The Sun God,* in which a magnificent specimen from the South Seas hated human society and was convinced of the futility of all art and human illusion, holding that there was something bigger behind it all, and that he must strive for it.

In this way, Jack matched his will to live and his feverish mind against his chronic pain. He felt himself purged through suffering, become a prophet of mankind through his many experiences. He planned a series of bold, truthful essays to expose the self-delusion of modern men. He would make them aware as he had been made

aware. He would tell them that, if some women were p
so were most men. Hypocrisy and secret sinning ruled s/
gods of the flag and the constitution and the law were tin gou.
struggle between capital and labor was absurd in an economy that
was managed inefficiently. Man was both a brute and an angel, who
chose to exist in a limited and cowardly way, chasing the dollar. If
he would only live by his finer passions and his rationality, he could
master the earth and harness the stars. Otherwise he would skulk
in the shadows like the helpless cave man, afraid of the ferocious
beasts in the open, terrified of nature's hostility.[19]

It was a bold concept of humanity, as extreme as Jack's own
manias and depressions, his heroic myths of himself and his periodic
revulsions from his own kind. For Upton Sinclair, he wrote a moving introduction to *The Cry for Justice,* an anthology of social protest.
He recognized that the world was filled with unfairness, cruelty,
and suffering, and he preached a gospel of understanding and
service by the strong through which they might help the weak to
become strong. The remedy for social ills did not lie in the faiths
of the jangling sects, but only in the individual's nobility of action
and love of mankind. "We know how gods are made," the introduction ended. "Comes now the time to make a world."[20]

Repelled by the quarrels and splits among the Socialist leaders,
and by the inertia of the working masses, Jack was arguing for old
humanist values. He resigned his membership in the Socialist Labor
Party, because the party had lost its fire and its emphasis on the class
struggle. "Liberty, freedom, and independence, are royal things
that cannot be presented to, nor thrust upon, races or classes."[21] If
races and classes could not rise up and take their liberty, they would
not know what to do with it even though superior individuals gave
it to them on a silver platter. Jack no longer believed in the aristocrats of the working class dragging the proletariat upward into a
Socialist government. He felt that he had tried to do that, and that
he had been disregarded. He had been preaching to the deaf and
the abject. "I gave a quarter of a century of the flower of my life
to the revolutionary movement, only to find that it was as supine
under the heel as it was a thousand centuries before Christ was

born. Will the proletariat save itself? If it won't, it is unsavable."[22]

Salvation now lay for Jack in awareness of himself and in the love of those close to him. He tried to come to terms with his rejection by his father and his mother, which had led to his rejection of his own daughters. Earlier he had tried to find out more about his father, William Henry Chaney, even persuading a friend to send him a long report about the old man's lifetime of "moral delinquencies."[23] This had only added to his dread of being tainted or insane, and thus to his public banging the drum about his Anglo-Saxon virtues. Now his night pad revealed a search for a solution in a projected novel called *Bastard of Youthful Attempt.* In it, the bastard, reborn and purged, would ride on his mother's horse out of the womb of the sea. Although he had been deprived all his life by being sent to prison, now he had escaped and returned. His true love would be for his half sister—the Eliza of the story. He would find out that he was a bastard and that she was not related to him, and all would end well.[24]

Jack did seem to love and depend on Eliza more and more. It was not only that he relied on her to run the ranch, but that she had been loyal and loving to him all her life. He trusted her utterly. Nobody else could ease his suspicion and despair. Although she herself was rather practical and unemotional, she did assure Jack of her love, and she did acknowledge that he had become the patriarch of his desires. He had done away with the specter of his father at last by becoming the father of all the families on the ranch. "Dear Daddy Man," she wrote to him,

> Thank you so much for the books—I love your books best of all I have—
>
> 1*st* Because you belong to me and you wrote them—
> 2*nd* Because you have made good—
> 3*rd* Because of all the good you do with the income derived from them.
>
> And last but not least for the thoughts written in the page for me alone and because I love you.[25]

His advance in awareness and understanding allowed him to forgive his daughter Joan. He had already written a fantasy, "The

Turtles of Tasman," in which a dark-eyed, flashing daughter came back to a ranch with her dying father in order to hear his stories of adventure and to light his cigars until he passed away in peace. Now Jack appealed to Joan to start getting to know him by letters since she could not visit his home. "Oh, my dear," he wrote, "I am very old, and very wise, and I can set you four-square to this four-square world." Soon he was telling her to put her grammar right and to learn how to do the breaststroke and crawl. He recommended diving as "first of all a psychological matter, after that, it becomes physical." He reminded her not to be too high-and-mighty, because she was doing well at high school and wanted to become an actress. He used to sweep the floors in that school, and he had been arrested nearby. "The only way to know life is by not ignoring life." Yet he praised her for wanting to keep dainty and clean. "One cannot maintain a high mind in a filthy body." He was proud of her again, and he wanted to see her.[26] They did meet late in 1915 in Oakland, and he did not test her loyalty by demanding that she come to the ranch and meet Charmian.

She was only fifteen, and she could not see how broken he was in health. Later, she thought that his physical collapse explained how tolerant and uncritical he finally became to her and her sister. During their reconciliation, there was just one row about doubling the girls' allowances, when he reverted to feeling that he was only a meal ticket for them. Yet he did agree to do this, if their mother would make over to him the insurance policies on his life. Joan did not know that he was planning a big novel about his relationship with her, to be written from her standpoint. He was finally acute enough to see that she was too young to comprehend how to cope with "her terrible radiant father's rare visits." She could not understand how Nakata might mean more to him than she did, because Nakata had stood by his master through sickness and danger. She would discover her mistake too late at twenty.[27]

One reason for Jack's turning back to Joan was, indeed, the fact that Nakata had left him. Nakata had given him loyal and loving service for seven years, and he had watched Jack acting as an amateur dentist in the South Seas. Now he wanted to become a professional dentist, and he had saved enough money to put himself through a training course in Oakland before setting up a practice in Honolulu. Jack could merely regret his decision, praise him for it, and replace him with another Japanese valet called Sekinè. It was part of Jack's ultimate maturity that he did not treat Nakata's action as treachery or desertion.

Finally, he was thrown back onto his relationship with Charmian. It had had its stresses, particularly during his two trips to New York and after her miscarriage in 1912. Yet as he knew that he was dying, Jack depended on her more and more. As his body thickened and his pains increased, he particularly admired her care of her body, which had never changed its shape. She might be five years older than he, but she had the spring and playfulness of a girl. Among his notes, there are four extraordinary pages on "Her Body." Apparently, nobody on the beach in Hawaii could say why Charmian's body was the best, even if she was forty-four years old, but the other women did not hate her for her boyish form because her camaraderie was not hoydenish or mannish, even in her maddest romping. She was an artist at molding herself into what she wished to be in any social situation. And she was always "flesh-proud and spirit-proud."[28]

Jack was no longer proud of his own flesh, and he could not keep up that fiction even in his writing. The fruit juice he swilled on his second trip to Hawaii in order to flush out the toxins made him fat, and he rarely stirred out of his kimono and his hammock. He felt too ill to walk more than a block, and he preferred to take the chauffeur and the car for the shortest excursion. His only exercise was swimming and body-surfing. On one occasion, he got cramp far out in the water, and it was Charmian who coolly brought him back to shore. His distractions were nightly bridge and poker parties with the smart set of Honolulu.

Charmian relaxed her watch over him, because she was sure of him and his need for her. Their relationship was reversed. Her diaries, which had always recorded their lovemaking, show that he was in no state to make love to her. In fact, he became jealous of her for the first time. The curious story "The Kanaka Surf" contains so much autobiographical detail, including the attack of cramp and

Charmian was still full of fun and games on her last trip to Hawaii with Jack in 1916.

some of the notes for "Her Body," that its description of the surrogate Charmian's flirtation with a wealthy planter can be taken at face value, even if the gossip that reached George Sterling was Jack's self-defensive boast of an affair with a nameless woman.[29] The plot of "The Kanaka Surf" is confirmed in Charmian's proposed autobiography *Charmette,* which deals with the flirtation as an act of policy. "Perhaps, in her marriage," it reads, "when her husband is unfaithful, and she finds that he has been for years, she lets him think she too is playing the game. Comes in late, looks him squarely in the eyes, and offers no explanation, nor does he dare ask. But she sees him suffer."

The notes on *Charmette* are also interesting because Charmian clearly understood her own role in Jack's world. She asked herself as Charmette whether she had spoiled her man by becoming his mouthpiece and his shadow. Could she have done differently and better? Could she have saved him from himself? Her peace of mind comes when she knows that she acted in the only possible way with her particular man and problem, which was to follow his strong desires. She even knows that she has lived her life in imitation of his ideal of her.

It was a fine ideal, but had little to do with Charmian's nature. She had taught herself from the books he read; she had followed his moralities and immoralities, his pessimism and his enthusiasms. These lessons had now become second nature.[30] She even signed herself "Mrs. Jack London," although she saw herself as the Eternal Kid who, as she put on years, still looked like a kid of a different kind. That was what Jack wanted, she believed, so that was how she behaved.

What Jack still tried to hide from her, or what she still tried to hide from herself, was just how sick he was. He kept a brave face on things, pretending laziness instead of illness, and he slept apart from her, in order to attend to his own wants and drug injections during the nights. She knew how depressed and isolated he felt in his insomnia; but she also knew that she must stand by, day and night, for his instant need.[31] He was both too proud to rely on her too much, yet too vulnerable in his agony not to cry out for comfort like a child in the dark. In Honolulu, she had him in her hands again, as she had him in her hands during his physical collapse on the *Snark*.

His recognition of his dependence on Charmian and Eliza and Joan, his laying to rest his father's rejection of him, his Jungian discovery that his nightmares might be the good myths of his unconscious, all helped Jack to write some of his better short stories in the last months of his life. He no longer identified himself with young Anglo-Saxon heroes braving the frozen wastes and bullying the lesser breeds, but with aged Hawaiian natives telling the tales and myths of their past to skeptical foreigners. Most of the stories in *On the Makaloa Mat* and *The Red One* are of ancient wisdom confounding modern materialism. One Hawaiian matriarch tells another of her two weeks of perfect barbaric love with a prince of the ancient royal line, while another prince of that blood, educated at Oxford and a trained skeptic, talks of diving into the burial lava cave of his ancestors—a psychic return to the womb. From the cave, the prince takes away the bones of two of the heroes of his people's sagas. It is not that he believes in the mystery stuff of old time, "And yet I saw in that cave things which I dare not name to you. . . . This is the twentieth century, and we stink of gasoline."[32]

So Jack began to reveal the power of his dreams and his unconscious rather than parading his socialism or his realism. In another of the late stories, "The Eternity of Forms," he specifically put his slogans from Bacon and Hobbes about materialism into the mouth of a liar and a murderer. And when the old fisherman in "The Water Baby" told him that the local Prometheus named Maui had lifted up the island from the sea by hooking it to heaven and had stopped men from walking on all fours by raising the sky, Jack did recall that a volcanic eruption had originally pushed up Hawaii from the Pacific, and that men were once brutes who walked on four feet. He acknowledged the prehistoric and scientific basis of myths, and he was liberated into the conscious description of his own unconscious. He now used his rooted fears as plots for his stories. He even tried to exorcise his lifelong fear and sense of loss regarding his mother in a comic story, "The Tears of Ah Kim," in which the good and successful son still endures his aged mother's endless beatings with a stick, but never cries out until the day he weeps from the joy of knowing that her blows have become too feeble to hurt him and that she must die soon.

Jack's last Alaskan tale, "Like Argus of the Ancient Times," carefully identified the old Tarwater of his youthful memories with the hero of classical myth. The old man sings the same ditty all the way to the far north:

> Like Argus of the ancient times,
>   We leave this modern Greece,
> Tum-tum, tum-tum, tum, tum, tum-tum,
>   To shear the Golden Fleece.

Greed was no longer the motive of Anglo-Saxon history; myth and the unconscious lay behind the quest for treasure. Tarwater's apparent reason for going to Alaska was to prove to his family that he was not finished, while the deeper cause lay in his dreams. When lost in the snows, half-dead with lethargy and cold, Tarwater,

> as in the delirium of drug or anaesthetic, recovered, within himself, the infantile mind of the child-man of the early world. It was in the dusk of Death's fluttery wings that Tarwater thus crouched, and, like his remote forebear, the child-man, went to myth-making, and sun-heroizing, himself hero-maker and the hero in quest of the immemorable treasure difficult of attainment.
>
> Either must he attain the treasure—for so ran the inexorable logic of the shadow-land of the unconscious—or else sink into the all-devouring sea, the blackness eater of the light that swallowed to extinction the sun each night. . . . But how to escape this monster of the dark that from within him slowly swallowed him? Too deep-sunk was he to dream of escape or feel the prod of desire to escape. For him reality had ceased.

So Jack reached down into his own unconscious and his knowledge that his death was near, and set it boldly on the page. The most haunting of his final stories was "The Red One." In it, an explorer is dying slowly, this time in the large hut of an old shaman in cannibal Melanesia. The explorer has passed through all the stages of savagery himself, and he waits for his inevitable death from the shaman's knife as he watches the old witch doctor cure the heads of other white men. Both explorer and shaman have left behind the desires of the body. "Where was the appetite of yesterday? the roasted flesh of the wild pig the hunter's arrow failed to slay? the maid, unwed and dead, ere the young man knew her?" Only one mystery remains unsolved, the melodious siren call that has lured the explorer into his particular heart of darkness. The shaman tells him that the bewitching note comes from The Red One, which is also The God-Voiced, The Sun Singer, and The Star-Born.

Before he dies, the explorer reaches the source of the mystery. His final discovery is not that of Conrad's Kurtz, "The horror! The horror!" It is another mystery. The siren sound comes in fact from a huge iridescent vermilion metallic sphere that has fallen to earth in the jungle, a marvelous messenger from outer space that has tumbled into the hands of savages, who have made it the idol of their blood sacrifices. "It was as if God's Word had fallen into the muck mire of the abyss underlying the bottom of hell; as if Jehovah's Commandments had been presented on carved stone to the monkeys of the monkey cage at the Zoo; as if the Sermon on the Mount had been preached in a roaring bedlam of lunatics."[33]

As the explorer yields his head to the shaman at the sound of The Red One, struck by the tribe like a dinner gong for their feast, he seems to gaze upon "the serene face of the Medusa, Truth." Yet what that truth was, the story does not tell—only that, in the total dichotomy between the hallucinatory message from the stars and the utter savagery of men, the boundaries of Jack's split personality lay. At last, he had the courage and the awareness to declare himself, as he prepared for his own death.

16

FORTY HORSES ABREAST

Satiety and possession are Death's horses;
they run in span.

—JACK LONDON

Jack has finally worn down as perfect
a human machine as the world seldom sees.

—GEORGE STERLING

The first intimation of death came in March of 1916 in Honolulu, before he wrote "The Red One." He woke Charmian one morning to tell her that he was dying of the pain in his bowels. The doctors diagnosed a calculus, an obstruction within his diseased kidneys. It was the first time that his poisoning by arsenic had led to nephritis, an inflammation and internal spasm which prevented his discharging the toxins in his body and threatened him with sudden death from uremia. His pyorrhea was still uncured and was spreading more poison from his gums through his swollen limbs. It was made worse by his insistence on living on *aku* or raw bonito, an occasional papaya, and feasts of barbecued pork at large *luau* parties. The doctors managed to ease the muscular spasm and allow him to discharge his wastes. Then they insisted on putting him on a diet of mild solids, to clear the pyorrhea and the poisons from his body. By April he was recovering, but he did not feel well enough to leave Hawaii until four months later.

The moment he felt better, he resumed his fatal diet of raw fish and meat. It had become an uncontrollable appetite by the time he was forty. Like Freud himself, who would not give up smoking cigars when he was dying of cancer of the throat, Jack persisted in gobbling underdone flesh as if he were a wolf. Charmian could not control him, and she could not force him to eat the vegetables which he needed to balance his diet. Even she attributed his refusal to put his body to rights as a "longing, at least of his *unconscious* mind, for cessation of effort to continue existence."[1] He seemed to be hiding something from her, even as he stressed his passion and need for her. What he was hiding was his knowledge that he must die soon from his wrecked kidneys and from the drugs he was taking in order to exist at all.

On his return in August to California, he went with George Sterling and Jimmy Hopper to the High Jinks at the Bohemian Grove, not so much a meeting of artists now as a gathering of wealthy *bon viveurs* playing at being bohemian. Charmian feared for his health and fell sick herself from anxiety. Jack returned after four days, having slept only two hours in the past sixty. He survived the strain; but he went down with a bad attack of gout in his swollen left leg at the September Fair in Sacramento. He could not leave his bed for seven days, and a doctor had to drive him back to the ranch. His friends and neighbors were shocked by his appearance and temper. His skin was gray, his body corpulent, his nerves on edge. Even his vaunted self-discipline was ragged. He found fault easily, he gave up his games with his guests, he lost the gleam in his eyes, he became morbidly suspicious. A nearby rancher's wife noticed that he was bloated and distressed and fatigued, his ankles swollen over his low shoes. Yet even during these last weeks, Finn Frolich claimed that Jack's brain was as active as ever, burning brightly at the end.

"I never saw a man in all my life with more magnetism, beautiful magnetism," Frolich testified. "If a preacher could have the love in his make up, and the life, God, this whole world would go religious. When he talked, he was marvelous. His hair was bushy, and he wore an eyeshade, and his eyes were big, and his mouth was just as sensitive and full of expression, and the words came out of him just rippling. It was something inside of him, his brain just ran sixty miles a minute, you couldn't follow him. He talked better than he wrote."[2]

Yet such spurts of energy and charisma came rarely now. Jack had suffered a psychic blow that crippled him even more effectively than his rotten kidneys and his swollen gums and legs. He had been worrying about his potency, and like Dick Forrest, he had transferred his dreams of virility to his great Shire stallion. Neuadd Hillside died from a rupture on October 22, 1916, and Jack and Charmian spent the evening weeping together. Their hope of having a son was extinct. Yet once again Jack appeared able to transcend his own sorrow and physical pain by planning a novel about Neuadd. He told Charmian, "He did not die in vain."

His pencil scrawled across the yellow pads on his night table. "Am I hard?" he asked himself. "I try not to be hard. But, oh, a strong man, with two strong arms, to be thrown down and his arms tied. . . . Here I am, a wreck, physically, with a thousand strong arms mentally, that are tied. Rheumatism. Who knows my suffering?" He then put down his dream, the breeding game of England. He planned to do on his ranch what the "god-enlightened old country breeders, here and there, had done for centuries." He would ignore the small minds surrounding him, "they of the one pigeon-hole and the two horses abreast." He would drive his forty horses abreast, his thousand horses abreast. He would comprehend everything there was to know, he would set it all down with his mastery of expression.

The new novel was to be called *Neuadd* after the dead stallion. Its owner would be a "strange scholar man, a rheumatic invalid on his bed of perpetual pain who knew the dirt of all the world, who loved books." The scholar would say curious things. When people questioned his wisdom in paying $10,000 for one stallion, he would say, "I wasn't buying horse. I was buying man, and I think I've bought a whole lot of man." The stallion would be put in harness, groomed for the show ring, pampered like a gentleman. It would be so gently treated that it would only know human beings as gods, nuzzling them vainly even in its death agony, as if they could save it. Messengers would come to the frail, sleepless scholar to tell of the death of the stallion. "Pain-wracked . . . on his back among his books and memories of the sensate world in which he had once been a sensate being," the scholar would write down the facts of Neuadd, so that men might know that horses were like men.[3]

He was again trying to transfer his pain and sense of loss into a nature story, as in *The Call of the Wild.* He no longer saw himself as the efficient, dominant rancher of *The Little Lady of the Big House,* in which the Shire stallion represented Eros and the sap of life; he now could only embody the spirit of study in a wasting war with the torments of the flesh. When the wild duck season opened in California, he gave up the vegetable diet again imposed on him after his rheumatic attack at the Sacramento Fair. He threw caution to the wind and defied his doctors, living entirely on two blood-red wild ducks a day—"a sure ticket to the grave," Charmian wrote later, "for a man in his condition."[4] On November 8, he had another kidney attack and passed matter in his urine. On November 10, he had an attack of food poisoning, which started a bout of dysentery. There was nothing Charmian could do to stop his passion for raw duck or to ease his pain, except to spend hour after hour massaging his swollen ankles. She became sick and sleepless herself, and he massaged her back in return.

Yet Jack's ambitions still flogged his body forward. Two days before his death, he managed to get on his horse and ride to the top of the hill overlooking the ranch, to gaze over some new land he wanted to buy because it was well watered. He had been taken to court by his neighbors, including Charmian's aunt, for diverting too much of the water supply of the valley into his irrigation dam. He now wanted to control the water without any possibility of litigation. He insisted on being the sole master of his soil.

He had also begun work on another novel, to be called *How We Die.* He proposed to take five subjective stories of men dying, to emphasize their withdrawal into themselves and to bring out their loneliness, their fear of death, their loss of illusions, their doubt of the goodness of the world, and the lack of sympathy of those near to them. One would be the story of a man Jack had seen hanged in 1900, another of a Russian soldier at the Battle of the Yalu, the third the slow death of the captain of the *Dirigo* from stomach cancer, the fourth the end of a businessman or an Arctic explorer, and the fifth the cool going of a materialist who shared Jack's belief that when he was dead, he would be as obliterated as a mosquito smashed by his fist.[5] Of these five deaths, that of the sea captain would be the most terrible. He would know that all things must die. He would know that he was no different from a rat starving in the steel hold of his ship. Only an invalid sailor would keep him alive in a grisly race to see which survived the longer. He would wonder at the abandon of his youth, when

> life was a thin-shelled egg, fragile as fairy glass; yet lightly and recklessly had he carried it in his hand, flung it in the air, a shining toy—And now, when he had grown to care for it; when he cherished and cuddled it—ran no risks, behold, it was fading, failing, oozing away from the mass of helpless wreckage that had once been his body, fleshed and filled with the heady stuff of life.[6]

Jack's own life was oozing away from his bowels in dysentery, which he refused to treat. On November 21, he woke up vomiting and spent the day in bed, taking a drug to sleep in the afternoon. When he woke in the evening, he shook off his stupor and spent an hour with Eliza discussing the future of the ranch. He still wanted to become the patriarch of a self-sufficient community, and planned to build a school and a store for the ranch hands and their families. His vision lasted halfway through his dinner with Charmian, then he became aggressive, then melancholy. As usual, he was eating underdone wild duck, although these days he was not drinking more than one cocktail. After dinner, he picked up the two wooden box-trays of books and papers that were his reading matter during his working nights. He looked for Charmian's sympathy, complaining of his burden. She pointed out that he made himself overwork. His ruthless schedule was self-imposed. He chose to slave through most of the nights under his green eyeshade. He forced himself when his body asked for rest.

For an hour, Jack lay with her on her couch in her glassed porch. He was very tired, but soon he left her for his study. His last words to her were strange and urgent: "Thank God, you're not afraid of anything!" She took a walk outside for an hour, then she came back to find him half-asleep over his books. So she went to her separate bedroom on the other side of the ranchhouse, where she slept heavily until eight o'clock the following morning. It was her first night of deep sleep for many days.

Jack had seen Eliza again after dinner, and she had said that she would carry out all his plans to make the ranch into a community. He had given her a hug, betting her that she would not and saying, "I'll go you, old girl." He was not seen outside his study and sleeping porch again, although one of the ranch hands believed he had heard Jack walking about during the night. Shortly before dawn the next morning, Jack injected himself with an overdose of drugs, not more than 12 ½ grains of morphine sulphate mixed with atropine sulphate. He fell into a deep coma and his face turned dark blue. At seven o'clock, he was found breathing heavily by Sekinè, who roused Eliza and Charmian. A local doctor, Allan Thomson from Sonoma, was the first to reach the ranch. He later stated that he found two empty phials of drugs on the floor, and he claimed that Jack had left on the night table some calculations for a lethal dose of morphine. He telephoned his assistant to bring remedies and a stomach pump to the ranch.[7]

The treatment given the dying Jack was for an overdose of morphine and for an attack of renal colic. Charmian herself wrote of the ranch hands waiting on call to walk the comatose figure of her husband up and down, so that he would not sink into a deadly lethargy. The two local doctors tried to use the stomach pump to wash out the poisons, but they could not because there was a stricture of the rectal muscles. Jack was given stimulants: massage and the usual methods of resuscitation were tried. He seemed almost beyond reaction. Charmian noticed that he did not want to be brought back to life. His willpower, what was left of it, was set on dying. When he was told that the new irrigation dam on the ranch had burst, he thumped the bed with his right fist in protest.

He tried to say hello to the doctors and gave his wife the ghost of a smile. Otherwise, he remained in a coma and his breathing became slow and irregular. He lingered on throughout the day, and he died in the evening on the couch of Charmian's porch, where she had had him carried.

Two specialists had been summoned from Oakland and San Francisco, Jack's surgeon, Dr. Porter, and another family physician called Shiels. They took over the handling of the case from the local doctors, Thomson and his assistant Hayes, and insisted on issuing a press bulletin. Thomson became angry at being superseded, accusing the two city doctors of being big shots and Charmian, who was probably in a state of shock, of being casual. On his sole testimony rests the subsequent theory that Jack had deliberately committed suicide, but this was not even suggested in the press bulletin nor on the final death certificate.

The bulletin read:

At 6.30 PM, November 21, 1916, Jack London partook of his dinner. He was taken during the night with what was supposed to be an acute attack of indigestion. This, however, proved to be a gastro-intestinal type of uremia. He lapsed into coma and died at 7:45 PM, November 22.[8]

According to Dr. Thomson's evidence taken twenty-one years after the event, the two specialists concocted the cause of death in order to avoid an inquest and an autopsy. In his opinion, they put the cart before the horse. The overdose of morphine and atropine had contracted Jack's muscles and had stopped him from emptying his bladder, as well as plunging him into coma. Uremia could have killed him only as a consequence of the overdose. Technically, two causes of his death could have been what Dr. Porter entered on the death certificate: "Uremia following renal colic," with a contributory cause: "Chronic interstitial nephritis." Yet in Thomson's later opinion, this verdict ignored the overdose of morphine and atropine which had allowed the toxins to build in the body and had prevented resuscitation. The fact that Sekinè immediately tidied away all the evidence in Jack's sleeping porch and study, and that his body was quickly cremated by his wife, made any further investigation of his death impossible.

Thomson's bias against the specialists and Charmian rendered his testimony suspect. The other main supporter of the suicide theory was George Sterling, who was not present and relied on hearsay. He had long since been jealous of Charmian, although he took a retainer from her to finish *The Assassination Bureau, Ltd.* He thought that she had deliberately separated Jack from his old friends, and he fell into conspiracy theories about her. He even suggested that Jack's death might be the result of foul play, because Jack had boasted to him of a love affair in Honolulu and had threatened to leave Charmian.[9] Jack might, indeed, have made some wild claim to prove that he was still free and virile, but he was far too sick and dependent on Charmian to consider leaving her. She could be reproached only for sleeping deeply on his final night after suffering from weeks of insomnia. Yet his last act had been one of consideration for her, wandering from bathroom to bathroom as far from her room as possible so as not to disturb her. "Dying by inches, then by leaps and bounds."[10] And she had slept.

The evidence against Jack's suicide was strong. Eliza was the first in the room after Sekinè. She saw neither of the empty phials of drugs. She was with the doctors throughout the daytime, when they were trying to revive Jack. She did not hear a word about suicide, and she believed the press release to be true.

Charmian herself always insisted that her husband had died slowly from the poisons accumulated in his system from his uremia, although a comatose death is rare following renal colic and common following an overdose of morphine. Thus finally the evidence rests on Dr. Thomson, who always asserted that his statements after the event were correct.

Suicide is ultimately a matter of intention, whether premeditated or on impulse. If Dr. Thomson was right and Jack left behind the calculations for an overdose of morphine, then it was a premeditated suicide. Yet even this evidence seems faulty. Thomson only spoke of it twenty-one years later and failed to sign his statement or to produce the paper with the calculations. An exhaustive search of Jack's medical library revealed only four medical books partially dealing with the properties of morphine. None of these books had been annotated or underlined by Jack himself, although he usually did so when he was interested in something. The calculation of a lethal dose of morphine remains inexact to this day, and it is an unlikely method of suicide. All in all, if Dr. Thomson saw some arithmetic on the night table, it was more likely to refer to 12 ½ percent royalties than grains of morphine for a fatal dose.

As for the two empty phials of drugs, they were probably there. Jack had shown the symptoms of a morphine overdose and he had been treated for one. He had a traveling medicine chest and hypodermic case, and he had frequently drugged himself against his recurrent pains. He had already built up a great tolerance to opium and its derivative morphine. It is certain enough that he did take some of the contents of the two bottles in the early morning of November 22, seeking to stop the intolerable agony in his guts. During the day of his struggle for life, Sekinè was known to have cleaned up his room and to have left it exactly as it should have been were Jack alive, only adding a single rose on the empty pillow.

Yet this act by Jack was not necessarily a chosen suicide. It did not seem to have been premeditated. He had just written to his daughter Joan, trying to arrange a meeting with her and her mother. He was planning a long trip to New York and another trip to study Oriental agriculture the following year. He was full of schemes for the future of the ranch. There were plots for a dozen books. There were many people to meet, much to do. Above all, he was a tidy man, and he never left unfinished business behind him.

If it was not premeditated, could it have been a suicide on impulse? He had once tried that by drowning, when he was young and crazed by alcohol. He had often talked of it in his books, especially in *Martin Eden*. In that work, he had written:

> There are times when I am light-headed from want of sleep—times when death, with its rest and sleep, is a positive lure to me; times when I am haunted by Longfellow's lines:
>
> > The sea is still and deep;
> > All things within its bosom sleep;
> > A single step and all is o'er,
> > A plunge, a bubble, and no more.

The Little Lady of the Big House had taken that single step and had finally been eased away by an injection of morphine. Although there was a longer step between literature and deed, Jack had been lightheaded from want of sleep and crazed from too much pain, and morphine was at his hand to use.

How much of the morphine he took is uncertain. He was already a walking corpse, only kept from collapse by the strength of his will and his constitution. His myth of himself was that he could put any amount of drink and drugs into his body and get away with it. Supermen do not die, even from an overdose. He had certainly made no preparations for dying, no last letters, no winding up of his affairs, no provision for tomorrow. There was a Colt .44 revolver beside his bed. He did not use it on himself like the Little Lady. His large injection before dawn seems to have been an impulse, not intended to be terminal. A needle-thrust at brief oblivion rather than a snatch at death, a quick remedy for a sudden agony. To the maker of his own myth, taking the remnants of two bottles of morphine and atropine capsules rather than two capsules might seem no more drastic than swallowing two bottles of whiskey rather than two glasses in his drinking days. His body had always stood it so far.

This time, it did not. In his coma, his will to die seemed stronger than his will to live. As he had written of Martin Eden's drowning: "Death did not hurt. It was life, the pangs of life, this awful, suffocating feeling; it was the last blow life could deal him."[11] Once he had lapsed into his coma, he intended to see his death through as he had seen his life through. In that, he provided an example from his "alternately treasured and detested" Schopenhauer, who had written that the sudden cessation of existence had a positive side to it, because only those with the will to live could be strong enough to destroy themselves. He did not even think that willing one's death was a bad thing. He supported the right to suicide and euthanasia and cremation. In that, he was a true Californian. He believed that the body should be always young and that, if it betrayed its owner, it should be scattered to dust and ashes. He believed in risking himself and working as if he could live for ever. For if the risk failed and the work turned sour, then there would be an end to his share of living, but the race would go on regardless. Until his last years, he wrote of men strong enough to deny disease and failure and age. They were nature's aristocrats, self-made men, the pioneers of the Californian dream. If the good life was merely the imposition of the human will, so could the good death be the ceasing of the will to live.

Jack's self-destruction did not take place that night. He had been slowly destroying himself for a decade by overwork and adventure, by excessive eating and heavy drinking and arsenic remedies. One thing that he did wish to leave behind him was his vision of the improved land. Charmian implored the four speakers at his funeral service—George Sterling, James Hopper, Frank Strawn-Hamilton, and Upton Sinclair—to speak of that. She wrote to them all to remind them that in his final years his one object and desire was to "make ten blades of grass grow where one grew before," to leave the land better than he had found it.[12] But the four speakers all thought that the ranch—and perhaps Charmian herself—had already buried the revolutionary and charismatic youth they had once loved. So they forgot his dreams of the land, and they spoke of their dreams of what he had been to them and was no longer.

17

POSTMORTEM AND
RESURRECTION

There is a standard of loyalty and woe to the biographer who deviates
from its prescribing lines! To be at peace with the reader he must be at
peace with his subject. A breach of loyalty in any work of a biographical
nature offends as does nothing else, the unwritten law for the creation
of personal history being that he alone who loves the life shall tell the
story. Else why do it?

ANNA STRUNSKY WALLING

At the death, many tried to claim Jack London as their own. The
Socialists were the most insistent, since they needed an American
proletarian writer with a huge following. When the Russian Revolution broke out in 1917 and the Bolsheviks were triumphant, they
too found in Jack's selected works the voice of the oppressed masses
of the United States. He became and remains the most widely read
American author in Russia. "How sad it is," Anna Strunsky Walling
wrote in her epitaph on him, "that Jack London should have passed
into the silence, out of the sight of the red banners waving over a
free people and out of the reach of the voices of millions singing
the Internationale!"[1] Ironically enough, both John Reed, who had
stolen Jack's radical thunder in Mexico, and Big Bill Haywood
were to meet their deaths in Russia and be buried beneath the walls
of the Kremlin. Had Jack lasted one more year so that he could
have visited the Bolsheviks, he might well have been the third
American rebel to have ended there rather than beneath a red
boulder on his ranch.

To his Socialist biographers thereafter, beginning with his daughter Joan and continuing through Philip Foner and Vil Bykov, Jack's story was to seem a simple one of the tragic corruption of his revolutionary ardor through the excesses of capitalism. They took him at face value when he talked of his lonely struggle from the slums against all the evils of industrialism. They presented him as a proletarian hero in his revolutionary period until the end of the first Russian Revolution of 1905. They praised his prophecies of fascism in *The Iron Heel*—Trotsky himself wrote that Jack was a better prophet than even Lenin or Rosa Luxemburg. They took Charmian to be the villainess who persuaded Jack to become a large ranch owner, finally spoilt by his own success. Only Joan, in her second unfinished and unpublished biography of her father, saw him crippled by his early years; she learned to marvel at how far he had overcome the legacy of his unhappy, lonely, and delinquent childhood. She claimed that, in the end, Jack recognized that the warp in his nature was not his mother's fault or Chaney's, but society's. The fatal wound of his upbringing, however, was incurable, and even socialism could not heal it.

Jack's final justification by his Socialist daughter, who died before she could complete the story of her reconciliation with her dead father, became part of the armory of later defenders of his myth. These were led by his widow Charmian, who produced a two-volume memoir of him in 1921. She was faithful to his legend beyond the call of duty, and she perpetuated it. She hid the fact that he was born a bastard, she stressed his superhuman struggle to become a writer, she blamed the oddities of his mother for any psychic disturbances in his character. She repeated all his changing myths about his origins, from his ancient lineage dating back to noble English families, to the veracity of his boys' fiction, the protean quality of his genius, the consistency of his evolutionary socialism, and the development of his life to fulfillment on the Beauty Ranch with her.

This official version was cut down by the gossip of the Crowd. Three people were the sources of most of the innuendo. The first was George Sterling, who continued to be jealous of Charmian for taking his beloved Wolf away from him. The second was Upton Sinclair, who was a puritan and a prohibitionist and a Socialist. The third was the spiteful Joseph Noel, whom Jack in the end had called a crazy liar. Sterling started the rumor that Jack had been about to leave Charmian for another woman, and that he had committed suicide or been poisoned, perhaps by Charmian. Upton Sinclair picked up this unfounded gossip and printed it in *Mammonart* and *Money Writes,* adding his own biased opinion that alcohol had finally killed the self-indulgent Jack, thus giving a moral twist to the Greek's jealous slanders. Moreover, he linked Jack's death to the suicides of many of the Carmel group, as a sermon against the sins of bohemianism.[2]

In truth, Jack had been the second of George Sterling's friends to die suddenly. (Ambrose Bierce had already disappeared in northern Mexico.) The first had been the writer Nora May French, who had killed herself and been cremated; her friends had fought for the privilege of scattering her ashes at Carmel. After Jack's death, the tragedies hastened. George Sterling's divorced wife Carrie took cyanide in 1918 to the recorded music of Chopin's *Funeral March.* George Herman Scheffauer, the poet and disciple of Bierce, killed himself and his mistress in postwar Berlin. Then in 1926, in the Bohemian Club, the aging Sterling swallowed the cyanide which he had carried for years in a phial in his breast pocket wrapped in an envelope marked "Peace."

Before his death, Jack had praised Edgar Lee Masters for writing the Great American Novel in his *Spoon River Anthology.* Now Masters wrote an epitaph for George Sterling and Jack London and the whole Crowd, which had larked at Piedmont and had dived for abalone so strenuously at Carmel. Masters thought that Sterling did not have the heart to go on. No more than Jack London could he stand the process of his own decay. "He had what might be called a Ponce de León complex. He wanted to be young forever, and the coming of old age struck him as a dishonor. . . . He seemed mantled in a terrible loneliness. He had survived his Crowd."[3]

Joseph Noel confirmed this false coherence in the deaths of many of the Crowd and spread the legend of a Suicide Club. Most

literary groups attract a gossip and a recorder. Some achieve a
Boswell, others suffer the Goncourts, while the Crowd were
afflicted with Joseph Noel. He had always loved George Sterling,
he had always been envious of Jack London and Ambrose Bierce.
His book about the three of them, *Footloose in Arcadia,* is the source
for nearly all of the scandal about Jack's life. He presented Jack's
story as that of a fine young Socialist falling into degeneration and
debauchery after his desertion of his first wife. This malevolent
gossip became the main reference for the denigrators of Jack's
reputation, particularly for Kevin Starr's brilliant and erratic exposé
of Jack's pretensions and inadequacies in *Americans and the California Dream.*

Yet Jack had been his own mythologizer, and Charmian had
aided and abetted his fond falsification of his own life. Just as
nations are said to get the governments they deserve, so Jack got
his Irving Stone. A fringe member of the Crowd, Rose Wilder
Lane, had already written a fictional magazine biography and a
novel about Jack, called *He Was a Man.*[4] Stone persuaded Charmian to give him access to nearly all the London papers in the
mid-thirties, and he produced a biographical novel called *Sailor on
Horseback.* It showed the same ambivalence as its subject, sometimes
following Jack's mythic persona so closely that it used his very
words about himself in what one critic called "bald piracy," sometimes muckraking so deeply into the gossip of the Crowd that it
spattered false dirt all over the golden image.[5] Stone did reveal the
truth about Jack's birth, and he was able to talk to many of Jack's
old friends while they were still alive. He was also responsible for
popularizing the version of Jack's suicide told by George Sterling
and Dr. Thomson. Yet all in all, he ended by overpraising and
undercutting his subject, either hypnotized by Jack's myth or determined to topple the idol.

Stone's biographical novel was commercially successful, and it
became the chief source for the mixture of fact and fiction of Jack's
later legend. It also caused the Jack London Papers to be restricted
for a long period of time by his heirs. Only Richard O'Connor has
since tried to write a full biography, and he did not use the exten-

sive family papers. The result was that he had to rely too heavily on Jack's own dramas about his life, on Charmian's hagiography, and on Stone's ambivalent novel. It was a book that should not have been written, but it was a gallant failure. Since its publication, the papers have been available to qualified scholars.

If Jack's heirs could find no biographer to describe their protean and self-mythologizing hero, his literary critics were thrown into an equal confusion upon his death. He had always despised critics as a breed. "What's it all worth?" he complained to an early friend who analyzed his work. "Cavil, and carp, and criticise, bark and snap, and what does it amount to? You're none the better for it. The world is not."[6] While he was alive, he could defend himself ferociously, if he bothered to waste the time. The critics who tangled with him personally found themselves punched off the page.[7] One of them dared to criticize Jack's use of the language, particularly of the word "fetch." Jack was proud of the strength of his prose, and he did not care too much about its precision. His answer to his critic was typical of the man:

> My kind kicks authority out of the path. Your kind puts mine in jail for violent assault on authority. My kind makes the living language. Your kind preserves the language my kind makes. Your kind and mine are always at war. We have been so in the past, and we shall be so in the future as long as languages *live* upon the planet. This is not sophistry; it is clubbing home the science of language, and is deeper than the deepest generalisations of the purist and the vulgarist. Think it over."[8]

Jack was right about what he said, but his command over the living language depended on his being alive. In his time, he was modern in his praise of evolution and socialism, and at the end he was ahead of contemporary thought in his study of Freud and Jung. He always saw himself as the interpreter between new scientific discovery and the mass mind, but his bad luck was to make the bedrock of his beliefs the theory of social evolution and determinism, which would become offensive to liberal thinkers because of the misuse made of it by totalitarian governments. The fashions in thought and language changed, and when he was dead, he could not adapt. So his reputation was slowly buried by the critics and writers of America.

His national image had depended on the extensive press coverage of all his doings and on the power of his personality in his encounters with reporters and famous people. From the grave, he could no longer defend his ideas passionately. His books had to speak for him, and their uneven quality and wide range made them uncertain and contradictory witnesses. By 1919, H. L. Mencken was asserting that no other popular writer of his time wrote better than Jack in his better books. "Here, indeed, are all the elements of sound fiction: clear thinking, a sense of character, the dramatic instinct, and, above all, the adept putting together of words—words charming and slyly significant, words arranged, in the French phrase, for the respiration and the ear."9 Yet Mencken was already assailing the propaganda element in Jack's work, the amateur Great Thinker who spoiled the effects of the literary artist.

Jack had created the image of the heroic *macho* writer, who lived his fiction and made a fiction of his living. He behaved like the Great American Novelist, even if he had not written the Great American Novel. Those who followed his self-dramatizing style of existence and his short, jerky, bald method of writing, such as Ernest Hemingway, forgot to acknowledge the inventor of the mode, which had more to do with Jack London's Alaska than the Paris of Gertrude Stein. Jack also got little thanks from Dos Passos or Steinbeck or Kerouac for pioneering the hobo novel in *The Road.* Norman Mailer has not praised the American writer who, straight from the shoulder, made prizefighting the subject of his best journalism and professional fiction. Only in a private letter at the time of Jack's death did Henry Miller admit that there was not another educated writer of equal courage and fiery energy in America; later in public, Miller forgot his earlier praise.10 Of the leading American writers of the next generation, only Eugene O'Neill had the grace to acknowledge that Jack London was a major source of his inspiration.

He had towered over his time like a colossus. When Sinclair

Lewis ran into him at Carmel, he called him "The Master" without irony. Yet his gargantuan self-projection produced an equally large reaction. As the dominant schools of British and American critics were based in London and New York, and as the philosophic fashions changed from social Darwinism to liberal reformism and Freudianism, a Californian upstart whose racism was as blatant as his apocalyptic sense of social justice was condemned to pinpricks and oblivion.

To his more sympathetic critics, such as Frederick Lewis Pattee and Maxwell Geismar, his obvious power and talent fell short of genius because of the tragic flaws in his thought. For them, the evolutionist too often dominated the mythologizer of the frontier. In an age which found its profundities in Joycean labyrinths, Proustian motivations, and Eliot's wasteland, Jack London's brutal northland seemed vulgar and crude. When the doctrine of the Aryan race also became loathsome to the American public, Jack appeared to be the John the Baptist of the Nazi superman was well as of the Bolshevik revolutionary. Even if his books were burned in Hitler's Germany because of his socialism, his belief in white supremacy made him suspect at home, while his popularity in Stalinist Russia seemed to confirm that he was the enemy of liberty and individuality. His works were consigned to the shelves of nurseries. He was regarded by most of the literary critics as a misguided man who had written a few good dog stories.

Such patronizing and misjudgment were ludicrous. Jack had been such an individualist in his life, he had been so relentlessly modern, scientific, and prophetic in his work, that his sentencing by the change of intellectual fashion after World War II appeared both inevitable and unjust. It was inevitable because he could no longer evolve, thus evolution condemned his works. It was unjust, because his life had been experimental and questing, so that his dismissal as a totalitarian or a children's writer was absurd. He had been his own worst enemy in his insistence that he was merely a farmer who needed a lot of money for the land, and who lit after inspiration with a club; but such a self-denying ordinance should not have dimmed the mytho-poetic magnificence of some of his books.

There was another irony in the situation. Although the major literary critics sneered at his reputation or neglected him wholly, many of his books continued to sell very well indeed, particularly in Russia, America, and France. In their youth, many public figures, such as the British Socialist Aneurin Bevan and the American physicist Isidor Rabi, read *The Iron Heel* and took their first step from the slum toward a radical hope and career. Jack's chosen image endured, as a bold proletarian who had slugged his way to success. Even Lenny Bruce, trapped in the U.S. navy and talking of "deep-sixing" a rusty steel cable off a ship, had to mention that it was a new technique never elaborated by Jack London, as though Jack's spirit still haunted American sailors.[11] No critical onslaught on him could kill off the affection of the masses for whom he had always said that he wrote.

In the past decade, intellectual fashion and literary criticism have begun to resurrect Jack London as a great American author, whom the people have never forgotten. The publication in 1965 of a large portion of his letters, edited by King Hendricks and Irving Shepard, made most of the critical and biographical writing about him appear absurd. His hidden nature, his delicate and romantic and playful and compassionate aspects, were evident in his correspondence with the few people whom he trusted enough to drop his heroic posture. Franklin Walker's biography, mainly dealing with Jack's Klondike experiences, presented him as a tormented man on the human scale, neither demigod nor gutter Lucifer. Since then, the bibliographical and critical work of a handful of scholars devoted to his reputation—such as Earle Labor, James McClintock, and Hensley Woodbridge—has accelerated his overdue resurrection.

Another trend in intellectual fashion has also come to his rescue. The increasing emphasis on the behavioral similarities between animals and human beings, pioneered by Konrad Lorenz and popularized by Robert Ardrey and Desmond Morris, has ushered in a hybrid "science," sociobiology. Even if Jack London was not the herald angel of American socialism or fascism, he was certainly the prophet of the correspondences between beasts and men. *The*

Call of the Wild, Before Adam, and *White Fang* are to sociobiology what *Uncle Tom's Cabin* is to the sociology of slavery. The evolution of fashion has rediscovered the fashion of evolution.

It is not known that Jack London also began before Lévi-Strauss and Chomsky an inquiry into the biological basis of language. In some notes for an essay, left unfinished before his death, he spoke of a world language for a world tribe. He claimed that there were common noises in all tribal languages for hunger, fear, anger, and the gurgle of love sounds. Numerals were universal, as were the bardic chants to the heavens which had so struck his ear in Hawaii. Misunderstanding was also universal, but it was chiefly the misunderstanding of languages, despite their origins in common appetites. He looked to the polyglot Pacific Islands to develop a language rooted in biology and human brotherhood at the end of the Great War.[12]

His powers of biological insight, political prophecy, and science fiction have made him curiously modern as a thinker, despite the dark corridors of his racist beliefs. In France especially, the revival of his reputation has been marked by the reprinting of nearly all his books. Paris has often been the resurrectionist of the victims of Anglo-Saxon prejudice—in this case, a master of Anglo-Saxon prejudice himself. Yet his emphasis on rationality and scientific discovery makes him attractive to a society which still uses the constructions of Descartes to appreciate the fantasies of Jules Verne.

Today we are blessed or plagued with more self-awareness than the activists of the frontier. The tools of psychiatry lie in our hands; but they cannot be used fully on a man who discovered psychiatry only at the end of his life. The first attempt to apply them to Jack was made in 1917, using *John Barleycorn* as material. The analyst Wilfred Lay came up with the conclusion that Jack's masculinity was suspect and that his personality exhibited traits of sado-masochism, homosexuality, and extraversion to a high degree.[13] These were pejorative terms to apply to a man who lived by his myths to an unusual extent in an age when few men analyzed their own motivations correctly. Nor can a man who believed so much

in revealing himself through his actions be judged too harshly for
his unconsidered motivations. His age preferred universal to private explanations. Herbert Spencer was his Freud.

Jack was a born rebel by inheritance and desire, and his personality demanded the immediate gratification of his opposed wants.
He had a dialectic of appetites without a synthesis of satisfaction.
When he protested that he was consistent, he wrenched his nature
and his beliefs into a pattern that had vehemence without coherence. In his books, he often split himself into two opposing characters, because he lived so uneasily within his single personality. In
The Sea-Wolf, he was both Wolf Larsen and Humphrey van Weyden, the brute ego in conflict with the social being. In "South of
the Slot," he made one man represent his own divided loyalties to
his working-class origins and personal aspirations. His hero played
the roles of university intellectual and labor leader, rich man and
poor man, as if Jack's own enthusiasm for all the aspects of his life
enabled him to live simultaneously on both sides of a conflict. He
could only be happy when he did what he wanted and damned the
consistency of his actions. At those rare times, he felt both the
mastery of himself and of the human condition, and he drove his
forty horses abreast.

He always complained that he had little imagination, so that
he had to take his plots from his own experience or from newspaper
reports. He could also have said that he strove to realize his dreams,
not to analyze them. As he thought himself larger than life, he tried
to do more than other men did. For a man who has a heroic vision
can do more than a man who knows himself too well and is afraid
to move. To deny weakness, to insist on excess and success is to live
at full stretch. Jack London lived nine lives and wrote more than
fifty books and founded a ranch and died at forty. A man like that
is worth his own myths.

Of course, the myths were too great for the person of one man.
At times, he seemed to be trying to live out the history of the whole
of mankind as well as to personify the American or the California
dream. He had the vaunting ambition of the self-taught; he was
always the poor boy in the public library who determines to read

every book on every shelf in order to add up the whole sum of human knowledge. It was a noble and futile aspiration, and a tragic one. It condemned a finite mind and body to an infinite dissatisfaction. Even mythologically, Jack was not the American Adam, the innocent in the wilderness, nor the spirit of Huckleberry Finn, the savage fleeing civilization, nor even the Horatio Alger hero, the assiduous kid determined to make good. Although he had elements of these three stereotypes, he was more of the incessant California pilgrim. However great his self-destruction and his corruption, his mind ranged on to a new vision of a new earth.

His inheritance was, indeed, the confusions and questings of the new Californians. His mother was a spiritualist, his probable father an astrologer; both of them tried to talk a living from the audiences of that state, where most radical theories come to roost before they die. Their son came from the first extensive generation to be born there, those who were formed by their raw state, those who re-formed it in their working image. As California settled its problems, so Jack London settled himself when he finally left the Socialist Labor Party and returned to the land. Like Billy and Saxon Roberts, his pilgrimage ended in the Valley of the Moon. With his curious gift for political prophecy, so brilliantly shown in *The Iron Heel,* he was leaving the struggle for industrial control proclaimed by Marx for the struggle to redeem the countryside proclaimed by Mao. The soil must be enriched before it could become the cooperative commonwealth of the revolution to be.

In a letter written just before his death, he declared himself primarily a farmer. "What am I doing? In few words, I am trying to do what the Chinese have done for forty centuries. . . . I am rebuilding worn-out hillside lands that were worked out and destroyed by our wasteful California pioneer farmers."[14] From the slums of the city, Jack London returned to the wreck of the country. His apocalypse of a red revolution matured into a vision of a green one. His forty horses abreast came to rest on his land.

ACKNOWLEDGMENTS

This book could not have been written without the kind permission of the late Irving Shepard, who allowed me access to all the Jack London material. His widow, his son Milo, and his daughter Joy have all been most hospitable and informative. I have been allowed to examine all the Jack London Papers as well as photographs and objects in their possession at the Jack London Ranch at Glen Ellen, and also at the Henry E. Huntington and Utah State University libraries. Although all the opinions in this biography are my own, I can only express my profound gratitude for the information and aid given to me by the Shepard family, who are the trustees of the Jack London material.

My second debt is to the library staff of the Henry E. Huntington Library, in particular to Jean Preston and Alan Jutzi. I spent the best part of a year there going through the London material, and all my difficult requests for obscure sources were met with unfailing speed and patience. I would also like to thank the library staff at the second leading collection of Londoniana at Utah State University, Logan. Furthermore, I am grateful to the staff of the various other libraries which I consulted, particularly at the Cresmer Collection at the University of Southern California, the Irving Stone Collection at the University of California at Los Angeles, the Bancroft Library at Berkeley, the Jack London Room at the Oakland Public Library, and the Holman-London Collection at the Jack London State Park, Glen Ellen. My gratitude also to the friendship and help of Ann O'Connor.

My third debt is to that growing band of scholars who have done so much to revive Jack London's reputation in the past twenty years. Although none of them has reviewed this book, their own writings, conversations with me, and criticism of my views have aided me considerably. I would have been unable to write this book without the pioneering work of the late King Hendricks, and of Earle Labor, James I. McClintock, Arthur Calder-Marshall, Alfred S. Shivers, Charles C. Walcutt, Franklin Walker, Kenneth S. Lynn, Hensley C. Woodbridge, Howard L. Lachtman, Robert Forrey, William Curtin, Clarice Stasz, and Katherine Littell. I would particularly like to thank Carolyn Willson for her generosity and original insights. For aid with Jack London research, all London scholars are in the debt of James E. Sisson and Russ Kingman. As for bibliographies of Jack London's works, the exhaustive lists compiled by Tony Bubka, James E. Sisson, Dale L. Walker, Hensley C. Woodbridge, John London, George H. Tweney, and David M. Hamilton have made my task easier than I had the right to expect.

I am also dependent on the previous biographies of Jack London, although I may disagree with many of their conclusions. Irving Stone was kind enough to grant me an interview and to make his papers deposited at UCLA available to me. The late Joan London, and Richard O'Connor and Kevin Starr, particularly provoked and stimulated my own perceptions, while Dr. Michael Barraclough checked my medical conclusions, and Frances Lindley made her just and wise editorial decisions.

In all, I would like to thank all those, living and dead, who believed Jack London to be an extraordinary and significant man and writer, and who took the trouble to record their opinions. A biographer is entirely dependent upon the testimony he can find. During my work on Jack London over the past two years, I have entered into an enclosed world of such engagement and welcome that I can only hope this book reflects something of the passion and complexity with which Jack London's life infuses all who know of him.

ANDREW SINCLAIR

Pasadena, 1975
Berkeley, 1976

NOTES TO CHAPTERS

In these notes, the Henry E. Huntington Library at San Marino, California, will be cited as *HL,* the University of California at Los Angles as *UCLA*, the University of Southern California as *USC,* and the Utah State University at Logan as *US.*

FOREWORD

1. Jack London, *The Little Lady of the Big House* (New York, 1915), p. 49.
2. *The Complete Works of Ralph Waldo Emerson* (12 vols., Boston, 1903–1904), VI, p. 255—quoted by Kevin Starr in his *Americans and the California Dream, 1850–1915* (New York, 1973), p. 66. Starr's book is a brilliant analysis of early California history, only marred by an audacious and hostile assault on the final years of Jack London on his ranch.
3. Stephen Powers, *Afoot and Alone* (Hartford, Conn., 1872), p. 315. For the economic feeling of the United States in the late nineteenth century, I have relied much on the insights of two of the professors who once taught me social history, Richard Hofstadter in *The Age of Reform* (New York, 1958), and David M. Potter in *People of Plenty* (Chicago, 1954).
4. Mark Twain, *Roughing It* (H. N. Smith, ed., New York, 1959), Part II, p. 132.
5 William H. Chaney to Jack London, June 4, 1897, Irving Stone Collection, *UCLA*.
6 There is an interesting article on the life of Chaney by Fulmer Mood, "An Astrologer from Down East," *New England Quarterly*, V, No. 4, 1932. See also Joan London, "W. H. Chaney: A Reappraisal." *American Book Collector*, XVII, November 1966.
7 See San Francisco *Chronicle* and *Bulletin*, June 4, 1875. Both Irving Stone and Richard O'Connor give extended accounts of the scandal of Jack London's birth, although it was largely irrelevant to his boyhood. Stone first published the details of the scandal and of Londons probable paternity in 1938. His version as been accepted by Joan London and most scholars since that time. The texts of part of Chaney's letters to Jack London are to be found in Irving Stone's *Sailor on Horseback* (Boston, 1938).

1. LOST BOYHOOD

1. See Jack London's notes for a projected autobiography, Cresmer Collection, *USC.*

2. See Rose Wilder Lane, "Life and Jack London," the first "biography" of Jack London, which ran in serial form in *Sunset, the Pacific Monthly* between October 1917 and May 1918. Although it is written in the form of fiction based upon fact, Mrs. Lane had access to most of Jack London's early circle of friends, particularly to Herman "Jim" Whitaker. Mrs. Lane later wrote a novel based on the same material called *He Was a Man* (New York, 1925). It was the forerunner of Irving Stone's "biographical novel," *Sailor on Horseback* (Boston, 1938).

3. Jack London to Judge R. B. Tappan, as reported by Henry L. Betten in the Alameda *Times-Star,* March 30, 1954.

4. *Idem.* Both Jack's boyhood friend, Frank Atherton, and Eliza Shepard testified that there was plenty of meat in the London household, even if money was short. Eliza also confirmed that the young Jack's favorite occupation was to go hunting for fish and game with John London.

5. Jack London, *John Barleycorn* (Bodley Head Collected edn., London, 1964), II, pp. 45–46.

6. Jack London to Marion Humble, December 11, 1914. See *Letters from Jack London* (K. Hendricks and I. Shepard, eds., New York, 1965), pp. 438–439.

7. James Hopper, later football player, war correspondent, and Carmel resident, quoted by Charmian London, *The Book of Jack London* (2 vols., New York, 1921), I, p. 60.

8. Frank Atherton wrote an unpublished memoir about his childhood with Jack London. A copy of the manuscript is in the possession of R. Kingman at the Jack London bookstore at Glen Ellen, California. The most useful sources on London's boyhood are to be found in the opening chapters and notes of Franklin Walker's unfinished biography of Jack London, the manuscript of which is deposited at the Huntington Library.

9. Jack London to Mabel Applegarth, November 30, 1898, *HL.* See also *Letters from Jack London,* pp. 4–8. At this time, Jack London was still near enough to his childhood not to overdramatize it too much, although he does extend his time in the cannery from several months to a year.

10. Jack London, *The Valley of the Moon* (New York, 1913), pp. 263–264.

11. Notes for an autobiography, "Jack Liverpool," Cresmer Collection, *USC.* In her second unpublished biography of her father, Joan London agreed that he had become a delinquent because he was an unhappy child, a lonely child, a lost and misunderstood child who felt he did not belong.

12. J. Noel, *Footloose in Arcadia* (New York, 1940), p. 20.

13. See Jack London, *The Cruise of the Dazzler* (Bodley Head Collected edn., II, London, 1964). Also see Jack London, *Tales of the Fish Patrol* (New York, 1905). In a long letter to the Corresponding Editor of the *Youth's Companion,*

March 9, 1903, Jack London admitted that most of his book was not his personal adventures. See also *Letters from Jack London,* pp. 147–149.

2. LAWLESS AS SNOW-FLAKES

1. See Jack London's notes for an unwritten novel to be called "The Mercy of the Sea . . . A fairly truthful narrative of things that happened," *HL.* Parts of his experiences appeared in *The Sea-Wolf,* and an expurgated version of the death of the Bricklayer in "That Dead Men Rise Up Never," *The Human Drift* (New York, 1917), pp. 35–51.
2. Jack London, *The Cruise of the Snark* (New York, 1911), pp. 4–5.
3. Jack London, *The Sea-Wolf* (Signet Classic edn., New York, 1964), p. 125.
4. San Francisco *Morning Call,* November 12, 1893.
5. See Jack London, *John Barleycorn, op. cit.,* pp. 124–136.
6. Jack London, *The Road* (Bodley Head Collected edn., London, 1964), II, p. 321.
7. Jack London, Tramp Diary, 1894, *US.* For a full analysis of the march, see Donald L. McMurry, *Coxey's Army—A Study of the Industrial Army Movement of 1894* (Boston, 1929). See also the excellent book by Frederick Feied, *No Pie in the Sky: The Hobo as American Cultural Hero in the Works of Jack London, John Dos Passos, and Jack Kerouac* (New York, 1964).
8. See Josiah Flynt [Willard], "Homosexuality Among Tramps," Appendix A in Havelock Ellis, *Studies in the Psychology of Sex: Sexual Inversion* (2nd rev. edn., Philadelphia, 1908), pp. 219–224.
9. Jack London, *The Road, op. cit.,* pp. 333–334. In his article on "The Road," printed in *Jack London Reports* (K. Hendricks and I. Shepard, eds., New York, 1970) pp. 311–321, London testifies to the misplaced devotion of the road kids and prushuns for their profesh and their jockers.
10. *Ibid.,* pp. 396, 410, 415.
11. For confirmation of this view, see Jack London to Charles Brown, Jr., July 28, 1914; also Jack London to Maurice Magnus, October 23, 1911. (Both are quoted in *Letters from Jack London,* pp. 354–355, 426). Magnus was a homosexual and a friend of D. H. Lawrence. He had written to Jack London complaining that his heroes Wolf Larsen and Burning Daylight seemed not to know women, and were perhaps homosexual.

    Perhaps the most interesting of those who claimed to have been on the road with Jack London was Leon Roy Livingston, who called himself "A-No. 1, The Famous Tramp," and in 1917 printed in Erie, Pennsylvania, an account of their apparent adventures called *From Coast to Coast with Jack London.* The author could not reply to it because he was dead, but the whole book seems to be a complete tramp fantasy. Its most cogent observation was that the tramps' section in Chicago was called the Abyss.
12. See Jack London's notes on the unwritten "Leith Clay-Randolph," *HL.*
13. Jack London, "The Tramp," *Jack London: American Rebel* (P. S. Foner, ed., New York, 1947), pp. 441–457. Richard Etulain, in his forthcoming intro-

duction to a collection of Jack London's hobo pieces, minimizes the effect which the road experiences had on the young tramp. To defend this contradiction of London's own testimony, Etulain ignores the importance of London's economic and Socialist pieces about the tramp, as well as playing down the effects of the jail experience.

14. Jack London, *John Barleycorn,* p. 46.

3. A FRANTIC PURSUIT OF KNOWLEDGE

1. Georgia Loring Bamford, *The Mystery of Jack London* (Oakland, Calif., 1931), pp. 17–20. The threat of a lawsuit by Charmian London caused this book officially to be withdrawn, but 1,000 copies from a truckload mysteriously appeared on the second-hand book market in Los Angeles.

2. See the file on the *Aegis* in *HL.*

3. Jack London, *Martin Eden* (Bodley Head Collected edn., London, 1965), III, p. 22.

4. Jack London to Anna Strunsky, undated, 1900, Anna Strunsky Walling Collection, *HL.*

5. See the interview with Jack London, "The Boy Socialist," in the San Francisco *Chronicle,* February 16, 1896. Also see the Oakland *Times,* May 9, July 29, August 12, August 24, 1896.

6. Jack London, *Martin Eden, op. cit.,* pp. 119–121. See also Richard Hofstadter, *Social Darwinism in American Thought* (rev. edn., Boston, 1955), p. 44. Hofstadter's important work remains essential in understanding the enormous influence of social Darwinism at the time. Also penetrating is Cynthia Eagle Russett, *Darwin in America: The Intellectual Response, 1865–1912* (San Francisco, 1976), particularly in the section dealing with Jack London.

7. Jack London to Cloudesley Johns, May 28, 1899, *HL.*

8. Jack London to Cloudesley Johns, July 5, April 17, 1899, *HL.* Quoted in *Letters from Jack London,* pp. 44, 27.

9. Jack London to Mabel Applegarth, November 30, 1898, *HL.* Quoted in *Letters from Jack London,* p. 7.

10. James Hopper, quoted in Charmian London, *The Book of Jack London, op. cit.,* I, p. 211.

11. David Starr Jordan, *The Days of a Man* (2 vols., New York, 1922), I, p. 460.

12. Jack London to Mabel Applegarth, November 30, 1898, *HL.* Quoted in *Letters from Jack London,* p. 7. See also Sibley S. Morrill, "Jack London UC Rebel of '96," *East Bay Magazine,* I, December 2, 1966.

13. See William H. Chaney to Jack London, June 4, 1897, Irving Stone Collection, *UCLA.*

14. See Jack London, *John Barleycorn,* p. 147. The first stanza of "Gold" shows just how bad the poem was:

> Strange was the alchemy through which thou passed,
>   Before, deep-sunk in earth and massive rock,
> Thou layest concealed whilst centuries o'er thee passed;

Nor felt the rush of life, the toil, the shock
Of man above thee torn with emotions wild;
Living, dying, existing but a space;
Enduring sorrows or with joys beguiled:
Crushing his fellows in that fierce onward race.
Where brute survived and true nobility was lost;
When souls pursuing hot desire were passion tossed.

15. From Jack London, "The Lover's Liturgy," *HL.* The poem was eventually printed without payment in Oakland's little literary magazine, *The Raven,* February 1901.
16. Jack London, untitled typescript on how he became a writer, ca. 1902, *HL.*
17. Jack London to Mabel Applegarth, November 27, 1898, *HL.* Quoted in *Letters from Jack London,* p. 4.
18. See Thomas Beer, *The Mauve Decade: American Life at the End of the Nineteenth Century* (New York, 1926), p. 224.
19. Frank Norris, "Sailing of the Excelsior," San Francisco *Wave,* July 31, 1897.

4. KLONDIKE AND PAYDIRT

1. All biographers of Jack London are in the debt of Franklin Walker for his thorough and penetrating book, *Jack London and the Klondike: The Genesis of an American Writer* (London, 1966). He examines in great detail the reality of London's trip to Alaska. For a general appreciation of the phenomenon of the Gold Rush, Pierre Berton's *The Klondike Fever: The Life and Death of the Last Great Gold Rush* (New York, 1958) remains the best account, ably supported by Kathryn Winslow's *Big Pan-Out: The Story of the Klondike Gold Rush* (New York, 1951). In addition to the biographical sources on Jack London, the diary of Fred Thompson of the trip to the Stewart River, and Jack London's own diary and account of the voyage downriver from Dawson City to the sea are essential reading. So are the manuscript memoirs of Emil Jensen and Marshall Bond, the original of which is in the Yale Library. Copies of all these sources are to be found in the Huntington Library.
2. Joaquin Miller, quoted in K. Winslow, *Big Pan-Out,* p. 116.
3. Charmian London, *The Book of Jack London,* I, p. 228.
4. Fred Thompson's diary, September 21, 1897, *HL.*
5. Jack London, "Through the Rapids on the Way to Klondike," *The Home Magazine,* June 1899. Irving Stone states in *Sailor on Horseback* that London earned $3,000 as a steersman at the White Horse Rapids, but the Thompson diary disproves this.
6. See letter of J. D. Dines, Mining Recorder, to Franklin Walker, August 31, 1954, enclosing a copy of Jack London's application for a placer mining claim on November 5, 1897, Franklin Walker Collection, *HL.*
7. See *The American Monthly Review of Reviews,* March 1898.
8. See Marshall Bond's memoir of Jack London, original in the Yale Library, copy in *HL.*

9. Edward E. P. Morgan in *God's Loaded Dice,* quoted by F. Walker, *Jack London and the Klondike*, pp. 111–112.

10. See Marshall Bond's memoir.

11. Jack London, "Housekeeping in the Klondike," *Harper's Bazaar,* September 15, 1900.

12. Quoted by Charmian London, *The Book of Jack London,* I, pp. 236, 238.

13. Jack London, "From Dawson to the Sea," Buffalo *Express,* June 4, 1899. The actual log of the trip down the Yukon is reprinted in full in Charmian London, *The Book of Jack London,* I, pp. 248–257.

14. Jack London, "The Gold Hunters of the North," *Revolution and Other Essays* (New York, 1910), p. 162. See also his article, "The Economics of the Klondike," *The American Monthly Review of Reviews*, January 1900.

5. MAKING A NAME

1. See Notebook No. 1 in the Jack London Collection gathered by King Hendricks for the Utah State University Library at Logan.

2. Jack London, *John Barleycorn,* p. 154.

3. Jack London to Mabel Applegarth, November 30, 1898, *HL.* See also *Letters from Jack London,* pp. 4–8.

4. For a longer exposition on the importance of "A Thousand Deaths," see Edwin B. Erbentraut, "A Thousand Deaths: Hyperbolic Anger," *Jack London Newsletter*, September-December 1971.

5. Jack London to the Corresponding Editor, *Youth's Companion,* January 7, 1899, *HL.* See also *Letters from Jack London,* pp. 11–12.

6. Three London essays, written at this period on the subject of how to break into the literary market, are called "Again the Literary Aspirant," "The Question of a Name," and "On the Writer's Philosophy of Life." The quotations are taken from these manuscripts in the Huntington Library, as are Jack's poems and jokes for *Town Topics.*

7. This memoir by Anna Strunsky is printed in Charmian London, *The Book of Jack London*, I, pp. 319–322.

8. Anna Strunsky (Walling) to Franklin Walker, March 16, 1953, Franklin Walker Collection, *HL.*

9. See the Elsie Whitaker Martinez transcript to Franklin Walker and Willa Klug Baum in the Bancroft Library, Berkeley.

10. Jessie Peixotto's memories of the young Jack London are to be found in the Irving Stone Collection, *UCLA.*

11. Jack London to Ninetta Eames, March 26, 1900, *HL.*

12. Jack London to Anna Strunsky, December 21, 1899, Walling Collection, *HL.* See also *Letters from Jack London,* pp. 76–77.

13. *Ibid.,* April 6, 1900, Walling Collection, *HL.*

14. Jack London to Ninetta Eames, April 3, 1900, quoted in Charmian London, *The Book of Jack London,* I, pp. 12–13. Mrs. Eames wrote a most flattering article on Jack London for the *Overland Monthly,* May 1900.

15. Jack London to Cloudesley Johns, February 16, 1900, *HL*.
16. Autobiography, "Who the Hell IS Cloudesley Johns?", manuscript, p. 214, *HL*.
17. Jack London to Idah M. Strobridge, June 17, 1900, Hoffman Collection, *HL*.
18. Jack London to Anna Strunsky, July 31, 1900, Walling Collection, *HL*. See also *Letters from Jack London,* p. 109.

6. THE CROWD AND THE CRACK

1. Jack London to Cloudesley Johns, October 3, 1899, *HL*. See also *Letters from Jack London,* pp. 59–60.
2. See Joan London, *Jack London and His Times* (New York, 1939), pp. 179–191. The author is particularly good on the circle of Oakland Socialists, who remained close to her all their lives. Her views are very much confirmed by Elsie Whitaker Martinez in the remarkable series of tape recordings made by Franklin Walker and Willa Klug Baum at Berkeley in 1969.
3. See Anna Strunsky (Walling) to Franklin Walker, March 16, 1953, Walker Collection, *HL*.
4. Jack London to Cloudesley Johns, July 11 or August 26, 1903, *HL*. See also *Letters from Jack London,* pp. 151–152.
5. Jack London to George Sterling, July 11, 1903, *HL*.
6. See Joan London, *Jack London and His Times,* p. 260.
7. Jack London to Anna Strunsky, March 22, 1902, Walling Collection, *HL*.
8. See Rose Wilder Lane, "Life and Jack London," *Sunset, the Pacific Monthly,* January 1918.
9. Jack London to Anna Strunsky, December 20, 1902, Walling Collection, *HL*.
10. Mrs. Mira Maclay to Irving Stone, May 29, 1937, Irving Stone Collection, *UCLA*.
11. See Jack London to Anna Strunsky, March 22, 1902, Walling Collection, *HL*. In his library preserved at the Huntington Library, Jack London had a copy of Victor Robinson's *An Essay on Hasheesh: Including Observations and Experiments* (New York, 1912). Robinson was a pharmaceutical chemist who quoted Jack's loved Herbert Spencer on the power of hashish in reviving ideas. He also quoted John Addington Symonds's words: "What is left for us modern men? We cannot be Greek now. . . . What is left? Hasheesh, I think: Hasheesh of one form or another." Experiments with hashish or cocaine were popular at the time, before the addictive effects of the drugs were well known. London himself was to depend heavily on opium derivatives at the end of his life, to ease his bodily pains.
12. Jack London to Cloudesley Johns, March 10, 1900, *HL*. See also *Letters from Jack London,* pp. 98–100.
13. Jack London to Elwyn Hoffman, October 27, 1900, Hoffman Collection, *HL*.
14. See Jack London to Cloudesley Johns, April 22, March 30, 1899, *HL*. In his brilliant literary analysis of Jack London's short stories, *White Logic* (Grand Rapids, Mich., 1975), pp. 20–24, James I. McClintock studies in depth London's debt to Kipling's style and to Herbert Spencer's *Philosophy of Style,* but

without bringing out the full effect of Kipling and Spencer on London's political and social thought.

15. Jack London, "The Law of Life," in *Children of the Frost* (New York, 1902), p. 41.
16. See Jack London, "These Bones Shall Rise Again," *Revolution, op. cit.,* pp. 181–193.
17. Jack London, "Phenomena of Literary Evolution," *The Bookman,* October 1900.
18. See Jack London, "The Salt of the Earth," manuscript, *HL.*
19. Jack London, "The Home-Coming of the Oregon," San Francisco *Examiner,* June 14, 1901, reprinted in King Hendricks and Irving Shepard, eds., *Jack London Reports,* pp. 305–310.
20. Jack London was particularly wounded by a lampoon by "Yorick" in *Town Talk,* November 30, 1901, which ran:

> Dear London: Do I hear aright,
> Or has some gray witch of the night
> Her evil spell upon me cast
> And to a nightmare chained me fast?
> You writing stuff for Willie Hearst?
>
> . . . Alas, for this degen'rate day
> When Genius grovels to its pay!
> When such a mind of sterling worth
> As gave "An Odyssey of the North"
> Shall stultify its brilliant thought
> Just that the nimble pence be caught . . .

21. Jack London to Cloudesley Johns, January 6, 1902, *HL.* See also *Letters from Jack London,* pp. 128–129.
22. Jack London in San Francisco *Examiner,* November 17, 1901.
23. Jack London to Cloudesley Johns, November 22, 1900, *HL.*
24. See Jack London, "What the Community Loses by the Competitive System," manuscript, *HL.*
25. Quoted in Joan London, *Jack London and His Times,* p. 207.
26. See Jack London, "The Class Struggle," *War of the Classes* (New York, 1905), pp. 3–49.
27. Jack London, "The Scab," *War of the Classes,* pp. 101–147.
28. "Jack London by Himself," pamphlet, *HL.*
29. George Brett to Jack London, December 3, 1902, *HL.*
30. See Notes for "A Great Novel: A Study of Marriage, in Two Parts," Cresmer Collection, *USC.*

7. HIS LONG SICKNESS

1. Jack London to Cloudesley Johns, October 17, 1900, *HL.* See also *Letters from Jack London,* pp. 113–114.

2. See Jack London and Anna Strunsky, *The Kempton-Wace Letters* (New York, 1903), pp. 25, 27, 64, 65, 78 and *passim.*

3. Jack London to Anna Strunsky, December 26, 1900, Walling Collection, *HL.* See also *Letters from Jack London*, pp. 118–119.

4. Jack London to Anna Strunsky, April 3 and October 3, 1901, Walling Collection, *HL.* Anna Strunsky wrote a glowing review of both *The Son of the Wolf* and *The God of His Fathers.* The first review, printed in the *Dilettante*, February 1901, was the more impressive and original in seeing the mythic and poetic quality hidden behind London's stark prose:

> In Mr. London's stories one feels a truth to detail, a truth to the life. It is as if the author knew no other country and no other people. But with it all he is suggestive as only the creative artist can be, leading the eye and heart on to other scenes and facts, until the reader is caught up in the white light of the Spirit of the Thing and its Romance. *In a Far Country* is a terrible story of degeneration and death. It is bold enough artistically to be classed with the extremest of extreme realist productions. Yet it is powerfully done and it is modified and temporized, the reader being made to feel the law behind the tragedy. There is no internal evidence of a Mephistophelian compact binding the author to any one school.

5. See Jack London to Anna Strunsky, January 5, February 5 and 11, 1902, Walling Collection, *HL.* She wrote a poem at the time called "Ambition," which showed the strong influence of his work ethic on her. The first verse ran:

> If I greaten he will love me
> I shall draw him with my eyes,
> I will hold him when they praise me
> He will dream me sweet his prize,
> Therefore toil I in the night.

6. Jack London to Anna Strunsky, June 10, 1902, Walling Collection, *HL.*

7. Jack London to Anna Strunsky, July 29, 1902, Walling Collection, *HL.*

8. Jack London to Anna Strunsky, September 28, December 20, 1902, Walling Collection, *HL.*

9. Jack London to Anna Strunsky, July 31, 1902, Walling Collection, *HL.* See also *Letters from Jack London*, pp. 136–137.

10. Jack London, *The People of the Abyss* (New York, 1903), pp. 43, 64, 109, and *passim.*

11. See Jack London to Cloudesley Johns, February 21, 1902, *HL.*

12. Jack London, *The People of the Abyss*, p. 288.

13. Jack London to George Sterling, August 22, 1902, *UCLA.* See also *Letters from Jack London*, p. 137.

14. *The Nation*, October 30, 1903.

15. Jack London, *The People of the Abyss*, p. 168. For a fuller examination of Jack London's sources and methods of work in writing this book, see Andrew

Sinclair, "A View of the Abyss," *Jack London Newsletter*, January–August 1977.

16. Jack London to Anna Strunsky, October 15, 1902, Walling Collection, *HL*.
17. Jack London to Anna Strunsky, December 20, 1902, Walling Collection, *HL*.
18. Julian Hawthorne in *Wilshire's Magazine*, February 1903.
19. See Jack London, *A Daughter of the Snows* (Philadelphia, 1902), pp. 37, 83, and 111.
20. The best critical writing on *The Call of the Wild* is summed up in the selected bibliography of the major literary critic of Jack London, Earle Labor, in his *Jack London* (New York, 1974), pp. 168–171. Labor's own criticism of *The Call of the Wild* and *White Fang* (pp. 69–81) is incisive and masterful. The other essential recent examination of London's Alaskan fiction is to be found in McClintock's *White Logic, op. cit.* The present book does not intend to cover in breadth the one field in which Jack London's achievement is fairly described and analyzed.
21. Quoted in Joan London, *Jack London and His Times*, p. 252.
22. See Ann Upton, "The Wolf in London's Mirror," *Jack London Newsletter*, September–December 1973, pp. 111–118.
23. See Jack London, "The Terrible and Tragic in Fiction," *The Critic*, June 1903.
24. Jack London, *Before Adam* (New York, 1906), p. 1.
25. See Cloudesley Johns's autobiography, manuscript, p. 258, *HL*. Johns also wrote a little poem to commemorate his trip on the *Spray* and sent it to his friend.

> Aboard the "Spray," wrestling o'er pawns and things,
>   Obscene and frantic when the queen is lost.
> And though acute the torture that it brings,
>   The nightly rubber's played at any cost.
>
> Oppressed with rage at futile sacrifice,
>   Nearing defeat in spite of trick and sham,
> Jack launches forth in accents unprecise
>   Words like "Jehovah," "Jesus Christ," "Goddam!"

26. Herman Scheffauer to Charmian London, June 8, 1926, *HL*.
27. Jack London, *The Sea-Wolf* (New York, 1904), pp. 115–116. For a discussion of the Nietzschean element in *The Sea-Wolf*, see C. C. Walcutt's "Jack London: Blond Beasts and Supermen," *American Literary Naturalism: A Divided Stream* (Minneapolis, Minn., 1956), pp. 87–113. In his recent *Nietzsche in Anglosaxony: A Study of Nietzsche's Impact on English and American Literature* (Leicester, Eng., 1972), pp. 163–170, Patrick Bridgwater exaggerates the influence of Nietzsche on *The Sea-Wolf* as he fails to evaluate London's small knowledge of the German philosopher before 1904. In *The Book of Jack London*, II, p. 31, Charmian London quotes a letter from Jack written on September 29, 1904, stating that he has been "getting hold of some of Nietzsche." (The original of this letter was at the Jack London Ranch at Glen

Ellen and is now at the Huntington Library.) Thus Bridgwater wrongly presumes that Larsen is a crass "biological Superman," when he is more of a Spencerian or Miltonic character. Lewis Mumford was equally at fault when he attacked Larsen as an infantile Superman, "the social platitude of the old West, transplanted into a literary epigram."

28. Quoted in Franklin Walker's excellent afterword to *The Sea-Wolf and Selected Stories* (Signet Classic edn., New York, 1964), p. 345.

29. Jack London, "Experiences," manuscript notes, *HL*.

30. For Jack London's later explanation of his actions to the Crowd in his effort to protect Charmian Kittredge's reputation, see his two letters to Carrie Sterling, September 15 and 29, 1905, reprinted in *Letters from Jack London*, pp. 180–189.

31. Jack London to Charmian Kittredge, August 31, 1903, transcript in Irving Stone Collection, *UCLA*, original now at *HL*. Due to the great kindness and generosity of Mr. Milo Shepard, who has inherited the duty of looking after the Jack London Papers after the sad death of his father, the papers of Jack and Charmian London once stored at the Jack London Ranch at Glen Ellen were made available to me. They have now been transferred to *HL*.

32. Jack London to Charmian Kittredge, July 1903, quoted in *The Book of Jack London*, II, p. 82.

33. From an undated letter from Jack London to Charmian, probably written in 1904, Jack London Ranch Collection, Glen Ellen, now at *HL*.

34. In his research, Franklin Walker went to the County Records on Divorce at the Alameda County Courthouse, and looked up the two restraining orders filed by Mrs. Elizabeth London against her husband on June 28 and July 11, 1904 (No. 21056), and the complaint filed by her on August 6, 1904 (No. 21138). The testimony quoted comes from these records and may be found in the Franklin Walker Collection, *HL*.

35. Chicago *Record Herald*, August 12, 1903; Detroit *Journal*, August 24, 1903.

36. Jack London to Anna Strunsky, July 23, 1904, Walling Collection, *HL*. See also *Letters from Jack London*, pp. 162–163.

37. Jack London to Charmian Kittredge, September 1 and 24, October 12 and 26, 1903, Jack London Ranch Collection, Glen Ellen, now at *HL*.

38. Cloudesley Johns to Jack London, September 2, 1903, *HL*.

39. Jack London to Anna Strunsky, April 3, 1901, Walling Collection, *HL*.

8. MATE-WOMAN AND ANCHOR

1. Jack London, *The Game* (New York, 1905), p. 103.

2. Jack London's dispatch from Antung, June 2, 1904, was reprinted in *Jack London Reports, op. cit.*, pp. 118–122.

3. *Ibid.*, May 1, 1904, p. 106. See also *Jack London: A Biography* (Boston, 1964) by Richard O'Connor. His chapter on London during the Russo-Japanese War is the best section in an uneven book.

4. For an autobiographical description of the voyage on the junk, see Jack London, "Small Boat Sailing," *The Human Drift* (New York, 1917), pp. 59–62.

5. See Frederick Palmer's memoirs, *With My Own Eyes,* also quoted by Richard O'Connor, *op. cit.,* p. 217.

6. Jack London to Charmian Kittredge, May 22, 1904, quoted in *Jack London Reports,* p. 24.

7. See Joan London, *Jack London and His Times,* p. 284.

8. Jack London, "The Yellow Peril," *Revolution,* pp. 220–237.

9. Jack London, "The Unparalleled Invasion," *The Strength of the Strong* (New York, 1914), pp. 71–100.

10. Jack London to Charmian Kittredge, July 8, 1904, transcript in Irving Stone Collection, *UCLA,* original now at *HL.*

11. See Jack London, *John Barleycorn,* pp. 163–164.

12. Although Charmian Kittredge's diaries for the important period of 1902 and 1903 have apparently been destroyed, her diaries exist for 1900, 1901, 1904, and thereafter. They show her practical and gushing nature, also her daily devotion to Jack London's work and person, and her frequent sicknesses from the effort of keeping up with his energy. They are deposited in the Huntington Library and at Utah State. Transcripts of portions from Charmian's earlier diaries, 1890–1895, also exist in the Irving Stone Collection, *UCLA.* They seem to have been collected merely to prove that she was inconstant and prone to love affairs in her youth. She herself confessed to Jack that she had once been a giddy butterfly.

13. Jack London to Charmian Kittredge, September 29, 1904, Jack London Ranch Collection, Glen Ellen, now at *HL.*

14. Jack London to Cloudesley Johns, October 31, 1899, *HL.*

15. Jack London to Edward DeWitt, September 23, 1914, *HL.*

16. Jack London to Blanche Partington, undated and August 30, 1904, Blanche Partington Collection, Bancroft Library, Berkeley.

17. George Sterling to Blanche Partington, December 9, 1904, Blanche Partington Collection, Bancroft Library, Berkeley.

18. See Charmian Kittredge's diaries for January 30, March 1 and 8, 1905, *HL.*

19. Charmian London to Blanche Partington, March 8, 1907, Blanche Partington Collection, Bancroft Library, Berkeley.

20. In *The Book of Jack London,* II, p. 32, Charmian revealed Jack London's obsession about his disease. "I was reminded by Jack of Nietzsche's ultimate fate. Oh, no—he was not 'playing to the gallery,' nor inviting sympathy to his spiritual dole. That was not his custom; he was but frankly, soul to soul, letting me know what was true of him at the time, and vouchsafing a glimpse at the worst symptom—his own uncaring attitude concerning it." Further evidence of Jack's obsessive worry over the nature of his "tumor" can be found in his library in two editions of S. G. Gant's authoritative work, *Diagnosis and Treatment of Diseases of the Rectum, Anus, and Contiguous Textures* (Philadelphia, 1897, and rev. edn., 1902). In these books, the lurid color

plates of the effects of the diseases are enough to plunge any sufferer into morbidity.

After the relief of finding little wrong with himself, Jack London wrote to Charmian a confidential poem, "My Gentle Nurse," which is still preserved in the London Collection at Utah State. Its last verse runs:

A month ago 'tis since I held,
This nurse upon my lap;
My doctor says—I fear he's right—
I have a dose of—piles.

21. See Charmian Kittredge's diaries for April 1 to 12, May 10, 13, and 15, 1905, *HL*. Elsie Martinez, who was Jim Whitaker's daughter and the wife of the leading artist of the Crowd, confirmed Jack's fickleness in 1905 in her oral interviews conducted by Franklin Walker and Willa Klug Baum at Berkeley in 1969.

22. See Jack London to Carrie Sterling, September 15 and 29, 1905, reprinted in *Letters from Jack London*, pp. 180–189. The married woman he briefly considered for an affair may well have been Ada Lee Bascom (Mrs. George Hamilton Marsden). Her name was linked publicly with his when they collaborated on a one-act play, *The Great Interrogation*, which was eventually staged at the Alcazar Theater in San Francisco on August 21, 1905.

23. Charmian Kittredge's diaries, July 15, 1905, *HL*.

24. Charmian Kittredge to Jack London, May 1904, transcript in the Irving Stone Collection, *UCLA*, original now at *HL*.

25. Jack London to George Sterling, June 1, 1905, *US*.

26. Charmian London to Blanche Partington, Honolulu, 1907, Blanche Partington Collection, Bancroft Library, Berkeley. For a full account of the first years at Carmel, see Franklin Walker, *The Seacoast of Bohemia: An Account of Early Carmel* (San Francisco, 1966).

27. Mary Austin, *Earth Horizon* (Boston, 1932), pp. 300–304.

28. Jack London, *The Valley of the Moon* (New York, 1913), p. 410.

29. *Ibid.*, pp. 413–414.

30. Jack London to George Sterling, May 28, 1905, *HL*, quoted in *Letters from Jack London*, pp. 171–172.

31. Jack London to George P. Brett, June 20, 1905, *HL*.

32. Jack London, "Planchette," *Moon-Face* (New York, 1906), p. 231. There is a competent monthly account of Jack's doings in 1905 in Lois Rather, *Jack London, 1905* (Oakland, Calif., 1974).

33. Jack London, *John Barleycorn*, p. 165.

34. Jack London, notes for "Jack Liverpool," Cresmer Collection, *UCLA*.

35. Jack London to George P. Brett, December 5, 1904, *HL*, quoted in *Letters from Jack London*, p. 166.

36. Jack London to Frederick I. Bamford, May 8, 1905, Holman-London Collection, Jack London State Park, Glen Ellen, Calif.

37. Jack London, notes for "Must Make a Book," *HL*.

9. EARTHQUAKE AND ESCAPE

1. Charmian Kittredge's diaries, August 19, 1905, *HL*.
2. See Austin Lewis to Irving Stone, notes in the Irving Stone Collection, *UCLA*.
3. Jack London to Charmian Kittredge, undated, 1905, Jack London Ranch Collection, Glen Ellen, now at *HL*.
4. See Scrapbook 7 in the Jack London Collection in the Huntington Library for the newspaper clippings showing the notoriety generated by Jack London's sudden remarriage and lecture tour in 1905. His admission of the value of the publicity is printed in the Oakland *Herald*, February 20, 1906.
5. See Charmian Kittredge London's diaries, October 31, November 19, 1905, *HL*.
6. See Jack London, "Revolution," *Revolution*, pp. 11–41.
7. See Joshua Wanhope, "In Memoriam," *New York Call*, November 24, 1916. Also quoted in Joan London, *Jack London and His Times*, p. 309.
8. Upton Sinclair, *The Jungle* (New York, 1905), p. 197.
9. The review is quoted in full in P. Foner, *Jack London: American Rebel*, pp. 104–106.
10. Jack London to Frederick I. Bamford, March 22, 1906, Holman-London Collection, Jack London State Park, Glen Ellen.
11. Jack London, "The Minions of Midas," *Moon-Face*, pp. 110–111.
12. Jack London to Elwyn Hoffman, September 18, 1901, Hoffman Collection, *HL*. One astute critical article on Jack London in the Oakland *Tribune*, May 11, 1905, accused him of wanting "to become the Marat of a Socialist uprising in this country."
13. Even Jack London admitted the initial failure of *The Iron Heel* with most American Socialists. He wrote to Lilla Brockway on December 11, 1914: "The IRON HEEL was sadly received by the Socialists in the United States . . . the great majority of Socialists were hurt by it, feeling that it had given a blow to the Socialist propaganda in the United States. They were more the easy-going, middle-of-the-road, opportunist Socialists."
14. Jack London, *The Iron Heel* (New York, 1908), p. 216n and *passim*. As a story of prehistoric man, *Before Adam* is the best in the genre except for William Golding's work of genius, *The Inheritors*.
15. Jack London to Elwyn Hoffman, June 17, 1900, Hoffman Collection, *HL*.
16. *New York World*, March 25, 1906. The authors of "Lost in the Land of the Midnight Sun" were Augustus Bridle and J. K. MacDonald; they had the story printed in *McClure's*, December 1901.
17. See *New York World*, April 29, 1906, for Jack London's reply to the charge of plagiarism. Other instances of borrowing to which Jack London admitted were his debt to Edgerton R. Young's *My Dogs in the Northland* for certain passages in *The Call of the Wild*, and to Frank Harris's article on "The Bishop of London and Public Morality" for Bishop Morehouse's vision in *The Iron Heel*.

18. See the Terre-Haute, Indiana, *Star,* May 2, 1906, and the Winnipeg *Tribune,* May 9, 1906.
19. See Jack London, "The Other Animals," *Revolution,* pp. 194–219.
20. Jack London to George P. Brett, January 28, 1907, *HL.* When George Sterling also protested at the publication of *The Road,* Jack London properly asked him: "Is it a lingering taint of the bourgeois in you that makes you object? Is it because of my shamelessness? For having done things in which I saw or see no shame? Do tell me."
21. Jack London to Charmian Kittredge, June 1903, quoted by her in *The Book of Jack London,* II, p. 79.
22. Jack London to Cloudesley Johns, October 4, 1905, *HL.* See also *Letters from Jack London,* pp. 189–190.
23. See Cloudesley Johns's autobiography, manuscript, p. 76, *HL.*
24. Jack London, "The Story of an Eye-Witness," *Collier's,* May 5, 1906, reprinted in *Jack London Reports,* pp. 351–357.
25. Jack London to Gaylord Wilshire, text of a letter quoted in *The Worker,* May 12, 1906.
26. Jack London, "The Dream of Debs," *The Strength of the Strong* (New York, 1914), p. 176.
27. Charmian London, *The Book of Jack London,* II, p. 155.
28. See Jack London, *The Cruise of the Snark* (New York, 1911), pp. 16–35, for the misadventures of the building and commissioning of the *Snark.*
29. Jack London to Arthur T. Vance, March 14, 1907, *HL.* See also *Letters from Jack London,* p. 243.
30. Quoted in Joan London, *Jack London and His Times,* p. 320.
31. Jack London, *The Cruise of the Snark,* foreword, pp. 3–7.
32. See Frank Pease on his meeting with Jack London, *Seven Arts,* March 1917.
33. Charmian London, *The Book of Jack London,* II, p. 157.
34. In her unpublished second biography of her father, Joan London has an interesting chapter on the episode of the pistol left by her father in the house at Piedmont, and another chapter on the character of Flora, whom she remembered as having the face and character of a strong man, humorless, opinionated, intelligent, extraordinary.
35. See "Jack London's Mother Tells Pauline Jacobson Where Her Son Got His Looks and Literary Ability," San Francisco *Bulletin,* July 22, 1906.

10. THE ILLUSION OF THE *SNARK*

1. Jack London, *The Cruise of the Snark* (New York, 1911), p. 55.
2. Jack London to Eliza Shepard, November 25, 1907, Irving Stone Collection, *UCLA.*
3. See Charmian London's diaries, February 6, 1908, *HL.*
4. See Charmian London to Ninetta Eames, September 4 and 9, 1907, *HL.*
5. Jack London to Ninetta Eames, July 25, 1907, *HL.* See also *Letters from Jack London,* pp. 246–250.

6. Jack London to George Sterling, November 24, 1907, *HL*. See also *Letters from Jack London*, pp. 252–253.

7. Jack London, *The Cruise of the Snark*, pp. 235–236.

8. Jack London, the logbook of the *Snark*, manuscript, June 28, 1908, *US*.

9. See Charmian London to Ninetta Eames Payne, July 9, 1908, *US*. See also Jack London, *The Cruise of the Snark*, pp. 326–327, and Martin Johnson, *Through the South Seas with Jack London* (New York, 1913), p. 329.

10. See Jack London, *Adventure* (New York, 1911), pp. 39–40, 104.

11. See Jack London's notes in the back cover of Josiah Flynt [Willard], *My Life* (New York, 1908), in which he complains of an arsenic slough on his cheek from an Australian hospital, *HL*. He was presumably given the arsenic in a compound against yaws, probably atoxyl or arsacetin.

12. Jack London to Ninetta Eames, June 8, 1909, *HL*.

13. Jack London's statement to his friends, "A Brief Explanation," undated, early 1909, Holman-London Collection, Jack London State Ranch, Glen Ellen.

14. Jimmy Hopper to George Sterling, April 15, 1909, *HL*.

15. Charmian London to Ninetta Eames, November 19, 1908, *US*.

16. See the interview with Jack London in *The Lone Hand*, Sydney, Australia, February 1, 1909.

17. Jack London, "Strike Methods: America and Australia," *The Australian Star*, January 14, 1909.

18. Jack London to the Editor of *The Socialist*, June 5, 1909, *US*.

11. THE BEAUTY RANCH

1. Jack London, "The Madness of John Harned," *The Night-Born* (New York, 1913), p. 60.

2. Jack London to Lillian Collins, April 26, 1910, *US*. See also *Letters from Jack London*, pp. 302–303.

3. Jack London to Alice Lyndon, July 29, 1909, *HL*. See also *Letters from Jack London*, pp. 281–282.

4. Jack London, *Burning Daylight* (New York, 1910), pp. 157–158.

5. Jack London to Zadel B. Gustafson, March 4, 1911, *HL*.

6. Jack London to Fannie K. Hamilton, December 6, 1909, *US*.

7. Charmian London, *The Book of Jack London*, II, p. 185.

8. See Willows, California, *Daily Journal*, August 31, 1911.

9. Jack London to George Brett, May 25, 1910, *HL*. See also *Letters from Jack London*, pp. 304–305.

10. Jack London to Blanche Partington, March 22, 1911, Bancroft Library, Berkeley.

11. Jack London, "The Somnambulists," *Revolution*, p. 49.

12. Jack London to W. E. Walling, November 30, 1909, *US*. See also *Letters from Jack London*, pp. 289–290.

13. See S. Thernstrom's important essay, "Urbanization, Migration, and Social Mobility in Late Nineteenth Century America," in *Toward a New Past: Dis-*

senting Essays in American History (B. J. Bernstein, ed., New York, 1967), pp. 158–175.

14. Jack London to Donald D. Horne, December 1, 1910, *US.* Reprinted in Jack London, "The Eternity of Forms," *The Turtles of Tasman* (New York, 1916), p. 72.
15. Jack London to Fannie K. Hamilton, December 6, 1909, *US.*
16. George Sterling to Mrs. Herbert Heron, November 3, 1909, Bancroft Library, Berkeley.
17. See Franklin Walker, *The Seacoast of Bohemia: An Account of Early Carmel* (San Francisco, 1966), pp. 90–95.
18. Jack London to Charmian London, undated, probably August 1910, *HL.*
19. George Sterling to Jack London, December 18, 1911, Bancroft Library, Berkeley.
20. Charmian London, *The Book of Jack London*, II, p. 193.
21. Jack London, Notes on "Psoriasis," *US.*
22. Jack London, Notes on "My Memoirs," *US.*

12. CONFESSIONAL

1. See Jack London to Jack Byrne, March 31, 1916, *US.* The company which declined to insure Jack London was Western State Life. London noted that the doctor who failed him died shortly afterwards.
2. The six works preserved in Jack London's library at the Huntington are E. L. Keyes, *The Venereal Diseases Including Stricture of the Male Urethra* (New York, 1880); Henry H. Morton, *Genito-Urinary Diseases and Syphilis* (2nd rev. edn., Philadelphia, 1908); William L. Holt, *The Venereal Peril: A Popular Treatise on Venereal Diseases: Their Nature, Course, Symptoms and Prevention* (W. J. Robinson, ed., New York, 1909); Victor G. Vecki, *The Prevention of Sexual Diseases* (W. J. Robinson, intro., New York, 1910); Professor E. Tomaszewski, *The Treatment of Syphilis with Salvarsan or 606* (W. J. Robinson, intro., New York, 1911); and William J. Robinson, *The Treatment of Gonorrhea and Its Complications in Men and Women for the General Practitioner* (New York, 1915).
3. Charmian London's diaries, December 2, 1910, *HL.*
4. See W. R. Gowers, *Diagnosis of Diseases of the Brain and of the Spinal Cord* (New York, 1885), pp. 172, 194, 195. Jack London's copy at the Huntington Library is marked by him on these pages. The George Sterling and Blanche Partington Papers, and Joseph Noel and Irving Stone in their works on London, supply more evidence for Jack's depressive fears.
5. Jack London, notes in Josiah Flynt [Willard], *My Life, op. cit., HL.*
6. For a defense of salvarsan as a wonder drug, see Estill D. Holland, "Salvarsan, or, A Case of 'I Told You So,' " *American Journal of Urology and Sexology,* April 1916. This article is preserved in a box marked "Medical" at the Jack London Ranch, now at the *HL.* The box contains other articles of interest to Jack London during the last years of his life. They give a good indication of his

medical preoccupations. There are about twenty articles on gonorrhea and venereal disease, also another twenty articles on pyorrhea. London had lost all his teeth by this time, and his rheumatic arthritis was aggravated by his poisoned gums as well as by his arsenic treatments. The few other medical articles in the box deal with dysentry, pellagra, alcoholism, and narcotic addiction—all subjects of minor concern to London. I am much indebted to Milo Shepard for showing me this box, also for producing the silver traveling pocket hypodermic case carried by Jack London before his death.

7. See Andrew Sinclair, *Prohibition: The Era of Excess* (Boston, 1962), pp. 70–75.
8. Jack London to T. A. Bostick, September 28, 1913, *HL*. See also *Letters from Jack London,* p. 401.
9. Jack London, *Martin Eden,* p. 176.
10. See Joan London's unpublished second biography of her father.
11. Charmian London, *The Book of Jack London*, II, pp. 209–211.
12. See Joan London's unpublished second biography of her father. Becky, however, always insisted that Jack put her through the window by accident.
13. Jack London to Bess London, January 8, 1911, *US*. See also *Letters from Jack London*, pp. 329–331. A copy of Jack London's will dated May 24, 1911, is at *HL*.
14. Ninetta Eames to Jack London, June 14, 1909, *US*.
15. Jack London, notes for "Jack Liverpool," Cresmer Collection, *USC*.
16. Charmian London to Ninetta Eames, November 19, 1908, *US*.
17. Jack London to George Brett, May 30, 1911, *HL*.
18. Jack London to Roland Phillips, January 18, 1912, *US*. See also *Letters from Jack London*, pp. 358–359.
19. Jack London to Edward Carpenter, March 27, 1914, *HL*.
20. Jack London, *The Valley of the Moon*, pp. 174, 310.
21. Jack London to Elwyn Hoffman, October 23, 1911, Hoffman Collection, *HL*.
22. Jack London to Anna Strunsky, January 21, 1900, *HL*. See also *Letters from Jack London*, pp. 84–85.
23. See Ed Morrell's interview with Irving Stone in the Irving Stone Collection, *UCLA*.
24. J. Noel, *Footloose in Arcadia*, p. 143.
25. Anna Strunsky Walling, "Memoirs of Jack London," *The Masses*, November 1917.
26. Jack London to Eliza Shepard, January 18, 1912, *US*.
27. Jack London, *John Barleycorn*, pp. 71–72.
28. Jack London to W. G. Beecroft, February 7, 1913, *US*.
29. Jack London to Romaine Fielding, February 4, 1915, *HL*.
30. Jack London, "Small-boat Sailing," April 15, 1911, reprinted in *The Human Drift* (New York, 1917), pp. 72–73.
31. Jack London in the *New York Evening World*, quoted by Charmian London, *The Book of Jack London*, II, p. 231.
32. Jack London in the Oakland *Tribune*, quoted by Charmian London, *The Book of Jack London*, II, p. 236.

33. Jack London, notes on "The American Abyss," *HL.*
34. Charmian London's diaries, March 4, 1912, *HL.*
35. Charmian London, *The Book of Jack London*, II, p. 245.

13 . DISGUST

1. Jack London to Charmian London, August 13, 1912, *HL.*
2. Jack London to Cloudesley Johns, 1899, quoted in Johns's autobiography, p. 32.
3. See Charmian London's diaries, February 23 and 25, 1914, *HL.*
4. Charmian London to Anna Strunsky Walling, November 14, 1913, Walling Collection, *HL.*
5. See Jack London to Joan London, August 24 and 29, September 5, and October 11, 1913, *US.* See also *Letters from Jack London.* pp. 394–397, 405–408.
6. See the appendix of Joan London's unpublished second biography of her father.
7. Joan London to Jack London, October 28, 1913, *US.*
8. See Jack London to Joan London, February 24, 1914, *US.* See also *Letters from Jack London*, pp. 414–417.
9. Jack London to Charles L. Marriott, June 24, 1913, *HL.*
10. Quoted in Irving Stone, *Sailor on Horseback*, p. 304.
11. Jack London to Frederick H. Robinson, September 5, 1913, *US.* See also *Letters from Jack London*, pp. 397–398.
12. Jack London to J. J. Hawley, June 26, 1913, *US.* See also *Letters from Jack London*, pp. 389–390.
13. Jack London to Hartwell S. Shippey, February 7, 1913, *US.* See also *Letters from Jack London,* pp. 370–371.
14. Jack London to George Brett, April 22, 1913, *HL.* See also *Letters from Jack London*, pp. 379–381.
15. Jack London to Roland Phillips, March 14, 1913, *HL.* See also *Letters from Jack London*, pp. 374–375.
16. See Jack London, *The Mutiny of the Elsinore* (New York, 1914), p. 371. See also Jack London, *The Little Lady of the Big House* (New York, 1916), p. 392.
17. Quoted in Charmian London, *The Book of Jack London*, II, p. 268.
18. Jack London, *The Star Rover* (New York, 1915), p. 286.
19. Jack London to Roland Phillips, March 26, 1914, *HL.* See also *Letters from Jack London,* pp. 418–419.
20. Jack London, notes on "Farthest Distant," *HL.*
21. Jack London to Eliza Shepard, December 2, 1913, *US.*
22. Jack London to Charmian London, January 24, 1914, *US.*
23. Jack London to Charmian London, January 29, 1914, *US.* See also *Letters from Jack London*, pp. 412–413.

14. MEXICAN CONFUSION

1. [Attributed to Jack London], *The Good Soldier,* pamphlet, *HL.*
2. For Jack London's articles on Mexico in May and June 1914, see *Jack London Reports, op. cit.,* pp. 126–210.
3. See John Reed, *Insurgent Mexico* (New York, 1969).
4. Ford Madox Ford, "Jack London," *Living Age,* January 1917.
5. Charmian London to Dr. W. S. Porter, July 22, 1914, *US.*
6. Jack London, "The Impossibility of War," *Overland Monthly,* March 1900.
7. Jack London to John M. Wright, September 7, 1915, *US.*
8. Jack London to H. Braam, December 11, 1914, *US.*
9. See Charmian London's diaries, 1914 and 1915 *passim, HL.*
10. Charmian London to Anna Strunsky Walling, undated, ? 1914, Walling Collection, *HL.*
11. Arthur T. Johnson, *California: An Englishman's Impressions of the Golden State* (New York, 1915), p. 298.
12. Quoted in J. Noel, *Footloose in Arcadia,* p. 168.
13. Jack London to Dr. F. Lydston, March 26, 1914, *HL.* See also *Letters from Jack London,* pp. 419–420.
14. Jack London, notes on "Socialist Autobiography," "One Phase Autobiography—Socialism," and "The Watcher in the Tower," *HL* and *US.*
15. See Jack London, notes for "Socialist Novel," "A Series of Socialist Lectures," "Disappearing Class," and "My Great Labor Novel," *US.*
16. Jack London to George Brett, December 26, 1914, *HL.* See also *Letters from Jack London,* pp. 440–441.
17. Jack London to George Brett, October 7, 1914, *HL.* See also *Letters from Jack London,* p. 432.
18. Jack London, *The Acorn Planter* (New York, 1916), p. 9.
19. Jack London to Walter S. Kerr, January 26, 1915, *HL.* See also *Letters from Jack London,* pp. 442–443.
20. Jack London to George Brett, February 18, 1915, *HL.* See also *Letters from Jack London,* pp. 449–450.

15. AN APPETITE FOR AWARENESS

1. Jack London's three articles for *Cosmopolitan* from Hawaii in 1916 are collected under the title of "My Hawaiian Aloha" in Charmian London, *The New Hawaii* (New York, 1923).
2. Charmian London to Anna Strunsky Walling, April 30, 1915, Walling Collection, *HL.*
3. Jack London, *Jerry of the Islands* (New York, 1917), p. 289.
4. Jack London, *Michael, Brother of Jerry* (New York, 1917), p. 309.
5. Jack London to Edward and Ninetta (Eames) Payne, June 28, 1916, *US.*
6. Eliza Shepard to Jack London, undated, 1915, *HL.*

7. The correspondence in the Huntington Library reveals that the Bowman Drug Company filled London's medicine chest according to his requirements, but that it needed a further prescription from Dr. W. S. Porter to give London fifty more capsules of opium and hyoscyamine.

8. Jack London to the Owl Drug Company of San Francisco, August 28, 1915, *HL.*

9. Jack London to Ethelda Hesser, September 21, 1915, *HL.* See also *Letters from Jack London*, pp. 460–461.

10. Jack London to Blanche Partington, December 2, 1915, Partington Collection, Bancroft Library, Berkeley.

11. Jack London to Richardson, October 9, 1913, *US.*

12. See the Jack London and Spiro Ophens correspondence, 1916, *US.*

13. See Jack London's copy of C. Jung, *Psychology of the Unconscious* (B. Hinkle, intro., New York, 1915), *HL.*

14. Charmian London, *The Book of Jack London,* II, p. 323.

15. See Jack London, notes on night pads and for "Cherry," *HL.* See also his notes on "Jack Liverpool," Cresmer Collection, *USC.*

16. Charmian London, *The Book of Jack London,* II, pp. 343–344.

17. Jack London, telegram to Charles G. Norris, April 15, 1914, text in *Letters from Jack London*, p. 421.

18. See Jack London's notes for his autobiography, to be called "Jack (or) Paul Liverpool," "My Biography," "Memoirs," "A Sailor on Horseback," at the *HL,* Cresmer Collection, *USC,* and *US.*

19. Jack London, notes on "Man," *US.*

20. Jack London, introduction to *The Cry for Justice: An Anthology of the Literature of Social Protest* (U. Sinclair, ed., Philadelphia, 1915).

21. Jack London to the members of the Local, Glen Ellen Socialist Labor Party, March 7, 1916, published in *Letters from Jack London,* pp. 466–467.

22. Jack London to William Davenport, secretary of the Socialist Party of the United States, September 21, 1916, *US.*

23. See Joe Trounson to Jack London, August 22, 1909, Irving Stone Collection, *UCLA.*

24. Jack London, notes on "Bastard of Youthful Attempt," *HL.*

25. Eliza Shepard to Jack London, undated, *US.*

26. Jack London to Joan London, February 4, August 2 and 25, September 18, 1915, *US.* See also *Letters from Jack London,* pp. 446–447, 455–60.

27. Jack London, notes on "Novel re Joan and Jack London—Big Novel," *HL.*

28. Jack London, notes on "Her Body," *HL.*

29. Jack London, "The Kanaka Surf," *On the Makaloa Mat* (New York, 1919), *passim.*

30. Charmian London, "Charmette," *HL.* These notes of her projected autobiographical novel appear to have been put together during the thirty years after 1913. My quotations and references are taken from what appear to be the earlier notes.

31. Charmian London, *The Book of Jack London*, II, p. 325.

32. Jack London, "Shin Bones," *On the Makaloa Mat,* p. 80.
33. See Jack London, *The Red One* (New York, 1918), pp. 129–130, 21, 37–38, 49.

16. FORTY HORSES ABREAST

1. Charmian London, *The Book of Jack London*, II, p. 331.
2. See Irving Stone's interviews with Mrs. Robert Hill and Finn Frolich, Irving Stone Collection, *UCLA.*
3. Jack London, notes on "Horses/Himself," "40 Horses Abreast," and "Horse Novel—Neuadd," *HL.*
4. Charmian London to Leonard Abbott, June 30, 1928, *HL.* She was telling Abbott, who claimed that Jack London committed suicide, that her husband had died of uremia.
5. Jack London to Ralph Kasper, June 25, 1914, *HL.* See also *Letters from Jack London,* p. 425.
6. Jack London, notes on "How We Die," *HL.*
7. The most important testimony on Jack London's death is Dr. Allan Milo Thomson's, given to Irving Stone in 1937 and preserved in the Irving Stone Collection at *UCLA.* Franklin Walker tracked down Dr. Thomson in Santa Rosa in 1953; through his wife, the doctor reaffirmed that his evidence to Irving Stone was true. Yet when C. Hartley Grattan had suggested thirteen years after London's death that it had been a suicide, Dr. Thomson had denied it, saying, "Jack London died of internal poisoning brought about through kidney trouble" (see San Francisco *Call,* February 15, 1929). Eight years later, the doctor from Sonoma gave Irving Stone the grounds to assert a theory of suicide. He showed evident bias against the two San Francisco doctors at the deathbed, and against Charmian London and Eliza Shepard. Joan London, however, largely believed his evidence in her biography of her father, and she told Franklin Walker that Dr. W. S. Porter's vehement denial to her of the possibility of an overdose of drugs made her believe Dr. Thomson even more than before. Dr. Porter did, however, admit to her that morphine poisoning might have been a contributory cause of her father's death.

   Charmian London's *The Book of Jack London*, II, pp. 381–394, deals fully with the events of his death from her point of view. Her testimony on the methods used by the doctors to resuscitate Jack London supports the thesis that he was suffering from narcosis, an overdose of morphine. In fact, Dr. Thomson's assertion that London had taken 12½ grains of morphine was only based on the assumption that both empty bottles of twenty-five tablets of ¼-grain each had been full when Jack London was supposed to have injected himself with them—they may have been nearly empty and the overdose small. Charmian London, however, was always determined to prove that uremia was the sole cause of her husband's death. She even commissioned a paper on the subject which is still preserved at the Huntington Library.

The other important assertions of London's suicide can be found in George Sterling's correspondence with Margaret Smith Cobb at the Stanford Library. He supported the Thomson thesis about London's death and supplied the motive of London's love of another woman in Honolulu or New York. Later in the correspondence, he seemed surprised that Charmian began to avoid him because of his spreading the story. Upton Sinclair's source of information for his assertions about Jack London's suicide in *Mammonart, Money Writes,* and *American Outpost* was George Sterling. The trouble with Sinclair as a witness is that he was so pleased at his longevity, which he attributed to health foods and teetotalism, that he could not hide his satisfaction and sermons on the subject of the short and dissipated lives of his rival Californian writers, Frank Norris and Jack London. When Joan London began her biography of her father, Upton Sinclair wrote to her on August 3, 1937, to say, "You are going to have a hard problem of how to deal with Jack's death. . . ." She inclined to the overdose theory, but she rightly refused to call the act suicide. Her verdict was the Scots verdict of not proven.

Joseph Noel's evidence of suicide in *Footloose in Arcadia* was, as usual, likely to be distorted because of his quarrels with London at the end of his life; he even claimed London was a member of an informal suicide club. There is a curious pamphlet by William McDevitt called *Jack London as Poet and Platform Man* and subtitled *Did Jack London Commit Suicide?* It was printed in San Francisco in a limited edition in 1947, but it contains no new information on the subject. Of more importance is the work done by Alfred Shivers of Northern Illinois University for his unpublished book on Jack London. He had the Jack London library checked for evidence that the author might have used his thirty-six medical books to calculate a lethal dose of morphine. No evidence was found, thus putting Dr. Thomson's testimony in question. Shivers's conclusions are published in *The Dalhousie Review,* Spring 1969, pp. 43–57, under the title, "Jack London: Not a Suicide."

Eliza Shepard's own testimony against the theory of suicide is most important. She wrote an injured letter to Irving Stone on September 2, 1937, protesting that she had never seen or heard any evidence of suicide, and she was not a liar. Stone ignored her testimony in *Sailor on Horseback,* as he ignored many other witnesses who conflicted with his interpretation of events.

8. San Francisco *Chronicle,* November 23, 1916.
9. See J. Noel, *Footloose in Arcadia,* pp. 272–273. Noel's evidence about Sterling, whom he admired, is more reliable than about Jack London. See also George Sterling to Margaret Smith Cobb, September 5, 1923, *HL* and Stanford Library.
10. Charmian London to Upton Sinclair, July 21, 1930, *HL.*
11. Jack London, *Martin Eden,* pp. 273, 406. Yet as Alfred Shivers has pointed out, youthful suicide attempts and suicide by the pen do not imply actual suicide for authors. Poe did not finally kill himself despite a previous attempt

by opium. Nor did Conrad, who had also tried suicide when young. It is tempting to overstress the death wish in writers.

12. See Charmian London's round robin to the speakers at the funeral, undated, 1916, *HL.*

17. POSTMORTEM AND RESURRECTION

1. Anna Strunsky Walling, "Memoirs of Jack London," *The Masses*, November 1917.
2. See Upton Sinclair, *Mammonart* (Pasadena, Calif., 1925), and *Money Writes* (New York, 1927).
3. See Edgar Lee Masters in the San Francisco *Examiner*, July 18, 1926.
4. See Rose Wilder Lane's "biography" of Jack London in *Sunset, the Pacific Monthly*, October 1917 to May 1918, and her novel *He Was a Man* (New York, 1925).
5. See "Jack London Rides Again," *Ken* magazine, August 1939. The criticism lists Irving Stone's reuse of London's own words from his stories.
6. Jack London to Elwyn Hoffman, February 1, 1902, Hoffman Collection, *HL.*
7. See Jack London's correspondence with Philo M. Buck, Jr., *US.*
8. Jack London to V. C. Gilman, November 14, 1911, *HL,* also published in *Letters from Jack London*, p. 356.
9. H. L. Mencken, *Prejudices: First Series* (New York, 1919), pp. 236–237.
10. Henry Miller to Charles Keeler, December 9, 1916, *HL.*
11. See Aneurin Bevan, *In Place of Fear* (New York, 1952), pp. 19, 214: "From Jack London's *Iron Heel* to the whole world of Marxist literature was an easy and fascinating trip." See also the profile of Isidor Rabi in *The New Yorker*, October 13, 1975, and Lenny Bruce's "autobiography," *How to Talk Dirty and Influence People*.
12. Jack London, notes on "Language," ca. 1915, *HL.*
13. See Wilfred Lay, "John Barleycorn Under Psychoanalysis," *The Bookman*, March 1917.
14. Jack London to Geddes Smith, October 31, 1916, *HL.* See also *Letters from Jack London*, pp. 478–479.

SELECTED BIBLIOGRAPHY

BOOKS BY JACK LONDON

The Abysmal Brute. New York, 1913.
The Acorn Planter. New York, 1916.
Adventure. New York, 1911.
Before Adam. New York, 1907.
Burning Daylight. New York, 1910.
The Call of the Wild. New York, 1903.
Children of the Frost. New York, 1902.
The Cruise of the Dazzler. New York, 1902.
The Cruise of the Snark. New York, 1911.
A Daughter of the Snows. Philadelphia, 1902.
Dutch Courage and Other Stories. New York, 1922.
The Faith of Men. New York, 1904.
The Game. New York, 1905.
The God of His Fathers. New York, 1901.
Hearts of Three. New York, 1920.
The House of Pride and Other Tales of Hawaii. New York, 1912.
The Human Drift. New York, 1917.
The Iron Heel. New York, 1908.
Jerry of the Islands. New York, 1917.
John Barleycorn. New York, 1913.
The Little Lady of the Big House. New York, 1916.
Lost Face. New York, 1910.
Love of Life and Other Stories. New York, 1907.
Martin Eden. New York, 1909.
Michael, Brother of Jerry. New York, 1917.
Moon-Face and Other Stories. New York, 1906.
The Mutiny of the Elsinore. New York, 1914.
The Night-Born. New York, 1913.
On the Makaloa Mat. New York, 1919.

The People of the Abyss. New York, 1903.
The Red One. New York, 1918.
Revolution and Other Essays. New York, 1910.
The Road. New York, 1907.
The Scarlet Plague. New York, 1915.
Scorn of Women. New York, 1906.
The Sea-Wolf. New York, 1904.
The Son of the Wolf. Boston, 1900.
A Son of the Sun. New York, 1912.
South Sea Tales. New York, 1911.
Smoke Bellew. New York, 1912.
The Star Rover. New York, 1915.
The Strength of the Strong. New York, 1914.
Tales of the Fish Patrol. New York, 1905.
Theft: A Play in Four Acts. New York, 1910.
The Turtles of Tasman. New York, 1916.
The Valley of the Moon. New York, 1913.
War of the Classes. New York, 1905.
When God Laughs and Other Stories. New York, 1911.
White Fang. New York, 1906.

BOOKS BY JACK LONDON AND OTHERS

London, Jack, and Strunsky, Anna. *The Kempton–Wace Letters*. New York, 1903.
London, Jack, completed by Robert L. Fish. *The Assassination Bureau, Ltd*. (New York, 1963).

BOOKS AND ARTICLES ABOUT JACK LONDON

Austin, Mary. *Earth Horizon*. Boston, 1932.
Bamford, Georgia Loring. *The Mystery of Jack London*. Oakland, Calif., 1931.
Bridgwater, Patrick. *Nietzsche In Anglosaxony: A Study of Nietzsche's Impact on English and American Literature*. Leicester, England, 1972.
Brown, Deming, *Soviet Attitudes Toward American Writing*. Princeton, N.J., 1962.
Feied, Frederick. *No Pie in the Sky*. New York, 1964.
Foner, Philip S. *Jack London: American Rebel*. New York, 1947.
Ford, Ford Madox. "Jack London." *Living Age*, January 1917.
Hendricks, King, *Jack London: Master Craftsman of the Short Story*. Logan, Utah, 1966.
Hendricks, King, and Shepard, Irving, eds. *Jack London Reports*. New York, 1970.
———. *Letters from Jack London*. New York, 1965.
Johnson, Martin. *Through the South Seas with Jack London*. New York, 1913.
Jordan, David Starr. *The Days of a Man*. 2 vols. New York, 1922.
Labor, Earle. *Jack London*. New York, 1974.
Lane, Rose Wilder. *He Was a Man*. New York, 1925.

————. "Life and Jack London." *Sunset, the Pacific Monthly*, October 1917 to May 1918.

Lay, Wilfred. "John Barleycorn Under Psychoanalysis." *The Bookman*, March 1917.

London, Charmian. *The Book of Jack London*. 2 vols. New York, 1921.

————. *The New Hawaii*. New York, 1923.

London, Joan. *Jack London and His Times*. New York, 1939.

Lynn, Kenneth S. *The Dream of Success*. Boston, 1955.

McClintock, James I. *White Logic*. Grand Rapids. Mich., 1975.

Noel, Joseph. *Footloose in Arcadia*. New York, 1940.

O'Connor, Richard. *Jack London: A Biography*. Boston, 1964.

Pattee, Frederick Lewis. *The Development of the American Short Story*. New York, 1923.

Russett, Cynthia Eagle. *Darwin in America: The Intellectual Response, 1865–1912*. San Francisco, 1976.

Shivers, Alfred. "Jack London: Not a Suicide." *The Dalhousie Review*, Spring 1969.

Sinclair, Upton. *Mammonart*. Pasadena, California, 1925.

————. *Money Writes*. New York, 1927.

Starr, Kevin. *Americans and the California Dream, 1850–1915*. New York, 1973.

Stone, Irving. *Sailor on Horseback*. Boston, 1938.

Walcutt, C. C. *American Literary Naturalism: A Divided Stream*. Minneapolis, 1956.

Walker, Dale L. *The Alien Worlds of Jack London*. Grand Rapids, Mich., 1973.

Walker, Franklin. *Jack London and the Klondike: The Genesis of an American Writer*. London, 1966.

Walker, Franklin. *The Seacoast of Bohemia: An Account of Early Carmel*. San Francisco, 1966.

Walling, Anna Strunsky. "Memoirs of Jack London." *The Masses*, November 1917.

BIBLIOGRAPHIES

Bubka, Tony. *A Jack London Bibliography: A Selection of Reports Printed in the San Francisco Bay Area Newspapers: 1896–1967*. M.A. Thesis, San Jose State College, 1968.

Walker, Dale L., and James E. Sisson III. *The Fiction of Jack London; a Chronological Bibliography*. El Paso, Texas, 1972.

Woodbridge, Hensley C., John London and George H. Tweney. *Jack London: A Bibliography* (Georgetown, California, 1906. Rev. edn., Millwood, New York, 1973).

INDEX